COLLABORATING TO COMPETE

COLLABORATING TO COMPETE

Using Strategic Alliances and Acquisitions in the Global Marketplace

Edited by

Joel Bleeke
David Ernst

McKinsey & Co., Inc.

John Wiley & Sons, Inc.
New York • Chichester • Brisbane • Toronto • Singapore

In recognition of the importance of preserving what has been
written, it is a policy of John Wiley & Sons, Inc., to have
books of enduring value published in the United States
printed on acid-free paper, and we exert our best efforts
to that end.

Chapters 5, 6, 7, 8, 9, 10, and 13 were reprinted from the *McKinsey
Quarterly* with permission.

This publication is designed to provide accurate and
authoritative information in regard to the subject
matter covered. It is sold with the understanding that
the publisher is not engaged in rendering legal, accounting,
or other professional services. If legal advice or other
expert assistance is required, the services of a competent
professional person should be sought. *From a Declaration
of Principles jointly adopted by a Committee of the
American Bar Association and a Committee of Publishers.*

Library of Congress Cataloging-in-Publication Data

Collaborating to compete : using strategic alliances and acquisitions
  in the global marketplace / Joel Bleeke, David Ernst, editors.
     p.   cm.
  Includes index.
  ISBN 0-471-58009-0 (cloth)
  1. Strategic alliances (Business). 2. Consolidation and merger of
corporations. 3. Competition, International. I. Bleeke, Joel.
II. Ernst, David, 1956–
HD69.S8C65 1992
658.1'6—dc20   92-23933

Printed in the United States of America

10 9 8 7 6 5 4 3 2 1

To our parents,

whose lifelong partnership has been an
inspiration to us in our work and private lives.

About the Editors

JOEL BLEEKE and DAVID ERNST are consultants at McKinsey & Co. For the past several years, they have worked extensively on issues of international management for McKinsey's clients in the United States, Europe, and Japan. The issues have included organization, operations, strategy, mergers, acquisitions, joint ventures, and alliances.

Bleeke and Ernst have also led McKinsey's efforts to learn from its international consulting experience. In addition to editing this book, they have authored six of the chapters.

Joel Bleeke is a director (senior partner) in McKinsey's Chicago office. He is recognized as a writer and speaker on management topics and has published more than 30 articles in the *Financial Times* (London), *Harvard Business Review, McKinsey Quarterly, The Wall Street Journal, President Magazine* (Japan), and other periodicals.

Mr. Bleeke holds an M.S. in finance with honors from Northwestern University's Kellogg Graduate School of Management and a J.D. from Northwestern University School of Law. He is a member of the Council of Foreign Relations, Economic Club, and University Club of Chicago.

David Ernst is a consultant based in McKinsey's Washington, D.C., office. His work in the areas of cross-border alliances, acquisitions, and deregulation has served as the basis for recent articles in the *Harvard Business Review, The McKinsey Quarterly,* and the *Financial Times.*

Mr. Ernst was formerly vice-president and a founding member of Evans Economics, Inc. Mr. Ernst has also worked with Chase

Econometrics and The Asia Foundation. Mr. Ernst received his M.A. and B.A. degrees in economics with honors from Tufts University. He is a member of the Japan Society and Asia Society, and serves on the Advisory Board of the Economic Strategy Institute, and the Board of Directors of the Washington, D.C., Boys and Girls Club.

About the Contributing Authors

ROGER ABRAVANEL is a director (senior partner) in McKinsey's Milan office. He was born in Libya and has studied and worked in several European countries, North and Central America and Japan. He has a degree in chemical engineering from Polytechnic of Milan and an M.B.A. from INSEAD. He has written and spoken extensively on the subject of cross-border alliances and Euro-change programs at the business unit level.

VARUN BERY is a consultant in the New York office. Mr. Bery was educated in India and the United Kingdom. He also has an A.B. degree from Yale University and an M.B.A. from Harvard Business School where he was a George F. Baker Scholar.

THOMAS A. BOWERS is a consultant in McKinsey's San Francisco office. He works mainly on strategy and organizational issues. He has extensive experience in Japan, where he has worked for both Japanese and non-Japanese clients on alliance and organization issues. He attended Stanford University as an undergraduate and has an M.B.A. from the Sloan School of Management, Massachusetts Institute of Technology.

HENRY DENERO is a former director in McKinsey's Los Angeles office. He is now vice chairman and CFO of Dayton Hudson.

HERBERT A. HENZLER is a director (senior partner) of McKinsey and chairman of McKinsey in Germany and Austria. Currently, Mr. Henzler's professional interest concentrates on international management, entrepreneurship, alliances and transformation of the Eastern European economies. He has been a part-time lecturer on international management at the University of Munich for the past six years, and he was awarded an honorary professorship in 1992.

Before joining McKinsey, Mr. Henzler was an assistant professor at Munich University, after post-graduate studies at the University of California, Berkeley. He holds a degree in business administration and a doctorate in statistics from the University of Munich.

WILLIAM E. HOOVER, JR. is a director (senior partner) in McKinsey's Copenhagen office. He has completed numerous projects in the area of valuation and value creation, most of which involved United States and/or continental acquisitions. Mr. Hoover holds a B.A. in mathematics and economics from Dartmouth College; an M.S. in economics from Jesus College, Oxford; and an M.B.A. from Harvard Business School. Mr. Hoover has also researched and taught at INSEAD.

JAMES A. ISONO is a partner in McKinsey's Chicago office. Mr. Isono obtained his M.B.A. concentrating in general management from Harvard Business School. He earned his B.S. from the University of Illinois at Chicago.

KEVIN K. JONES is a partner in McKinsey's Tokyo office where he has worked both with Japanese companies expanding internationally and with foreign companies seeking to strengthen their positions in Japan and in the region. Kevin Jones graduated from INSEAD in France. Before that he worked with Dunlop as a systems analyst and as a consultant for PA Management Consultants, Ltd.

EDWARD KRUBASIK is a director (senior partner) in McKinsey's Munich office, specializing in innovation and technology management. Mr. Krubasik holds an M.B.A. from INSEAD and a Ph.D. in physics from the University of Karlsruhe. Before joining McKinsey in 1973, he conducted experimental and theoretical nuclear physics research projects in Europe and the United States. He is the author of a number of articles on technology management.

HARTMUT LAUTENSCHLAGER is a consultant in McKinsey's Sydney office. Before joining McKinsey, Hartmut worked as a manager at Robert Bosch, the large German supplier of components and systems for the automotive industry.

MAGNUS NICOLIN is a former consultant at McKinsey's Stockholm office. He was born in Sweden. He earned his B.A. from the Stockholm School of Economics and his M.B.A. from the Wharton School at University of Pennsylvania. Mr. Nicolin has worked on many international strategy and operations management assignments in Sweden, the United Kingdom, France, and the United States.

KENICHI OHMAE is chairman of McKinsey's offices in Japan. *The Financial Times* in London has called him "Japan's only management guru." Mr. Ohmae is author of *The Borderless World, Beyond National Borders: Reflections on Japan the World, Triad Power: The Coming Shape of Global Competition,* and *The Mind of the Strategist.* He has published editorials and articles in *Newsweek International, The Wall Street Journal, New York Times, Washington Post,* and *Harvard Business Review.* Mr. Ohmae is a graduate of Waseda University and the Tokyo Institute of Technology. He holds a Ph.D. in nuclear engineering from the Massachusetts Institute of Technology.

HOBART K. ROBINSON is a partner in McKinsey's Stockholm office. In early 1981, Mr. Robinson joined Brink's Inc., the world's largest security transportation company, as president and chief executive officer, where he served until year-end 1984, at which time he rejoined McKinsey in New York. He is now serving Scandinavian clients in the industrial and transportation sectors on issues concerning corporate and product/market strategy, operations, and organization. Mr. Robinson earned an A.B. from Williams College in 1959 and an M.B.A. from the Columbia University Graduate School of Business in 1964. He also served as a lieutenant in the U.S. Navy from 1959 through 1962.

WALTER E. SHILL is a consultant in McKinsey's Tokyo office where he has worked extensively with U.S. and European companies to develop strategies for entering and competing in the Japanese market. He has worked and studied in Japan since 1985 when he did research on the automotive industry. He has an M.B.A. and M.A. in East Asian Studies from the University of Virginia and an undergraduate engineering degree.

DOUGLAS D. WEINBERG was an international management specialist with McKinsey from 1987 to 1990. He has a B.A. from Princeton in political science. Currently, he is a student at the University of Chicago, where he is receiving a J.D. and an M.A. in international relations.

Acknowledgments

This book is about international collaboration. But it is itself the product of intensive collaboration by our partners in McKinsey offices around the world. Literally dozens of people have shared their time and experience to create a book that represents our collective best thinking on how to succeed in cross-border alliances and acquisitions.

The project began not as an effort to write a book, but as an attempt to go beyond well-trodden anecdotes to systematically understand what drives the cross-border strategies of the largest companies around the world. Thanks must go to Fred Gluck, Ken Ohmae, Herb Henzler, Ted Hall, and Christian Caspar for their comments and encouragement in the early phase of this work. Jim Isono and Doug Weinberg also played an important role in shaping our early efforts.

Along the way, we have benefited immensely from the reactions of our colleagues to early drafts of the chapters in this book. We leaned heavily on Eric Friberg, David Meen, and Dominique Turcq in Brussels, Ryuji Yasuda in Tokyo, Wilhelm Rall in Stuttgart, Roger Morrison in London, Lukas Mühlemann in Zurich, Tino Puri and Amir Mahini in New York, Roger Abravanel in Milan, and Ron Farmer in Toronto.

Outside McKinsey, Rosabeth Moss Kanter and Nan Stone at *Harvard Business Review* helped to challenge and clarify our thinking, as did Guy de Jonquieres at the *Financial Times*.

Special thanks to Stuart Flack, Alan Kantrow, and Bill Matassoni for their contributions to editing and producing this book.

We would also like to thank Ann Robertson, Kathy Knauss, and Betsy Green of McKinsey's Washington, D.C., office, who helped us in preparing data and analyses, and Ann Palms and Dianna Morrison, who typed the manuscript.

Finally, we want to thank Lisa Richardson and Jennifer Ernst, who supported us throughout this effort and who unselfishly sacrificed weekends so that we could complete this book.

J.B.
D.E.

Foreword

When I wrote *Triad Power* in 1985, I included charts that showed a proliferation of alliances, joint ventures, and other collaborative arrangements
in several industries; dozens of agreements had already been reached in
the auto and electronics industries. These charts looked like the webs of
an unartistic spider: company A linked to company B, B allied with C
and D, D in turn partnered with companies A and E.

Many of these partnerships were poorly conceived and executed. The
failures have led some business observers to conclude that alliances are
dangerous, and that they serve only as Trojan horses that let competitors,
namely Japanese companies, grab the home market or steal valuable technologies.

But cooperation continues. Moreover, as my McKinsey colleagues
point out in this book, cross-border collaborations have been successful
about half the time, and twice as frequently as domestic diversification
strategies. Alliances will continue to be an important strategic option
because the new reality of competing in global markets makes it necessary. Companies need to share costs, skills, and access to markets. Senior
managers will, therefore, need to learn to *design relationships* with foreign
companies.

Corporate relationship design violates much of what we think we
have learned about strategy; for example, that control is the key to success. In relationships, the key is common purpose and communication.
We have been taught to set specific goals, but in relationships goals
evolve. Common wisdom says cut your losses if a deal begins to sour,

but relationships often start slowly; happiness and success lie years, not months, in the future.

When potential partners discuss an alliance, they tend to think only in terms of equity shares, tax consequences, options to buy or sell, and legal issues. This is not design. The first step in the process is finding a partner who can contribute what you need and who needs what you can contribute. Let's say there is an American company that has a drug to combat high blood pressure, but no presence in Japan; and a Japanese drug company that sees a demand for a high blood pressure drug in the Japanese market, but has no such drug in its product line.

We have the basis for a partnership, but the relationship has yet to be designed. There are all kinds of possibilities. It can be a straightforward license agreement confined to a single product. It could encompass many products. The design might involve setting up a third company, with both partners contributing people and assets. Some time later, the partnership might extend into research and development. It might allow the Japanese company access to the U.S. market for its unique products. It might allow the U.S. company access to the rest of the Asian market, and so on. Areas of potential conflict (overlapping products, markets, etc.) must be designed *out* of the relationship, or the partners will have to give up all of the competitive interests to the new venture. But you can't have it both ways. So, too, with certain functions; don't expect salespeople to adopt a collaborative outlook toward your new partner.

There are many possible variations. As in genetic engineering, you need to design the concept of the future creature so that you know exactly which chromosomes to modify and manipulate. For any two partners, only a few basic types of corporate relationships are possible. This is as much a matter of intuition as it is analysis.

By far, the most important element is communication. The most carefully designed relationship will crumble without good, frequent communication. In many alliances, the two chief executive officers (CEOs) get together once a year to talk things over. This seems reasonable, but it is far too infrequent, especially in the early, fragile years of relationship. Even in a mature relationship, top management should meet at least four times a year to review what has been accomplished and the opportunities and obstacles that lie ahead. *Where* they meet is important as well. If it's an alliance between U.S. and Japanese companies, they should meet at least once in Japan, once in the United States, and once in Hawaii, the middle ground. This may seem like a lot and it is, but it's necessary.

Good management processes and systems alone do not ensure communication. Relationships take an enormous amount of time and attention from top managers. It is challenging to change the culture of existing companies to create a new one. Managers need to meet and speak often so that when there is a problem, and there are *always* problems, then the problem is shared. Without this steady, forthright communication one partner is bound to say to the other, "Why didn't you tell me of this? Why haven't you fixed it already?" Lack of communication can destroy even the most symbiotic corporate relationship.

Good relationships depend on communication and the ease of communication depends on similar values. The values of two partners must be in synch. This has nothing to do with geography. It has to do with the people at the top, and what their true interests and objectives are. In what order do they care about their people, customers, and financials? How do they think about the future, their ideals? I once observed two chairmen argue for hours about whether to leave a package when a customer wasn't home, yet they were of one mind on the importance of customer service. And sure enough, the alliance worked. On the other hand, I have advised against many potential relationships, even though the two parties originally wanted to go ahead, because this inner harmony was absent.

While both companies have to share strong values, paradoxically, they have to be able to adapt many tested approaches and tactics to the country and culture in which the alliance will operate. Mastering this flexibility is perhaps the most difficult skill of all.

Given all these pitfalls, it is easy to see why alliances have fared poorly. During the 1980s, many CEOs concluded that growth depended on finding partners. They also saw the scarcity of good ones. So they jumped into joint ventures and all kinds of deals without much chance of making them work. This time around they have to do better, and they will if they understand how to choose a partner and how to design a durable relationship that can grow.

KENICHI OHMAE

Contents

PART TWO

THE REGIONS:
JAPAN, UNITED STATES, EUROPE   107

1

The Death of the Predator

Joel Bleeke and David Ernst

For most global businesses, the days of flat-out, predatory competition are over. The traditional drive to pit one company against the rest of an industry, to pit supplier against supplier, distributor against distributor, on and on through every aspect of a business, no longer guarantees the lowest cost, best products or services, or highest profits for winners of this Darwinian game. In fact, the exact opposite is true. In businesses as diverse as pharmaceuticals, jet engines, banking, and computers, managers have learned that fighting long, head-to-head battles leaves their companies financially exhausted, intellectually depleted, and vulnerable to the next wave of competition and innovation.

In place of predation, many multinational companies are learning that they must collaborate to compete. This theme appears throughout the essays in this book. Multinationals can create highest value for customers and stakeholders by selectively sharing and trading control, costs, capital, access to markets, information, and technology with competitors and suppliers alike. Competition does not vanish. The computer and commercial aircraft markets are still brutally competitive.

Instead of competing blindly, companies should increasingly compete only in those precise areas where they have a durable advantage or where participation is necessary to preserve industry power or capture value. In packaged goods, that power comes from controlling distribution; in pharmaceuticals, having blockbuster drugs and access to doctors. Managers are beginning to see that many necessary elements of a global business are so costly (like R&D in semiconductors), so generic (like assembly), or so impenetrable (like some of the Asian markets) that it makes no sense to have a traditional competitive stance. The best approach is to find partners who already have the cash, scale, skills, or access you seek.

When a company reaches across borders, its ability and willingness to collaborate is the best predictor of success. The more equal the partnership, the brighter its future. This means that both partners must be strong financially and in the product or function that they bring to the venture. Of 49 alliances that we examined in detail, two thirds of those between equally matched strong partners succeeded, while about 60% of those involving unequal partners failed. So too with ownership. Fifty-fifty partnerships had the highest rate of success of any deal structure that we have examined.

The purpose of this book is to provide managers, regulators, and others with a resource that can be used to think about whether, how, and with whom to approach cross-border acquisitions and alliances—and to offer some insights into patterns followed by winners. It is a strategic and operational guide, not an academic work or a technical manual to financial, legal, or accounting issues of cross-border linkages, and it is based on hundreds of case studies from around the world, conducted by us and our colleagues in Asia, Europe, and America.

The need for better understanding of cross-border alliances and acquisitions is increasingly clear. Cross-border linkages are booming, driven by globalization, Europe 1992, the opening of Eastern European and Asian markets, and an increased need for foreign sales to cover the large fixed costs of playing in high-technology businesses. Go-it-alone strategies often take too long, cost too much, or fail to provide insider access to markets. Yet large numbers of strategic alliances and cross-border acquisitions are failing. When we examined the cross-border alliances and acquisitions of the largest 150 companies in the United States, Europe, and Japan, we found that only half of these linkages succeed. The average life expectancy for most alliances is approximately seven years. Common lessons from the wide experience of many companies in cross-border strategies are beginning to emerge.

We've organized this book into two Parts designed to capture the most important dimensions that must be explored in crafting cross-border strategy: "Manager's Choice," which maps the landscape, the strategic options, and the structures available; and "The Regions," which examines how these strategies and structures interact with the peculiarities of the Japanese, U.S., and European markets.

In "Manager's Choice," we first present (in Chapter 2) the results of our year-long study of the alliances of the largest companies in the United States, Europe, and Japan, pointing to some success factors that are common to all cross-border alliances. Ken Ohmae (Chapter 3) explains why entente goes against the grain with most managers, and offers his insight into the thinking that can help make them succeed. Ed Krubasik and Hartmut Lautenschlager (Chapter 4) summarize some common success factors for high-tech alliances. Varun Bery and Thomas Bowers (Chapter 5) use a case example to show how a flawed alliance can be reenergized. Finally, since M&A is usually a prime alternative to alliances, we summarize the results of a parallel study of what it takes to win in cross-border acquisitions—also based on the activity of the largest companies around the Triad (Chapter 6).

As you will see, there is a way to impose order on the seeming chaos of transnational strategy. For each situation, industry and player, there is a best structure and partner for a given set of goals. Defining those goals, choosing a partner and negotiating that structure takes a great deal more time, patience, and tolerance for ambiguity than many managers expect. Second-best solutions are often not solutions at all. Mergers do not substitute for alliances, or vice versa. In nearly all cases, these two approaches should be used in fundamentally different situations. Choosing the right path and understanding what it takes to stay on the path are requisite for success.

In "The Regions," we draw on the expertise of our partners around the world to clarify how cross-border strategy approaches need to be tuned to meet the unique situation of each region. The main challenge in cross-border linkages is to leverage effectively global scale or skills while becoming an insider in a specific geographic market. In achieving this, there are some requirements for success that are common across the regions. But the specific challenges differ in Japan, the United States, and Europe because of government regulations and industry structure. Equally important, players from each of the regions (and individual countries) bring different strengths, backgrounds, and objectives. Things change so much from country to country, there can be no single recipe for success. No individual author (or two authors) could realistically be expert in all regional twists across a broad range of countries.

Consequently, this book, culled from our writing and that of our colleagues in the *Harvard Business Review* and the *McKinsey Quarterly*, brings together McKinsey's current thinking on the subject of cross-border alliances and acquisitions as an exercise in global collaboration. The importance of regional factors is clear from the geographic diversity of authors—Herb Henzler, Ed Krubasik, and Hartmut Lautenschlager are German, Roger Abravanel is Italian, Magnus Nicolin is Swedish, Bart Robinson and Bill Hoover are Americans living in Scandinavia, Ken Ohmae is Japanese, and we are from different parts of America.

For many companies, penetrating Japan is the ultimate challenge. Kevin Jones and Walt Shill, in Chapters 8 and 9, write on the "mid-life crises" faced by many Western companies operating in Japan, and look at how successful Western companies are able to "ally for advantage." These chapters are based on personal experience and a data base of roughly 1,000 joint ventures and subsidiaries of foreign companies operating in Japan.

We next focus on the large and complex market of the United States. Although the success of Japanese companies in autos and consumer electronics is widely recognized, Japanese companies have often had poor performance in banking, telecom, electrical equipment, and home appliances. In Chapter 10, "Creating the Hyphenated Corporation," Henry DeNero points to six key gaps faced by Japanese multinational corporations in the United States and offers prescriptions for improvement. Looking at the experience of Scandinavian companies in the United States, Chapters 11 and 12 ("Winning Strategies in the Competitive Markets of the United States," and "Making Successful U.S. Acquisitions"), by consultants in our Stockholm and Copenhagen offices, illustrate the barriers faced by European companies in the United States and the approaches taken by winners.

The dramatic restructuring of Asia and Europe—both East and West—requires managers to build and use a new set of competitive skills. Many European and Asian companies that have previously relied on profitability from protected home markets will need to use alliances and acquisitions to respond to new threats from global or Pan-European competitors. The appropriate responses will differ depending on the nature of the business. Chapter 13, "Alliance versus Acquisition: Strategic Choices for European National Champions," by Roger Abravanel (of our Milan office) and David Ernst, illustrates the specific options that are available with a rich set of case studies. In Chapter 14, Joel Bleeke reviews the lessons of two decades of deregulation in the United States to chart a 10-year road map of the shifting competitive challenges that managers in newly opening markets will face during the first and second halves of the 1990s. In Chapter 15, Herb Henzler, who heads our German offices, argues that alliances enhance competition and can accelerate learning between companies.

In general, three themes weave through all the chapters in this book. First, as we have mentioned, companies are learning that they must collaborate to compete. This requires different measurements of "success" from those used for traditional competition. Second, alliances between companies that are potential competitors represent an arbitrage of skills, market access, and capital between the companies. Maintaining a fair balance in this arbitrage is essential for success. Finally, it is important for managers to develop a vision of international strategy and to see cross-border acquisitions and alliances as a flexible sequence of actions—not one-off deals driven by temporary competitive or financial benefit. The remainder of this chapter discusses each of these three themes in more detail.

COLLABORATE TO COMPETE

This book is based on the premise that cross-border strategies of the future will be increasingly founded more on collaboration than on pure competition, and that collaboration is best thought of as the negotiation and arbitrage of skills, access, and capital. A look at the top companies around the world illustrates the increasing importance of the collaborative mind-set. Motorola, Siemens, and Sony all have multiple alliances; so do General Motors, Daimler, and Toyota. In Japan alone, Royal Dutch Shell has more than 30 joint ventures; IBM more than 35.

Old measures such as financial hurdles and strategic goals only have meaning in the new context of collaboration. As markets become increasingly competitive, managers are beginning to measure success based on the scarcest resources—including skills and access, not only capital. In the global marketplace, maximizing the value of skills and access can often be achieved only if managers are willing to share ownership with and learn from companies much *different* from their own. Success increasingly comes in proportion to a company's willingness to accept differences.

Successful collaboration also requires flexibility. Most alliances that endure are redefined in terms of geographic or product scope. The success rate for alliances that have changed their scope over time is more than twice that of alliances where the scope has not evolved. Alliances with legal or financial structures that do not permit change are nearly certain to fail.

In this new world, even acquisitions—the old tools of the predator—take on a more collaborative color. Postmerger integration is no longer a process of forced conversion—particularly for cross-border mergers and acquisitions (M&A), where typically the acquirer cannot fold the acquiree into large existing operations. Any company worth acquiring across borders needs to offer something that can be preserved after the merger, especially if the acquirer has only modest presence in the target country. Sharing responsibility with managers of the acquired company does not come easily to people reared with the traditional competitive mind-set. Yet this is exactly what managers must do.

However, the notion of collaboration as competition applies differently depending on the nature of the linkage. In cross-border M&A, the main challenge is to transfer competence across borders, while selectively reaping synergies through consolidation. In our analysis of what it takes to succeed in cross-border M&A, we found that 11 of 14 successful cross-border M&A programs were characterized by a high degree of systems and skills transfer either to or from the target. The successful companies did this in several ways: They identified and retained key managers in the acquired company, used systems to monitor and improve performance, and used the merger or acquisition as an opportunity to take the "best of both" companies or even to aim at world-class performance levels. By contrast, skills transfer was insignificant in all of the 10 failed cross-border acquisitions programs.

ALLIANCES AS ARBITRAGE
(OR, SLEEPING WITH THE ENEMY)

If all markets were equally accessible, all management equally skilled, all information readily available, and all balance sheets equally solid, there would be little need for collaboration among competitors. But they are not, so companies increasingly benefit by trading these "chips" across borders.

The global arbitrage reflected in cross-border alliances and acquisitions takes place at a slower pace than in capital markets, but the mechanism is similar. Each player uses the quirks, irrational differences, and inefficiencies in the marketplace as well as each company's advantages to mutual benefit. This concept applies mostly to alliances, but cross-border acquisitions can also be viewed as an extreme example of arbitrage: all cash or shares from the buyer, for all the skills, products, and access of the other company.

Both big and small companies benefit from cross-border arbitrage. Already-global companies like Nestlé seek access to new markets for their products. Smaller companies use cross-border linkages to leverage specific product or distribution capabilities, while allying with global players who can cover the high fixed costs of worldwide marketing and sales or R&D in high-tech businesses. And companies of all sizes increasingly use alliances, joint ventures, and acquisitions to stake out future strategic options (the equivalent of financial futures and options in the world's capital markets).

To see how this complex arbitrage interaction works, let's simplify the world for a moment. Typically, companies from each of three regions of the Triad (Asia, Europe, and North America) bring a distinctive bargaining position. Japanese and other Pacific Rim companies offer cash and access to their markets in exchange for skills in manufacturing, R&D, or technology. Looking at the cross-border pattern of arbitrage over the past three years, for example, Japanese companies accounted for 363 acquisitions of high-technology companies in the United States—or two thirds of the foreign acquisitions of high-tech companies in the United States.

Since the U.S. market is relatively open, U.S. companies generally offer skills in exchange for cash. European companies offer access to their burgeoning markets in exchange for cash and skills; or trade cash and skills for access to Eastern European markets.

Many deals follow this stereotypical pattern. It is no surprise to see Amdahl and Fujitsu teaming up in computers; with Fujitsu trading capital and manufacturing skills for Amdahl's expertise in mainframe design and architecture. Or GE and SNECMA collaborating to form one of the world's leading players in jet engines. Specific deals may deviate, but all cross-border collaboration involves bargaining with the same three chips: skills, cash, and access. General Motors and Ford can offer access to the U.S. auto market to partners who can teach them the subtleties of team production or fill gaps in their product lines. So GM has partnered with Toyota, Isuzu, and Suzuki; and Ford, with Mazda.

Successful alliance partners follow several patterns in handling the inherent tensions of arbitraging with potential competitors. To begin with, they approach the negotiation phase with a win–win situation. As one executive said, "Do not sit down to negotiate a deal—build links between the companies."

Successful partners also build in conflict-resolution mechanisms such as powerful boards of directors (for joint ventures), and frequent communication between top management of the parent companies and the alliance. The CEOs of the parent companies need to be absolutely clear on where cooperation is expected—and where the "old rules" of competition will apply.

In approaching alliances as arbitrage, managers should recognize that the value of "chips" is likely to change over time. The key is to maximize your bargaining power—that is, the value of your company's contribution to the alliance—while also being ready to renegotiate the alliance as necessary. Some of the best alliances have had built-in timetables for reassessing partner contributions *and* clear rules for valuing the contributions going forward.

CROSS-BORDER ALLIANCES AND ACQUISITIONS AS A SEQUENCE OF ACTIONS

Beyond the themes of collaboration and arbitrage involved in individual deals, a third thread woven throughout this book is that cross-border alliances and acquisitions need to be viewed as a *sequence* of actions in the context of overall international strategy—not as one-off transactions. Companies that take a purely financial, deal-driven approach to cross-border alliances and acquisitions usually wind up in trouble.

Looking at cross-border M&A, the most successful companies make a series of acquisitions that build presence in core businesses over time in the target country. One consumer goods company, for example, made an "anchor" acquisition of a leading brand to establish a solid presence in an important European market, then used its enhanced distribution clout to ensure the acceptance of several brands that were subsequently acquired.

In our study of the cross-border acquisition programs of the largest Triad companies, successful acquirers had nearly twice the average and median number of purchases as unsuccessful companies. Through initial acquisitions, the acquirer refines M&A skills and becomes more comfortable with, and proficient at, using M&A for international expansion. And by completing a sequence of transactions, particularly in the same geography, it is possible to gain economies through integrating operations and eliminating overlapping functions.

It is important to think about cross-border alliances, as well as acquisitions, as a part of a sequence of actions. Most alliances evolve over time, so the initial charter and contract often are not meaningful within a few years. Since trouble is the rule, not the exception, and since two thirds of all cross-border alliances run into management trouble during the first few years, alliances require a willingness by partners to rethink their situation on a constant basis—and renegotiate as necessary.

Alliances should usually be considered as an intermediate strategic device that needs other transactions surrounding it. Approximately half of all cross-border alliances terminate within seven years, so it is critical that managers have a point of view early on "what's next?"

Most terminating alliances are purchased by one of the partners, and termination need not mean failure. But the high rate of termination does suggest that both parties should think hard early on about likely roles as a buyer or seller—the probabilities are high that alliance partners will eventually be one or the other.

The companies that can bring the largest short-term synergies to an alliance are often those companies that will most likely be direct competitors in the long-term. So if the desired sequence of management action does not include selling the business, a different, more complementary partner may need to be found at the offset. Understanding the probable sequence of transactions is therefore important in selecting even early alliance or acquisition partners. As our colleagues in Japan remind us, nothing is worse in cross-border alliances or acquisitions than to have "two partners in the same bed with different dreams."

PART
ONE

MANAGER'S
CHOICE

Managers looking to enter foreign markets appear to have a bounty of choices. They can go it alone. They can use licensing agreements, mergers, acquisitions, or some type of strategic alliance. In practice, however, strategic reality and corporate culture seem to conspire to close those options down fast. Going it alone can be costly and time consuming. Licensing is only a short-term fix. Merger and acquisition (M&A) is often prohibited by antitrust laws or barriers to foreign ownership. The collaborative approach necessary for alliances is difficult to master and cuts against the cultural grain of many companies. The manager's choice becomes no choice at all.

There is a way out of this dilemma. Managers can overcome some of these strategic and cultural constraints by consciously adopting new expectations about control, organization, flexibility, and time frames for their forays overseas. Implicit in each vehicle—go it alone, licensing, M&A, or alliances—is a unique set of expectations that must be adopted to give the vehicle its best chance of success. These new expectations come together in a characteristic mind-set that underpins each vehicle. Managers can

11

reopen their options by adopting new mind-sets. This can allow aggressive cultures to cooperate and cooperative cultures to be aggressive. It is the only way into many of the world's most important markets.

Part One helps managers choose and understand the appropriate mind-set for their strategic situation, the company's culture, and—if partners are required—their partner's culture. These choices of mind-set are the most important choices that managers make. Mismatching mind-sets almost assures failure. We focus on two mind-sets—alliance and acquisition—because they are the most complex and difficult for most companies to master.

Given this difficulty and complexity, some companies have mistakenly fixated on only one mind-set for all their cross-border efforts. One U.S. machinery company "only will do a joint venture if we can't do an acquisition." A European electronics company has pursued a long string of joint venture partners over the past few years, even though most of these deals have now failed. The truth is that no single strategy vehicle or mind-set can ensure success over time. Everything is tailored to the specific situation. This is the essence of the choice facing managers.

Heineken, the world's second largest beer company, shows the tailored approach in action. With product sales in 150 countries, Heineken produces and markets beer using a broad range of approaches: joint ventures and partnerships, wholly owned breweries, licenses to third parties, and distribution agreements. Heineken's web of cross-border alliances and acquisitions is not unusual. Other leading global companies, such as Asea Brown Boveri, Corning Glass, and Fujitsu, have also used both cross-border alliances and acquisitions extensively in building their position. In fact, most successful global companies use a portfolio of cross-border vehicles and mind-sets, tailored to strategic objectives and to the requirements of each geographic market.

UNDERSTANDING CULTURE

Mind-sets can help managers reopen their choices, but culture and strategy still determine much of what is possible and desirable. To understand the role that culture plays in cross-border alliances and acquisitions, it is useful to think of four types of companies:

- *Type 1:* Can transfer skills but not receive them. This type of corporation has strong, transferable skills, systems, and culture.

Management style is usually top-down. These companies are "universal donors"—they make good acquirers but are likely to encounter difficulties in their alliances when flexibility is needed.

- *Type 2:* Can transfer or receive skills. This type of organization is better able to work with partners because of an open management structure and flexible systems. These companies excel at collaboration, internally and externally. Examples include Motorola and Corning.

- *Type 3:* Can neither transfer nor receive skills. These companies have unique cultures and strong internal networks. However, their distinctive cultures often make it difficult to execute either acquisitions or alliances because of a "we–they" mentality. Examples include many service and professional firms.

- *Type 4:* Can receive but not transfer skills. These companies are good at learning through alliances but are not able to integrate foreign staff into the organizational structure. Because of limited foreign exposure, they do not have the capability to actively manage the staff of acquired firms to add value. Thus alliances are better suited than acquisitions to these companies. Many Japanese companies would fit into this category.

These culture types are not the last word on what a company is or is not capable of achieving. Many companies, like Heineken, have been able to use a range of cross-border vehicles, supported by multiple mind-sets. But if a company has a single constraining culture, managers may need to focus first on the broadening of mind-set before a full range of vehicles will have a reasonable chance of success. Alliances are appropriate in very different situations from acquisitions, so flexibility in mind-set and match between mindset and vehicle becomes essential.

CHOOSING VEHICLES

Strategic issues also define what choices are attractive in specific situations. Where the goal is to reach out into uncharted territory, alliances have a much higher success rate than acquisitions. As noted in Chapter 2, over 60% of alliances involving partners in nonoverlapping geographic markets succeed, while only 8% of cross-border acquisitions in nonoverlapping geographic markets succeed.

In contrast, when geographies are overlapping between the partners, cross-border acquisitions have a higher success rate than alliances. "Succeeding in Cross-Border Mergers and Acquisitions" (Chapter 6) clearly shows the importance of building on local presence.

The reason for this difference between alliances and acquisitions is straightforward. The potential for merger synergies is greatest where both partners have significant overlapping geographic positions. Our experience suggests that the important sources of synergies in cross-border M&A are consolidation on a national basis, for example, eliminating redundant headquarters staff or improving sales force coverage and skills transfers across borders. By contrast, strong overlapping geographic markets frequently suggest trouble for alliances: The overlap creates the potential for conflict and an unstable alliance position.

The different requirements for success in cross-border alliances versus acquisitions suggest that it is important for managers to differentiate between "acquisition thinking" and "alliance thinking." Using "acquisition thinking" for cross-border alliances, for example, is nearly certain to lead to failure—the keys to success in alliances are complementary activities and well-matched functional strengths, while the keys to success in acquisitions are often overlapping activities within countries and skills transfers between countries. Similarly, companies that have become accustomed to alliances often fail in their cross-border acquisitions in part because their "alliance thinking" does not put adequate emphasis on the disciplines required for supportive integration and skills transfer. Successful Japanese alliance partners, for example, have been notably unsuccessful in many of their cross-border acquisitions.

This distinction between alliances and acquisitions should not imply that acquirers can avoid the collaborative mind-set. Quite the contrary. Unlike many domestic acquisitions, cross-border acquisitions often offer limited opportunities to reduce redundant costs. Much of their value is based, therefore, on the sharing of skills, products, and customers across national borders.

CHOOSING PARTNERS

The difference between acquisition and alliance thinking is particularly clear in choosing partners. Alliance partners should be complementary in the products, geographic presence or functional skills that they bring to the venture. In Chapter 4, Edward Krubasik and Hartmut

Lautenschlager point to some important areas for complementarity between technology partners: product lines that cover key regions and segments, sales coverage of regions and channels, and innovation potential. Managers assessing alliance partners need to ask additional questions: Are potential partners likely to be direct competitors? How will the relative bargaining power of alliance partners change over time?

The lowest success rate for alliances is when two partners bring competing products to the same shared distribution channel. Yet this is exactly the situation that often leads to success in acquisitions, where one of the keys is to identify geographic, functional, or product overlaps among partners to ensure that acquisition premiums can be recovered.

The importance of this distinction between complementary partners and overlapping partners was demonstrated recently by a consumer financial services company that was considering distribution of its product using cross-border alliances through another consumer financial services firm's distribution channels. Given the direct overlap between product lines and potential future competition between the partners, selecting a partner from an industry away from financial services such as retailing where the potential for direct competition was less may have offered greater long-term partnership rewards. Yet choosing a partner with direct overlap would have been ideal if this were an acquisition instead of an alliance.

In addition to these differences, partners for alliances and acquisitions also need to be screened along several common dimensions. First, what strengths do potential partners bring—in terms of operating performance and geographic presence? Second, how compatible are potential partners? An otherwise attractive alliance between two large automotive components manufacturers failed because "one company focused on making components, while the other focused on making money."

In choosing partners, it is important that each partner be strong in the functions it brings to the partnership. Many of the cross-border alliances developing today are combinations among the weak in an attempt to become strong. This is particularly true in industries such as international airlines where nearly 100 strategic alliances and cross-border marketing managements are in place. The chapters in Part One suggest that companies forming alliances and acquisitions meet with success at least two thirds of the time when the acquisition targets or alliance partners have above-average return on equity, return on assets, and functional strengths. This compares with roughly a 60% failure rate for linkages with weak partners.

NO CHOICE IS FOREVER

The concept of "choosing" between alliances and acquisitions, or between alternative forms of alliance, needs to be viewed not as a one-time event but as a continuing process. Managers have significant choices to make as alliances evolve. These choices can lead down entirely different strategic paths. In the case discussed by Varun Bery and Thomas A. Bowers in Chapter 5, a U.S. and a Japanese company reassessed their failing alliance and decided to restructure it as a much broader 50-50 joint venture. In a different outcome, Crédit Suisse bought out its joint venture with First Boston to consolidate its control over the business. Sandoz and Bayer have recently dissolved their alliance in Japan to pursue strategies of independent growth.

The need to stay flexible is particularly important given the reality that most terminating alliances eventually end in acquisition. The partner who is an ideal alliance partner will seldom be an ideal acquisition candidate. If acquisition becomes the endpoint for the alliance, therefore, it is particularly important during the alliance to ensure both collaboration and the foundation for eventual integration.

2

The Way to Win in Cross-Border Alliances

Joel Bleeke and David Ernst

In the face of newly opening markets, intensified competition, and the need for increased scale, many chief executive officers (CEOs) have put the formation of cross-border alliances on their agendas for the 1990s. To international managers, the strategic benefits are compelling: Alliances are an expedient way to crack new markets, to gain skills, technology, or products, and to share fixed costs and resources. Yet, a lot of the war stories suggest that alliances are all but doomed to failure, and CEOs setting up cross-border alliances or dealing with early problems find little is systematically known about how to make alliances succeed.

To better understand cross-border alliances and what it takes to make them work, we examined the partnerships of 150 top companies ranked by market value (50 each from the United States, Europe, and Japan). The 49 strategic alliances that we studied in detail varied widely in size, location, industry, and structure. Some were established to speed entry into a new market, others to develop and commercialize new products; still others to gain skills or share costs.

Our analysis found that although cross-border alliances pose many challenges, they are in fact viable vehicles for international strategy. While two thirds of cross-border alliances run into serious managerial or financial trouble within the first two years, many overcome their problems. Of the 49 we analyzed, 51% were successful for both partners. Only 33% resulted in failure for both.

How can managers maximize their chances of success in these ventures? What wisdom can be derived from the experiences to date? Here are a few of our findings:

- Arguments over whether cross-border alliances or cross-border acquisitions are superior are beside the point; both have roughly a 50% rate of success. But acquisitions work well for core businesses and existing geographic areas, while alliances are more effective for edging into related businesses or new geographic markets.

- Alliances between strong and weak companies rarely work. They do not provide the missing skills needed for growth, and they lead to mediocre performance.

- The hallmark of successful alliances that endure is their ability to evolve beyond initial expectations and objectives. This requires autonomy for the venture and flexibility on the part of the parents.

- Alliances with an even split of financial ownership are more likely to succeed than those in which one partner holds a majority interest. What matters is clear management control, not financial ownership.

- More than 75% of the alliances that terminated ended with an acquisition by one of the parents.

All of these findings have implications for creating and managing successful cross-border alliances.

RELATED BUSINESSES,
NEW GEOGRAPHIC MARKETS

Both cross-border alliances and cross-border acquisitions are good vehicles for international strategy and have similar success rates (51% and 57% respectively). But that doesn't mean they are interchangeable. When used to expand core businesses, both cross-border alliances and acquisitions work well. But for expanding existing businesses into new geographic regions or for edging out into new businesses, cross-border alliances work better.

When moving into new geographic markets, managers should try to structure alliances to capitalize on the distinctive geographic positions of the partners. Some 62% of the alliances that involved partners with different geographic strengths succeeded (see Exhibit 2.1). This is very different from the finding for cross-border acquisitions: The success rate was just 8% when the acquirer and the target company did not have significant overlapping presences in the same geographic markets.

Crédit Suisse-First Boston, a joint venture formed in 1978 to expand both companies' positions in the Eurobond market, shows the benefits of using alliances to leverage complementary geographic strengths. First Boston provided access to U.S. corporate issuers of bonds and possessed the skills for structuring new financial vehicles like convertible Eurobonds. Crédit Suisse provided the capability to place issues with investors in Europe. This combination allowed the joint venture to assume a leading role in the rapidly growing Eurobond markets in the early 1980s. (The joint venture was bought out by Crédit Suisse in 1988 after First Boston began to experience financial problems, which were partly due to increasing competitiveness in the Eurobond markets.)

To build the position of core businesses in existing geographic markets, managers should use acquisitions instead of alliances. For acquisitions focused on existing markets, the success rate was 94%. For alliances in which partners had overlapping geographic positions, it was 25%. When both partners have a presence in the same geographic markets, alliances often lead to competitive conflicts. In one cross-border venture to manufacture and sell telecommunications products in the United States, one of the parents continued to sell a competing product line through a separate sales force. In theory, the two sales forces were targeting different customer segments, but because they were poorly coordinated, they ended up competing against each other. Within two years, the venture was acquired by one of the parents, and the sales forces were combined.

In the few instances in which companies have tried to use acquisitions instead of alliances to diversify abroad, they have had trouble withstanding the financial and operational strain. Not surprisingly, most companies pass up the challenge of making an acquisition to enter a new business overseas. Of the 28 cross-border acquisition programs in our study, 22 were focused on geographic expansion of core businesses; in 13 of the 16 successful programs, the acquirer already had a substantial presence in the target countries and was expanding a core business.

Overlap Helps Mergers and Acquisitions . . .

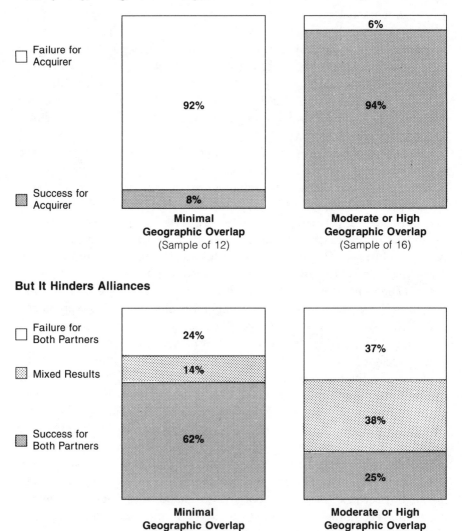

But It Hinders Alliances

Exhibit 2.1 Managers should consider geographic overlap when choosing between crossborder M&A alliances.

Managers should avoid acquisitions outside the core business, especially in new geographic markets, because they are extremely challenging and often fail. Take, for example, the British service company that acquired a Canadian electronics manufacturer to try to become a global player in the office automation industry. The Canadian company, a large second-tier player, was under intense competitive pressure: Demand was soft, prices were falling, and competitors were merging to gain economies of scale. Under the new parent, the Canadian company took several steps, including rationalizing manufacturing operations to cut costs and spinning off a small subsidiary. But the U.K. company, with little direct experience in the North American market, was unable to make the needed improvements in distribution and sales, which had been weak before the merger. The new parent also had no manufacturing facilities in North America and so was unable to expand volume to drive down costs. Finally, after absorbing five years of operating losses and losing a considerable amount of senior management's time, the parent decided to divest the business at a fraction of its purchase price.

Unlike cross-border acquisitions, cross-border alliances can work well for moving into new or related businesses. Corning's well-publicized joint venture with Siemens to produce fiber-optic cable is an example of a successful move into a related business. The Siecor joint venture, started in 1977, succeeded for many reasons. For one thing, the parents brought complementary skills and capabilities. Corning had developed and patented processes to manufacture high-quality optical fibers. Siemens had capital, scale, and worldwide distribution of telecommunications cable. Siemens also brought the manufacturing technology and equipment to produce cable from fiber. The alliance had distinct advantages over an acquisition. It allowed the creation of an enterprise focused on commercializing fiber-optic cable, and it relieved some of the financial pressure by dividing the investment. Moreover, neither company had to recoup an acquisition premium.

EQUAL STRENGTH

It stands to reason that alliances between two strong partners are a safer bet than alliances between two weak partners. But many strong companies actually seek smaller or weaker companies to partner with in order to control the venture. Weaker companies often seek a strong partner to get them out of trouble or to build their skills. Our analysis suggests that these strategies do not work well because the "weak link" becomes a drag on the venture's competitiveness and causes friction between the parents. Alliances in which one partner is consistently strong in the functions it brings to the venture while the other is not strong succeeded only one third of the time. Similarly, alliances between two financially strong performers or between a strong and an average performer (based on industry averages for return on equity and return on assets in the five years preceding the alliance) had a success rate of 67% versus 39% for alliances involving two weaker players.

When one partner is weak, managing the alliance seems to be too great a distraction from improvements needed in other parts of the business. When unbalanced partnerships do succeed, it is usually because the strong partner brings the capability that is crucial to the venture; it pulls the weaker partner along for a while before acquiring it or finding another partner.

One U.S. pharmaceutical company underestimated the importance of having a strong joint venture partner when it paired with a relatively weak Japanese player. The U.S. company had a large share in its domestic market, a good portfolio of drugs, and strong research and development (R&D) capabilities. Seeking to expand its position in Japan, it partnered with a second-tier company with a large sales force rather than one of the leading Japanese pharmaceutical companies, which might have had products that competed more directly.

The joint venture failed for several reasons. First, the sales force of the Japanese company was poorly managed and was unable to meet its targets for distributing the drugs of the Western partners. Second, over time, the Japanese partner was simply unable to push drugs that had been successful in other markets through Japan's development and approval process. It did not have insider contacts to guide the approval process, and it lacked the management resources and the capital to invest in commercialization. Even the excellent products and top-tier position of the Western partner could not compensate for its partner's shortcomings.

Most alliances formed chiefly to build the skills of a weaker partner meet with failure or mixed results. Only when the alliance has a solid business rationale other than self-improvement and a viable combined business system that draws on strengths from each partner can skills be transferred successfully.

Consider a joint venture between a weak European auto company seeking to improve its manufacturing effectiveness and a strong Japanese auto manufacturer. The Japanese manufacturer, which wanted

---

How We Defined Success

To be considered successful, an alliance had to pass two tests: both partners achieved their ingoing strategic objectives and both recovered their financial costs of capital. Progress on the strategic objectives was based on market share, sales volume, new product development, or other criteria specific to the alliance. Our evaluation of financial and strategic success relied heavily on access to unpublished financial results and on interviews with company insiders and industry experts, as well as public information.

For acquisition programs exceeding 20% of the acquirer's market value, we assessed whether the acquirer was able to maintain or improve its return on equity and return on assets. For smaller acquisition programs, we conducted interviews and assessed financial results to determine whether the return equaled or exceeded the companies' cost of capital.

We should note that these financial criteria for success are distinctly American. Most Japanese and many European companies have longer term, less financially oriented means for judging their purchases.

---

to produce a new compact car for the European market, was to provide design, body parts, and manufacturing technology—areas in which it excelled. The European partner was to provide capacity in an existing auto plant and local management. The European company was, however, financially strained and distracted by problems in its other car lines, and management was unable to give the new venture the time and energy it required. The venture ultimately failed, selling only 20% as many cars as projected.

Although skills transfer should not be the primary purpose of a joint venture, it often occurs naturally, and if the partners both bring specific strengths, both will benefit. In the GM-Suzuki joint venture in Canada, for example, both parents have contributed and gained. The alliance, CAMI Automotive, Inc., was formed to manufacture low-end cars for the U.S. market. The plant, run by Suzuki management, produces the Geo Metro/ Suzuki Swift, the smallest, highest gas-mileage GM car sold in North America, as well as the Geo Tracker/Suzuki Sidekick sport utility vehicle. Through CAMI, Suzuki has gained access to GM's dealer network and an expanded market for parts and components. GM avoided the cost of developing low-end cars and obtained models it needed to help revitalize the lower end of the Chevrolet product line and to improve GM's average fuel economy rating. And the CAMI factory, which promises to be one of the most productive plants in North America once it reaches full capacity, has been a test bed for GM to learn how Japanese carmakers use work teams, run flexible assembly lines, and manage quality control.

While it is important that partners have complementary skills and capabilities, an even balance of strength is also crucial. This is especially true in product-for-market swaps. When one partner brings product or technology and the other brings access to desirable markets, there is often a certain amount of suspicion. Each partner fears that the other will try to usurp its proprietary advantage. Such fears are hardly unwarranted, since many prospective partners are competitors in some business arenas to begin with. A European chemical company formed a venture with a large Japanese company to produce and market its product to food manufacturers in Japan in the early 1980s. Within less than 10 years, the Japanese partner had absorbed the production process technology and become its partner's biggest threat in the United States and Europe.

While it is effective for partners to bring complementary skills to the table—strong R&D paired with well-developed manufacturing processes, innovative products paired with solid and established distribution and sales capabilities—the strongest alliances exist when each partner brings both products and an established market presence in different geographic markets. The Toshiba-Motorola alliance is an example of getting the balance right: Toshiba brought expertise in Dynamic Random Access Memories (DRAMs) and access to Japan; Motorola brought expertise in microprocessors and access to the U.S. market. These alliances seem to have a more stable balance of power because neither partner relies solely on the other for technical expertise, products, or market entry. Fully 75% of the alliances serving at least two major markets— Europe, Japan, or the United States—succeeded. Only 43% succeeded when the venture focused on a single market—when, for example, one company traded products for its partner's access to customers.

AUTONOMY AND FLEXIBILITY

The flexibility to evolve is a hallmark of successful alliances. Flexibility allows joint ventures to overcome problems and to adapt to changes over time. If they are to evolve, alliances also need the capacity to resolve conflicts. A partnership is best able to resolve or avoid conflicts when it has its own management team and a strong board with operational decision-making authority.

Flexibility is important because it is inevitable that the objectives, resources, and relative power of the parents will gradually change. Even the most astute parent companies cannot anticipate these trends and other events that will occur during the life of the alliance. Somewhere along the line, joint ventures are likely to find that their markets are shifting, new technologies are emerging, or customers' needs are changing. Also, the strategies, skills, and resources of the parents may change. And once alliances are up and running, they often discover new opportunities like a new market for their products or a new way to leverage their expertise.

Flexibility is also needed to overcome problems, which many alliances encounter in one form or another early on. Some 67% of the alliances in our sample ran into trouble in the first two years, and those that had the flexibility to evolve were better able to recover. Many joint ventures have trouble meeting their initial goals, often because the expectations or projections at the outset were overly optimistic. An R&D venture to develop a new plastics-recycling process was unable to meet cost targets because the partners had seriously underestimated the investments required to commercialize the new technology. And the president of an automotive joint venture reflected on his similar experience this way: "If I were doing it over again, I'd insist on a more rigorous feasibility study. It is easy to be optimistic. Because of the reputation and experience of our parent companies, we figured we could get our automotive system specified in customers' cars rapidly. Not so. In the eyes of the customer, we were a new supplier of a safety-critical product and had to undergo seven or eight stringent engineering tests and validation steps with improvements and corrective action at each step. This took a minimum of two years with each customer. That's not to mention the fact that the investment levels were much higher than we expected."

The link between flexibility and success is strong. Nearly 40% of the alliances in our sample gradually broadened the scope of their initial charter. Some expanded into new geographic or product markets, others required major investments. Of those alliances that had evolved, 79% were successful and 89% are ongoing. In contrast, of the alliances whose scope remained unchanged, only 33% were successful and more than half have terminated.

The CFM International venture created by GE and Snecma in 1974 to collaborate on the development of jet engines is among those that evolved and flourished. The two companies initially focused on jointly developing and manufacturing the CFM56 engine, with 20,000 to 30,000 pounds of thrust. Subsequently, the two partners expanded their collaboration to spread the costs of developing a wider range of engines, including the larger CF6 series of engines. By 1991, the alliance had booked orders and commitments for more than 10,000 engines worth about $39 billion.

Similarly, GMF Robotics was set up in 1982 by GM and Fanuc to develop robotics for the auto industry. The venture has gradually broadened its focus and now sells robotics to nonautomotive customers in industries like food processing and computer manufacturing. And Toshiba and Motorola, building on an existing relationship, agreed in 1986 to create a joint venture to manufacture microprocessors and memory chips in Japan, and they continue to discuss other ways of expanding on their initial agreement.

Unlike the GM-Snecma, GM-Fanuc, and Toshiba-Motorola alliances, one joint venture between a U.S. and a foreign company to serve the minicomputer market in the United States did not deviate from its original plan and suffered because of it. The joint venture was conceived largely as a sales organization to sell to the U.S. market minicomputers designed and manufactured by the parent companies. The sales-oriented joint venture quickly fell behind in adapting products for the rapidly changing needs of banking customers in the United States. Friction quickly developed between the partners, and ultimately, the venture floundered and was bought out. In hindsight, the joint venture might have recovered had its scope been expanded to include product development, manufacturing, and sales for a broader range of minicomputer products the parents offered.

Negotiating every aspect of the alliance in excruciating detail and spelling out the rules in legal documents will not guarantee healthy evolution. But there are ways to build in flexibility, namely by giving the alliance a strong president, a full business system of its own (R&D, manufacturing, marketing, sales, and distribution), complete decision-making power on operating issues, a powerful board, and a sense of identity. As the president of a successful U.S.-based joint venture put it, "The best way for parents to make a joint venture work is to give it the resources it needs, put someone they trust in charge, and leave him or her alone to do the job."

Parent companies typically retain responsibility for decisions about equity financing and overall governance structure, but operating decisions are best made by managers whose sole focus is the joint venture. This kind of hands-off approach requires that the parent companies structure and perceive the alliance as an entity in and of itself and not as part of either ongoing business. Ensuring that the alliance does not need to depend on either parent for basic operating functions reinforces the separateness and also simplifies coordination of those activities.

Giving the alliance strong leadership further encourages autonomy. Managers of successful alliances embrace their authority and build employee loyalty to the joint venture rather than to the parent companies. Such loyalty is not always easy to cultivate in light of the fact that key employees usually are drawn from the parent companies and are likely to return there. But strong leaders can win the support they need to operate as a freestanding business. Early on in the Toshiba-Motorola alliance, for example, engineers were reluctant to share semiconductor production technology with people who just months before had been their competitors. When senior management realized what was going on, it met with mid-level managers to convince them that the relationship was good for both parent companies overall, even though each specific area might not be benefiting.

Establishing a high-powered board is important. Sometimes alliances slip from top management's attention, which may be understandable since they are not really part of the parent companies' everyday operations. In other cases, lack of a strong board for the venture creates delays as key decisions are passed up and down the parent organizations' chains of command.

There are some exceptions to the rule about managerial autonomy. When joint ventures are formed to share R&D costs, for instance, parents often need to stay closely involved to ensure that the R&D program fits with their customer needs and manufacturing capabilities. And when alliances are formed to coordinate activities performed by the partners at different stages in the value chain, the coordination may best be done directly between the parents without creating a separate joint venture organization. In these cases, a different rule applies: the responsibilities of each party must be clearly defined.

In the 50-50 venture between Petroleos de Venezuela (PDVSA) and Veba Oil, for example, PDVSA provided 50% of the crude oil supply, while Veba provided the other 50% and took clear responsibility for downstream refining and marketing. In Boeing's partnership with Fuji, Mitsubishi, Kawasaki, and Aeritalia to produce the Boeing 767, a separate joint venture entity was not created, and Boeing held overall control for coordination and management. These alliances would not be viable businesses without critical functions of the parents.

FIFTY-FIFTY OWNERSHIP

In structuring alliances, the issue of financial ownership should be separated from managerial control. In contrast to the conventional wisdom
that 50-50 ownership spells failure because of stalled decision making,
alliances with an even split of financial ownership are actually more
likely to succeed than those in which one partner holds a majority interest (see Exhibit 2.2). When one parent has a majority stake, it tends to
dominate decision making and put its own interests above those of its
partner, or for that matter, of the joint venture itself. Both partners tend
to be worse off as a consequence.

The autonomy and flexibility most alliances need are easiest to achieve
when neither parent's investment outweighs the other's. Our evidence
shows that joint ventures with an even split of ownership have a higher
success rate (60%) than those in which one partner holds a majority stake
(31%). For one thing, when ownership is even, it is more likely that the
joint venture will be set up as a separate entity with its own strong management. But 50-50 ownership is important for another reason: It builds
trust by ensuring that each partner is concerned about the other's success,
or in the words of Stephen Levy, former head of Japan operations and a
board member at Motorola, "Each partner has a stake in *mutual* success."

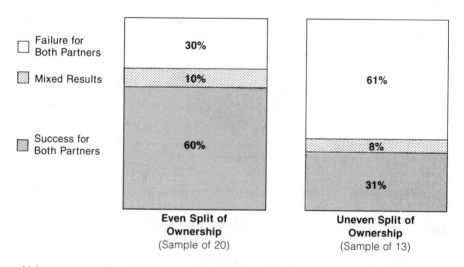

	Even Split of Ownership (Sample of 20)	Uneven Split of Ownership (Sample of 13)
Failure for Both Partners	30%	61%
Mixed Results	10%	8%
Success for Both Partners	60%	31%

(Joint ventures only; excludes parent-to-parent equity stakes and nonequity alliances.)

Exhibit 2.2   Fifty-fifty alliances are more likely to succeed.

When ownership is uneven, one parent typically exercises control, sometimes in ways that are not in the minority partner's interests. One majority partner shifted excess employees to the venture. When the bloated payroll contributed to cash flow problems, the partners had a showdown. Eventually, the minority partner gained more say in operating decisions, but only after threatening to withdraw from the venture.

Alliances that are not 50-50 can, of course, succeed. One way to boost the odds of success is to realize that the alliance is a win-win situation rather than a zero-sum game. In the 49 alliances we analyzed closely, only 3 resulted in success for one partner and failure for the other. In "unfair" alliances, both partners typically fail since the poorly compensated partner has little incentive to follow through on commitments. Indeed, it is particularly important to protect the interests of a minority partner. This is exactly the philosophy of the quickly expanding TRW-Koyo Steering Systems joint venture, which was established to serve Japanese transplant automakers in the United States. Although TRW owned 51%, Arvind Korde, president of TRW-Koyo Steering Systems, treated it as if it were a 50-50 partnership. In Korde's words, the earmark of the venture's success was that, "At times, both TRW and Koyo thought I was too sensitive to the other partner."

TERMINATION BY ACQUISITION

Most alliances terminate, even successful ones. We found that, of the ventures that terminated, more than 75% were acquired by one of the partners. Yet companies don't always prepare for the eventual ending of their alliances, and some are caught off guard when the other partner is in a better position to buy it. If the seller didn't anticipate such an outcome, the acquisition can compromise its long-term strategic interests. Says the CEO of a global communications company, "One of the most important elements of global strategy is the balance between intermediate-term and long-term initiatives. Joint ventures may fill intermediate-term needs but may also mortgage the long-term global future."

Alliances often terminate after meeting the partners' goals. Two Western-Japanese alliances—Sandoz-Sankyo and Bayer-Takeda—demonstrate the point that termination is not equivalent to failure. Both Sandoz and Bayer left their ventures after having achieved their goal of establishing independent businesses in Japan; both are ranked among the top 25 players in the Japanese pharmaceutical industry. Their Japanese partners, both of which are among the largest Japanese players, also benefited by gaining access to strong-selling drugs their Western partners had developed.

By 1990, when Sandoz and Sankyo agreed to dissolve their alliance, Sankyo was selling 22 Sandoz drugs, which took in ¥82 billion in revenues. Sandoz and Sankyo are continuing to cooperate with each other and are planning a phased withdrawal over four years of five key Sandoz drugs from Sankyo's sales channels. Sankyo is also helping Sandoz build its marketing force by sending personnel to Sandoz's Japan operations.

Similarly, Bayer, which owns 75.6% of Bayer Yakuhin, a joint venture in which Takeda owns 14.6% and Yoshitomi Pharmaceuticals owns 9.8%, recently dissolved its 80-year sales agreement with Takeda in order to sell Bayer-brand pharmaceuticals through its own channels. Takeda had previously sold an estimated ¥60 billion worth of Bayer drugs annually on a consignment basis.

Some joint ventures end less amicably and fairly. Shifts in the parents' geographic position, functional strengths, and technological position can make one parent emerge as the "natural buyer" (see Exhibit 2.3). By the time that happens, it may be too late for the seller to protect its interests. Take, for instance, the alliance between two specialty chemical companies. One was to provide product formulas and manufacturing know-how; the other was to provide marketing and distribution to its existing industrial customers. Over a 10-year period, though, the "sales" partner was able to improve on the basic process technology to tailor products to its customers. Then in a clear position of strength, since its people had the customer relationships and knew the technology, it offered to buy out the business. The "technology" partner, faced with the threat that its partner would go it alone anyway if it refused to sell, divested its share. The seller made a handsome profit but ended up with zero position in a major market and little chance of reentering in the future.

Often the natural buyer is the company that is most willing to invest to build the joint venture. Here companies that have deep pockets and look to strategic results, not financial returns, as the measure of success are at an advantage. It is important that alliance negotiators understand the differing goals and perspectives of potential partners as they form cross-border ventures. Western managers in particular often fail to balance the attractiveness of Japanese capital with the possibility that Japanese partners may become buyers of the business. Japanese companies are often able to pay more for their acquisitions because they have a lower cost of capital and longer time horizons for investments. But our research suggests that Japanese companies do not earn back even their

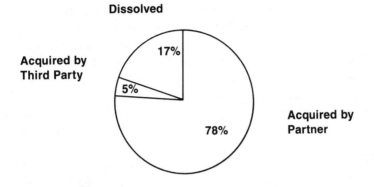

(Sample of 18 terminated partnerships.)

Partnership	Start Date	Acquired By	Acquisition Date
Asahi-Dow	1952	Asahi	1982
Merck-Banyu	1954	Merck	1983
Crédit Suisse-First Boston	1978	Crédit Suisse	1988
Toshiba-Rank	1978	Toshiba	1980
Fujitsu-TRW	1980	Fujitsu	1983
Du Pont-Philips (PD Magnetics)	1981	Philips	1988
Fiat-Rockwell	1981	Rockwell	1987
Mitsubishi-Verbatim	1982	Mitsubishi	1990
VW-Seat	1982	VW	1990
Sony-CBS (Digital Audio Disc Corporation)	1983	Sony	1985
Siemens-Telecom Plus International	1984	Siemens	1987
NatWest-Banca March	1985	NatWest	1989
Nestlé-Rothmans	1986	Nestlé	1988
Fujitsu-GTE	1987	Fujitsu	1988

Exhibit 2.3   Alliances are usually acquired by a major partner.

own relatively low cost of capital in two thirds of cross-border acquisition programs. And a survey of 90 mid-level managers at 25 leading Japanese companies found that 85% of the respondents thought that entering new businesses or improving the position of existing ones is more important than financial gain. This is in sharp contrast to the profit orientation of many Western executives.

These factors suggest that Japanese partners are often well positioned to buy the joint venture. Indeed, a separate study by the McKinsey & Company Tokyo office including more than 700 alliances between Japanese and non-Japanese companies indicated that Japanese partners have been the acquirers in approximately 70% of the terminating alliances.

One steel joint venture between U.S. and Japanese partners is typical. Over time, the U.S. investors have been unwilling to sink additional capital into modernizing factories, but the Japanese have been, and their stake has grown with each additional investment. As the business continues to require additional capital, the U.S. partner is likely to be reduced to a distinct minority.

The tendency of Japanese companies to be buyers of their ventures can be good news for Western partners that want to improve position or develop products before divesting a business. But it may make for a troubled relationship: If the Western company is looking for an early return, it is likely to seek the largest, hence most threatening, Japanese players as partners and rely on them to manage the venture. The venture may be profitable, but the Western partner's contribution to the business may shrink over time, and the Japanese company might eventually buy its partner out.

If, however, the non-Japanese partner continues to contribute in a significant way, the joint venture can grow and change. One example of a successful and enduring U.S.-Japanese alliance is Fujitsu-Amdahl. Fujitsu initially brought capital and manufacturing skills to the party, while Amdahl brought expertise in mainframe design and architecture, as well as an established local name in the United States. Since 1972, Fujitsu has increased its equity stake in Amdahl to about 44% but has agreed not to increase its ownership beyond 49.5% through April 1994. With Fujitsu's help as a financial backer and component supplier, Amdahl has been able to meet the rising ante to develop new mainframe machines, and its rank among U.S. computer companies has risen from nineteenth in 1980 to thirteenth in 1990.

Companies can retain the option to buy the venture by holding a 50% or greater stake. In addition, they should be actively involved in the ongoing operation of the joint venture. And they should be sure to place people in positions where they can learn the critical skills the venture needs to operate independently. There are reasons, though, to choose to be the seller. If, for instance, a company is exiting a business, a joint venture allows the eventual buyer to learn the business before taking it over.

Intellectual property rights and proprietary technologies are ticklish areas in an ongoing alliance, but they become even more sensitive when the partners separate. Legal protections go only so far. Successful alliance partners tend to use several different structural tactics to meet this challenge. First, they isolate sensitive technologies from the venture. For example, GE modularized the production of high value-added engine-core components to protect its know-how from Snecma. Similarly, Boeing retained control of overall design and assembly of key components in its alliances with Mitsubishi, Fuji, Kawasaki, and Aeritalia.

Manager's Choice: Expand Abroad or Diversify at Home?

Expanding at home in core businesses is often the most appealing growth strategy. But in many mature industries, it is not an option. Managers are left with the choice of diversifying at home or expanding abroad. On the one hand, most CEOs remember the "sins of the seventies"—the rash of acquisitions conglomerates made in a wide range of unrelated businesses, which left a legacy of poor business performance. On the other hand, given the added challenges of managing across borders, many managers are reluctant to make cross-border acquisitions or alliances.

In fact, we found that expanding through cross-border alliances or acquisitions is often a much more attractive option than diversifying by acquiring domestically. Cross-border alliances and acquisitions have a success rate of somewhat better than 50%, compared with the success rate of about 25% for home-country diversification programs.*

Why? In cross-border alliances, partners can avoid acquisition premiums while combining their strengths to target core or related businesses. And most cross-border acquirers focus their sights on core businesses, where there is more opportunity to add value than in related businesses.

---

* Data on domestic mergers and acquisitions are from a 1986 McKinsey study of 200 top companies.

Second, some companies centralize contact points between the joint venture and the parents. This is relatively easy in highly centralized companies—like Japanese businesses—but poses a challenge in more open and decentralized organizations, like many in the West. Third, fixed costs that are so high they must be shared and complementary staff make it hard for either partner to succeed without the other. Both Toshiba's and Motorola's strategic position would be damaged if either terminated the alliance because the two companies have such a high level of interdependence in the form of shared factories, shared distribution, and complementary specialized skills.

Strategic alliances are tough to pull off, but they are often necessary. Greenfield strategies take a long time, acquisition targets aren't always available, and simpler approaches like licensing may not be responsive enough. While every alliance is unique, there is a lot to be learned from the lessons of existing partnerships.

But managers need to remember that alliances by their nature are laden with tensions. No matter how well structured they are, most alliances get into trouble at one point or another. Strong companies make attractive partners, but they also present a competitive threat over time. The objectives and styles of parents will differ. Neither 50-50 nor majority ownership is a guarantee of fair or good management decisions. And as the venture grows, tensions will arise between the parents and between each parent and the venture.

These inherent tensions require more flexibility on the part of the parents than many other business strategies. Alliance managers should not only structure the alliance to minimize these tensions but also be prepared to rebalance the alliance—or exit smoothly—when it gets into trouble. Meeting the requirements of change, after all, is the main requirement for success in alliances.

3

The Global Logic of Strategic Alliances

Kenichi Ohmae

Companies are just beginning to learn what nations have always known: In a complex, uncertain world filled with dangerous opponents, it is best not to go it alone. Great powers operating across broad theaters of engagement have traditionally made common cause with others whose interests ran parallel with their own. No shame in that. Entente—the striking of an alliance—is a responsible part of every good strategist's repertoire. In today's competitive environment, this is also true for corporate managers.

But managers have been slow to experiment with genuinely strategic alliances. A joint venture here and there, yes, of course. A long-term contractual relationship, certainly. But the forging of entente, rarely. A real alliance compromises the fundamental independence of economic actors, and managers don't like that. After all, for them, management has come to mean total control. Alliances mean sharing control. The one precludes the other.

In stable competitive environments, this allergy to loss of control exacts little penalty. Not so, however, in a changeable world of rapidly globalizing markets and industries—a world of converging consumer tastes, rapidly spreading technology, escalating fixed costs, and growing protectionism. I'd go further. Globalization mandates alliances, makes them absolutely essential to strategy. Uncomfortable, perhaps—but that's the way it is. Like it or not, the simultaneous developments that go under the name of globalization make alliances—entente—necessary.

Why, then, the reluctance of so many companies either to experiment with alliances or to stick with them long enough to learn how to make them work? To some extent, both foot dragging and early exit are born of fear—fear that the alliance will turn out to be a Trojan horse that affords potential competitors easy access to home markets. But there is also an impression that alliances represent, at best, a convenience, a quick-and-dirty means of entry into foreign markets. These attitudes make managers skittish and impatient.

Unless you understand the long-run strategic value of entente, you will grow frustrated when it proves—as it must—not to be a cheap and easy way of responding to the uncertainties of globalization. If you expect more of your partners than is reasonable, you will blame them too quickly when things do not go as planned. Chances are your impatience will make you much less tolerant of them than you would be of your own subsidiary overseas.

When you expect convenience, you rarely have much patience for the messy and demanding work of building a strong competitive position. Nor do you remember all the up-front overseas investments that you did *not* have to make. And without memory or patience, you risk precipitating exactly what you fear most: an unhappy or unsatisfied partner that decides to bow out of the alliance and try to tackle your markets on its own.

Alliances are not tools of convenience. They are important, even critical, instruments of serving customers in a global environment. Glaxo, the British pharmaceutical company, for example, did not want to establish a full business system in each country where it did business. Especially given its costly commitment to topflight research and development (R&D), it did not see how it could—or why it should—build an extensive sales and service network to cover all the hospitals in Japan and the United States. So it decided to link up with first-class partners in Japan, swap its best drugs with them, and focus its own resources on generating greater sales from its established network in Europe. *That* kind of value creation and delivery is what alliances make possible.

Few companies operating in the Triad of Japan, the United States, and Europe can offer such topflight levels of value to all their customers all the time all by themselves. They need partners. They need entente. They might wish things were otherwise. But deep down they know better. Or they should.

THE CALIFORNIAZATION OF NEED

To understand why alliances are a necessity and not just a fad or a fashion, you first have to understand *why* globalization makes them essential as vehicles for customer-oriented value.

The explanation begins with a central, demonstrable fact: the convergence of consumer needs and preferences. Whatever their nationality, consumers in the Triad increasingly receive the same information, seek the same kinds of life-styles, and desire the same kinds of products. They all want the best products available, at the lowest prices possible. Everyone, in a sense, wants to live—and shop—in California.

Economic nationalism flourishes during election campaigns and affects what legislatures do and what particular interest groups ask for. But when individuals vote with their pocketbooks—when they walk into a store or showroom anywhere in the Triad—they leave behind the rhetoric and the mudslinging and the trappings of nationalism.

Do you write with a Waterman or a Mont Blanc pen or travel with a Vuitton suitcase because of national sentiments? Of course not. It does not matter if you live in Europe or Japan or the United States. You buy these pens or pieces of luggage because they represent the kind of value that you're looking for.

At the cash register, you don't care about country of origin or country of residence. You don't think about employment figures or trade deficits. You don't worry about where the product was made. It does not matter to you that a "British" sneaker by Reebok (now an American-owned company) was made in Korea, a German sneaker by Adidas was made in Taiwan, or a French ski by Rossignol was made in Spain. All you care about is the product's quality, price, design, value, and appeal to you as a consumer.

This is just as true for industrial customers. The market for IBM computers or Toshiba laptops is not defined by geographic borders but by the inherent appeal of the product to users, regardless of where they live. And with the proliferation of trade journals, trade shows, and electronic data bases, users have regular access to the same sources of product information.

Chip makers buy Nikon steppers because they are the best, not because they are made by a Japanese company. Manufacturers buy Tralfa industrial robots for the same reason and not because they happen to be Norwegian. The same goes for robots made by DeVilbiss in the United States. Companies around the world use IBM's materials resource planning and computer-integrated manufacturing systems to shorten production times and cut work-in-process. Because of the demands of contemporary production modes, they use Fujitsu Fanuc's machine tools made in Japan. In fact, this one company dominates the numerically controlled (NC) machine-tool market worldwide: Its marketshare in Japan is 70%; around the globe, 50%. This is neither accident nor fashion. These NC machines deliver value, and everyone knows it. But the national identity of these products has effectively disappeared.

THE DISPERSION OF TECHNOLOGY

Today's products rely on so many different critical technologies that most companies can no longer maintain cutting-edge sophistication in all of them. The business software that made IBM PCs such an instant hit— 1-2-3—was not, of course, an IBM product. It was a creation of Lotus Development Corporation. Most of the components in the popular-priced IBM PC itself were outsourced as well. IBM simply could not have developed the machine in anywhere near the time it did if it had tried to keep it 100% proprietary. In fact, the heart of IBM's accomplishment with the PC lay precisely in its decision—and its ability—to approach the development effort as a process of managing multiple external vendors.

Lotus provided applications software, and Microsoft wrote the operating system on an Intel microprocessor. Of course, Lotus, Microsoft, and Intel don't want to sell only to IBM. Naturally, they want to sell their products to as wide a range of customers as possible. Just as IBM needs to rely on an army of external vendors, so each vendor needs to sell to a broad array of customers. The inevitable result is the rapid dispersion of technology. No one company can do it all, simultaneously. No one company can keep all the relevant technologies in-house, as General Motors (GM) did during the 1930s and 1940s. And that means no one can truly keep all critical technologies out of the hands of competitors around the globe.

Even original equipment manufacturers with captive technology are not immune to this dispersion. NEC may develop a state-of-the-art memory chip for its own mainframes, but it can sell five times the volume to other computer makers. This generates cash, lowers unit costs, and builds up the experience needed to push the technology still further. It also gets them better information about its products: External customers provide tougher feedback than do internal divisions. To be a world-class producer, NEC must provide the best new technology to global customers.

In short order, the technology becomes generally available, making time even more of a critical element in global strategy. Nothing stays proprietary for long. And no one player can master everything. Thus, operating globally means operating with partners—and that in turn means a further spread of technology.

THE IMPORTANCE OF FIXED COSTS

The convergence of customer need, together with this relentless dispersion of technology, has changed the logic by which managers have to steer. In the past, for example, you tried to build sustainable competitive advantage by establishing dominance in all of your business system's critical areas. You created barriers to entry where you could, locked away market share whenever possible, and used every bit of proprietary expertise, every collection of nonreplicable assets to shore up the wall separating you from competitors. The name of the game in most industries was simply beating the competition. If you discovered an ounce of advantage, you strengthened it with a pound of proprietary skill or knowledge. Then you used it to support the defensive wall you were building against competitors.

The forces of globalization turn this logic on its head. You can't meet the value-based needs of customers in the Triad entirely on your own. You can't do without the technology and skills of others. You can't even keep your own technology to yourself for very long. Having a superior technology is important, of course, but it is not sufficient to guarantee success in the market. Meeting customer needs is the key—no matter what the source of the technology. No wall you erect stands tall. No door you slam stays shut. And no road you follow is inexpensive.

To compete in the global arena, you have to incur—and somehow find a way to defray—immense fixed costs. You can't play a variable-cost game any more. You need partners who can help you amortize your fixed costs, and with them you need to define strategies that allow you to maximize the contribution to your fixed costs.

The evidence for this lesson is overwhelming. As automation has driven the labor content out of production, manufacturing has increasingly become a fixed-cost activity. And because the cost of developing break-through ideas and turning them into marketable products has skyrock-eted, R&D has become a fixed cost too. In pharmaceuticals, for instance, when it can cost over $100 million to come up with an effective new drug, R&D is no longer a variable-cost game. And you can't count on being able to license a new drug—a variable cost—from companies not operating in your primary markets. Not unless you have your own pro-prietary drug to offer in return. With globalization, all major players in your industry are—or may become—direct competitors. You can't be sure in advance that they (or you) will want to share a particular piece of technology. You need partners, but you need your own people and your own labs too. That's fixed cost.

In much the same way, building and maintaining a brand name is a fixed cost. For many products, a brand name has no value at all if brand recognition falls below certain levels. When a company decides to buy a paper copier, for example, it usually calls up two or three producers in the order of their brand familiarity. If your copier is not among them, you don't even get a chance to try to sell your product. You simply *have* to be there to enjoy a high level of awareness among customers. And that means you have to pay for the privilege.

Trying to save money on brand promotion makes no sense if what you're selling is a consumer "pull" product: You spend a little money but not enough to realize any "pull" benefits. And a half-baked, half-supported brand is worse than no brand at all. With some products, you can better use the same money to enhance commissions so that the sales force will push them. In branded competition, if you want to play, you have to ante up the fixed costs of doing so.

The past decade saw a comparable movement toward fixed costs in sales and distribution networks. Sure, you can try to play the variable-cost game by going through dealers. You can, at least, to an extent. But your sales force still has to provide the support, the training, and the manuals. And all these are fixed costs.

You can also try to make some of these costs variable on your own. You can chase low-cost labor, for example, by moving production to developing countries, but that won't get you very far these days. In the past, you could make costs variable with your computers and management information systems by time-sharing. But experience has shown that you can't use time-sharing if you want a system that's dedicated to your own needs, a system capable of providing competitive advantage. So today, information technology is pretty much a fixed cost. Over the long term, of course, all these fixed costs become variable through adjustments in investment levels. But for the short term, they remain fixed. And the need to bolster contribution to them points in a single, clear direction: toward the forging of alliances to share fixed costs.

This is a fundamental change from the competitive world of 15 or even 10 years ago. And it demands a new logic for management action. In a variable-cost environment, the primary focus for managers is on boosting profits by reducing the cost of materials, wages, and labor hours. In a fixed-cost environment, the focus switches to maximizing marginal contribution to fixed cost—that is, to boosting sales.

This new logic forces managers to amortize their fixed costs over a much larger market base—and this adds yet more fuel to the drive toward globalization. It also forces managers to rethink their strategies as they search for ways to maximize contribution to these fixed costs. Finally, this logic mandates entente—alliances that both enable and facilitate global, contribution-based strategies.

In practice, this means that if you don't have to invest in your own overseas sales force, you don't do it. If you run a pharmaceutical company with a good drug to distribute in Japan but no sales force to do it, find someone in Japan who also has a good product but no sales force in your country. You get double the profit by putting two strong drugs through your fixed-cost sales network, and so does your new ally. Why duplicate such huge expenses all down the line? Why go head-to-head? Why not join forces to maximize contribution to each other's fixed costs?

Maximizing the contribution to fixed costs does not come naturally. Tradition and pride make companies want to be the best at everything, to do everything themselves. But companies can no longer afford this solitary stance. Take the machine-tool market. If a German manufacturer clearly excels in custom-made segments, why should highly automated Japanese producers like Mori Seiki and Yamazaki tackle those segments too? Why not tie up with the Germans and let them dominate those segments worldwide? Why not try to supply them with certain common components that you can make better—or more cheaply—than they do? Why not disaggregate the product and the business system and put together an alliance that delivers the most value to customers while making the greatest contribution to both partners' fixed costs?

Why not do this? Companyism gets in the way. So does a competitor-focused approach to strategy. So does not knowing what it takes to operate globally and how alliances help with fixed costs. Managers must overcome these obstacles. And that will not happen by chance.

DANGERS OF EQUITY

Global alliances are not the only valid mechanisms for boosting contribution to fixed costs. A strong brand umbrella can always cover additional products. You can always give heightened attention to, say, an expensive distribution system that you've already built in Japan or Europe. And there is always the possibility of buying a foreign company. Experience shows, however, that you should look hard—and early—at forging alliances. In a world of imperfect options, they are often the fastest, least risky, and most profitable way to go global.

You can expand brands and build up distribution yourself—you can do everything yourself—with enough time, money, and luck. But all three are in short supply. In particular, you simply do not have the time to establish new markets one by one throughout the Triad. The "cascade" model of expansion no longer works. Today you have to be in all important markets simultaneously if you are going to keep competitors from establishing their positions. Globalization will not wait. You need alliances and you need them now. But not the traditional kind.

In the past, companies commonly approached international expansion by doing it on their own, acquiring others, or establishing joint ventures. Now, the latter two approaches carry important equity-related concerns. Let equity—the classic instrument of capitalism—into the picture, and you start to worry about control and return on investment. There is pressure to get money back fast for the money you put in and dividends from the paper you hold.

It's a reflex. The analysts expect it of you. So do the business press, colleagues, and stockholders. They'll nod politely when you talk about improved sales or long-term strategic benefits. But what everybody really wants in short order is chart-topping return on investment (ROI).

No one's going to argue that dividends aren't nice to tuck in your pocket. Of course they are. But the pressure to put them there can wreak havoc with your initial goals, especially if they include competing successfully in global markets by maximizing the contribution to fixed costs.

Managers must also overcome the popular misconception that total control increases chances of success. Companies that have enjoyed successful joint ventures for years can have things quickly go sour when they move to a literal, equity- and contract-based mode of ownership. Naturally, details vary with the particular case, but the slide into disarray and disappointment usually starts with the typical arguments that broke up one transnational chemical joint venture:

Soon-to-Be New Owner (NO): You guys never make decisions in time.

Soon-to-Be Former Partner (FP): Speedy decisions are not everything. Consensus is more important.

NO: Well, just tell the dealers that our products are the best in the world. Tell them that they sell everywhere except here.

FP: But the dealers complain that your products are just okay, not great. Even worse, they are not really tailored to the needs or aesthetic preferences of local customers.

NO: Nonsense. What customers buy, everywhere in the world, is the physical performance of the product. No one matches us in performance.

FP: Perhaps. Still, the dealers report that your products are not neatly packaged and often have scratches on the surface.

NO: But that has no effect on performance.

FP: Tell that to the dealers. They say they cannot readily see—or sell— the performance difference you're talking about, so they have to fall back on aesthetics, where your products are weak. We'll have to reduce price.

NO: Don't you dare. We succeeded in the United States and in Europe by keeping our prices at least 5% above those of our competitors. If we're having trouble in Japan it's because of you. Your obvious lack of effort, knowledge, even confidence in our products—that's what keeps them from selling. Besides, your parent keeps on sending our joint venture group a bunch of bumbling old incompetents for managers. We rarely get the good people. Maybe the idea is to kill off our relationships entirely so they can start up a unit of their own making imitation products.

FP: Well, if you feel that way, there is not much point in our continuing on together.

NO: Glad you said that. We'll buy up the other 50% of the equity and go it on our own.

FP: Good luck. By the way, how many Japanese-speaking managers do you have in your company—that is, after we pull out all the "bumbling old incompetents" from our joint venture?

NO: None. But don't worry. We'll just hire a bunch of headhunters and get started up in record time.

This is a disaster waiting—no, rushing—to happen. Back when this arrangement was a functioning joint venture, however, both partners, and especially the middle managers, really made an effort to have things work. Under a cloud of 100% control, things are different. You can buy a company's equity, but you cannot buy the mind or the spirit or the initiative or the devotion of its people. Nor can you just go hire replacements. In different environments, the availability of key professional services— managerial, legal, and so on—varies considerably.

The lesson is painful but inescapable: having control does not necessarily mean a better managed company. You cannot manage a global company through control. In fact, control is the last resort. It's what you fall back on when everything else fails and you're willing to risk the demoralization of workers and managers.

This need for control is deeply rooted. The tradition of Western capitalism lies behind it, a tradition that has long taught managers the dangerously incorrect arithmetic that equates 51% with 100% and 49% with 0%. Yes, of course, 51% buys you full legal control. But it is control of activities in a foreign market, about which you may know little as you sit far removed from the needs of customers in your red-carpeted office in Manhattan, Tokyo, or Frankfurt.

When Americans and Europeans come to Japan, they all want 51%. That's the magic number because it ensures majority position and control over personnel, brand decisions, and investment choices. But good partnerships, like good marriages, don't work on the basis of ownership or control. It takes effort and commitment and enthusiasm from both sides if either is to realize the hoped-for benefits. You cannot own a successful partner any more than you can own a husband or a wife.

In time, as the relationship between partners deepens and as mutual trust and confidence build, there may come a point when it no longer makes sense to remain two separate entities. Strategy, values, and culture might all match up so well that both sides want to finish the work of combination. Hewlett-Packard's presence in Japan started out in 1963, for example, as a 51-49 joint venture with Yokogawa Electric. Over two decades, enough confidence had built up that in 1983, Yokogawa Electric gave Hewlett-Packard another 24%.

The point is, it took two decades for Hewlett-Packard to reach a significant ownership position. Control was never the objective. All along, the objective was simply to do things right and serve customers well by learning how to operate as a genuine insider in Japan. As a result,

Hewlett-Packard now owns 75% of a $750 million company in Japan that earns 6.6% net profit after tax.

An emphasis on control through equity, however, immediately poisons the relationship. Instead of focusing on contribution to fixed costs, one company imperialistically tells the other, "Look, I've got a big equity stake in you. You don't give me all the dividends I want, so get busy and distribute my product. I'm not going to distribute yours, though. Remember, you work for me." This kind of attitude problem prevents the development of intercompany management skills, which are critical for success in today's global environment.

Equity by itself is not the problem in building successful alliances. In Japan, we have a lot of "group companies," known as *keiretsu*, where an equity stake of, say, 3% to 5% keeps both partners interested in each other's welfare without threatening either's autonomy. Stopping that far short of a controlling position keeps the equity holder from treating the other company as if it were a subsidiary. Small equity investments like these may be the way to go.

Joint ventures may also work, but there are two obstacles that can trip them up. First, there is a contract, and contracts—even at their best—can only reflect an understanding of costs and markets and technologies at the moment companies sign them. When things change, as they always do, the partners don't really try to compromise and adjust. They look to the contract and start pointing fingers. After all, managers are human. They are sweet on their own companies and tolerant of their own mistakes. Tolerance goes way down when partners cause mistakes.

The second problem with joint ventures is that parent companies behave as parents everywhere often do. They don't give their children the breathing space—or the time—they need to grow. Nor do they react too kindly when their children want to expand, especially if it's into areas the parents want to keep for themselves. "Keep your hands off" is the message they send, and that's not a good way to motivate anyone, let alone their own children.

This is not to say that joint ventures cannot work. Many work quite well. Fuji Xerox, for example, a very successful 50-50 arrangement between Rank Xerox and Fuji Film, earns high profits on its $3 billion annual sales and attracts some of the best people in Japan to work for it. Equally important, it has enough autonomy to get actively involved in new areas like digital-imaging technology, even though both parents have strong interests there themselves. The head of Fuji Xerox, Yotaro

1. Treat the collaboration as a personal commitment. It's people that make partnerships work.

2. Anticipate that it will take up management time. If you can't spare the time, don't start it.

3. Mutual respect and trust are essential. If you don't trust the people you are negotiating with, forget it.

4. Remember that both partners must get something out of it (money, eventually). Mutual benefit is vital. This will probably mean you've got to give something up. Recognize this from the outset.

5. Make sure you tie up a tight legal contract. Don't put off resolving unpleasant or contentious issues until "later." Once signed, however, the contract should be put away. If you refer to it, something is wrong with the relationship.

6. Recognize that during the course of a collaboration, circumstances and markets change. Recognize your partner's problems and be flexible.

7. Make sure you and your partner have mutual expectations of the collaboration and its time scale. One happy and one unhappy partner is a formula for failure.

8. Get to know your opposite numbers at all levels socially. Friends take longer to fall out.

9. Appreciate that cultures—both geographic and corporate—are different. Don't expect a partner to act or respond identically to you. Find out the true reason for a particular response.

10. Recognize your partner's interests and independence.

11. Even if the arrangement is tactical in your eyes, make sure you have corporate approval. Your tactical activity may be a key piece in an overall strategic jigsaw puzzle. With corporate commitment to the partnership, you can act with the positive authority needed in these relationships.

12. Celebrate achievement together. It's a shared elation, and you'll have earned it!

Postscript

Two further things to bear in mind:

1. If you're negotiating a product OEM deal, look for a quid pro quo. Remember that another product may offer more in return.

2. Joint development agreements must include joint marketing arrangements. You need the largest market possible to recover development costs and to get volume/margin benefits.

Kobayashi, who is the son of the founder of Fuji Film, became a member board of Xerox, which has benefited greatly from Fuji Xerox's experience in battling the Japanese companies that have attacked Xerox's position in the medium- to low-end copier segments in the United States.

On balance, however, most parents are not so tolerant of their joint ventures' own ambitions. There have to be better ways to go global than a regular sacrifice of the firstborn. There are.

Going global is what parents should do together—through alliances that address the issue of fixed costs. They work. Nissan distributes Volkswagens in Japan; Volkswagen sells Nissan's four-wheel drive cars in Europe. Mazda and Ford swap cars in the Triad; GM and Toyota both collaborate and compete in the United States and Australia. Continental Tyre, General Tire (now owned by Continental), Yokohama Rubber, and Toyo Tire share R&D and swap production. In the United States, for example, General Tire supplies several Japanese transplants on behalf of Yokohama and Toyo, both of which supply tires on behalf of General and Continental to car companies in Japan. No equity changes hands.

In the pharmaceutical industry, where both ends of the business system (R&D and distribution) represent unusually high fixed costs, companies regularly allow their strong products to be distributed by (potential) competitors with excellent distribution systems in key foreign markets. In the United States, Marion Laboratories distributes Tanabe's Herbesser and Chugai's Ulcerlmin; Merck, Yamanouchi's Gaster; Eli Lilly, Fujisawa's Cefamezin. In Japan, Shionogi distributes Lilly's Ceclor as Kefral (1988 sales: $700 million). Sankyo distributes Squibb's Capoten; Takeda, Bayer's Adalat; Fujisawa, SmithKlines's Tagamet. Sales in Japan of each of these medicines last year were on the order of $300 million.

The distribution of drugs is a labor- and relationship-intensive process. It takes a force of more than 1,000 detail people to have any real effect on Japanese medicine. Thus, unless you are committed to building and sustaining such a fixed cost in Japan, it makes sense to collaborate with someone who has such a force already in place—and who can reciprocate elsewhere in the Triad.

Despite the typical "United States versus Japan" political rhetoric, the semiconductor industry has given rise to many forms of alliances. Most companies feel shorthanded in their R&D, so they swap licenses aggressively. Different forces prompted cooperative arrangements in the nuclear industry. General Electric, Toshiba, Hitachi, ASEA, AMU, and KWU (Siemens) banded together during the late 1970s to develop an improved nuclear boiling-water reactor. They shared their upstream R&D on a

global basis but kept downstream construction and local customer relationships to themselves. During the 1980s, the first three (core) members
of the alliance continued their R&D collaboration and, in fact, developed
an advanced boiling-water reactor concept. This time around, they split
the orders from Tokyo Electric Power, among others, one third each. As
confidence builds, the activities open to joint participation can begin to
encompass the entire business system.

Hitachi Kenki, a maker of construction equipment, has a loose alliance
in hydraulic excavators with Deere & Company in North America and
with Fiat Allis in Europe. Because Hitachi's product line was too narrow
for it to set up its own distribution networks throughout the Triad, it tied
up with partners who have strong networks already in place, as well as
good additional products of their own, like bulldozers and wheel loaders,
to fill in the gaps in Hitachi's product line. So effective have these arrangements been that the partners are now even committed to the joint development of a new wheel loader.

In the oligopolistic sheet glass industry, there is a noteworthy alliance
between PPG and Asahi Glass, which began in 1966 with a joint venture
in Japan to produce polyvinyl chloride. In 1985, the same pair formed a
joint automotive-glass venture in the United States in hopes of capturing
the business of Japanese automakers with U.S. production facilities. They
built a second such plant in 1988. That same year they set up a chloride
and caustic soda joint venture in Indonesia, along with some local participants and Mitsubishi Trading Company. During all this time, however,
they remained fierce global competitors in the sheet glass business.

Another long-term relationship is the one between Brown Shoe and
Nippon Shoe, which introduced a new technology back in 1962 to produce
Brown's "Regal" shoes. The relationship grew to encompass several other
brands of Brown's shoes. For Brown, this proved to be a most effective way
to participate in a Japanese market for leather goods that would be otherwise closed to them for both social reasons (historically, Japanese tanners
have been granted special privileges) and reasons of appropriate skill
(Brown's expertise in, for example, managing its own retail chains is not
so relevant in an environment where sky-high real estate prices make direct company ownership of retail shops prohibitively expensive).

There are more examples, but the pattern is obvious: a prudent, non-
equity-dependent set of arrangements through which globally active companies can maximize the contribution to their fixed costs. No surprise
here. These alliances are an important part of the way companies get back
to strategy.

THE LOGIC OF ENTENTE

One clear change of mind necessary to make alliances work is a shift from a focus on ROI to a focus on ROS (return on sales). An ROS orientation means that managers will concern themselves with the ongoing business benefits of the alliance, not just sit around and wait for a healthy return on their initial investment. Indeed, equity investments almost always have an overtone of one company trying to control another with money. But few businesses succeed because of control. Most make it because of motivation, entrepreneurship, customer relationships, creativity, persistence, and attention to the "softer" aspects of organization, such as values and skills.

An alliance is a lot like a marriage. There may be no formal contract. There is no buying and selling of equity. There are few, if any, rigidly binding provisions. It is a loose, evolving kind of relationship. Sure, there are guidelines and expectations. But no one expects a precise, measured return on the initial commitment. Both partners bring to an alliance a faith that they will be stronger together than either would be separately. Both believe that each has unique skills and functional abilities the other lacks. And both have to work diligently over time to make the union successful.

When one partner is weak or lazy or won't make an effort to explore what the two can do together, things can come apart. One-sidedness and asymmetry of effort and attention doom a relationship. If a wife goes out and becomes the family's breadwinner *and* does all the housework *and* raises the children *and* runs the errands *and* cooks the meals, sooner or later she will rebel. Quite right. If the husband were in the same position, he'd rebel too. As soon as either partner starts to feel that the situation is unfair or uneven, it will begin to come apart. Alliances are like that. They work only when the partners do.

It's hard work. It's all too easy for doubts to start to grow. A British whiskey company used a Japanese distributor until it felt it had gained enough experience to start its own sales operation in Japan. Japanese copier makers and automobile producers have done this to their U.S. partners. It happens. There's always the danger that a partner is not really in it for the long haul.

But the odds run the other way. There is a tremendous cost—and risk—in establishing your own distribution, logistics, manufacturing, sales, and R&D in every key market around the globe. It takes time to build skills in your own people and develop good relations with vendors and customers. Nine times out of ten, you will want to stay in the alliance.

Inchcape, a British trading house with a strong regional base in Asia, distributes Toyota cars in China, Hong Kong, Singapore, elsewhere in the Pacific region, and in several European countries. It also distributes Ricoh copiers in Hong Kong and Thailand. This arrangement benefits the Japanese producers, which get access to important parts of the world without having to set up their own distribution networks. It also benefits Inchcape, which can leverage its traditional British connections in Asia while adding new, globally competitive products to its distribution pipeline to replace the less attractive offerings of declining U.K.-based industries.

In practice, though, companies do start to have doubts. Say you've started up a Japanese alliance, not invested all that much, and been able to boost your production at home because of sales in Japan. Then you look at the actual cash flow from those sales, and it doesn't seem all that great. So you compare it with a competitor's results—a competitor that has gone into Japan entirely on its own. It's likely that you've forgotten how little effort you've put in when compared with the blood, sweat, and tears of your competitor. All you look at are the results.

All of a sudden you start to feel cheated; you remember every little inconvenience and frustration. You yield to the great temptation to compare apples with oranges, to moan about revenues while forgetting fixed costs. You start to question just how much the alliance is really doing for you.

It's a bit like going to a marriage counselor and complaining about the inconveniences of marriage because, had you not married, you could be dating anyone you like. You focus on what you think you're missing, on the inconveniences, and forget entirely about the benefits of being married. It's a psychological process. Alliance partners can easily fall into this kind of destructive pattern of thought, complaining about the annoyances of coordination, of working together, of not having free rein. They forget the benefits.

Actually, they forget to *look* for the benefits. And most accounting and control systems only make this worse. For instance, if you are running your own international sales operation in Japan, you know where to look for accurate measures of performance. You know how to read an income statement, figure out the return on invested capital, consolidate the performance of subsidiaries.

But when you're operating through a partner in Japan and you're asking yourself how that Japanese operation is doing, you forget to look for the benefits at home in the contribution to the fixed costs of R&D, manufacturing, and brand image. The financials don't highlight them; they usually don't even capture them. Most of the time, these contributions—like the extra production volume for OEM export—are simply invisible, below the line of sight.

Companies in the United States, in particular, often have large, dominant home-country operations. As a result, they report the revenues generated by imports from their overseas partners as their own domestic sales. In fact, they think of what they're doing not as importing but as managing procurement. Exports get recorded as overseas sales of the domestic divisions. In either case, the contribution of the foreign partner gets lost in the categories used by the U.S.-based accounting system.

It takes real dedication to track down the domestic benefits of a global alliance. And you're not even going to look for them if you spend all your time complaining. The relationship is never going to last. That's too bad, of course, if the alliance really does contribute something of value. But even when alliances are good, you can outgrow them. Needs change, and today's partner might not be the best or the most suitable tomorrow.

Financial institutions shift about like this all the time. If you're placing a major issue, you may need to tie up with a Swiss bank with deep pockets. If you need help with retail distribution, you may turn to Merrill Lynch or Shearson Lehman Hutton. In Japan, Nomura Securities may be the best partner because of its size and retail strength. You don't need to be good at everything yourself as long as you can find a partner who compensates for your weak points.

Managing multiple partners is more difficult in manufacturing industries but still quite doable. IBM in the United States has a few important allies; in Japan it has teamed up with just about everyone possible. (There has even been a book published in Japanese, entitled *IBM's Alliance Strategy in Japan*.) It has links with Ricoh in distribution and sales of low-end computers, with Nippon Steel in systems integration, with Fuji Bank in financial systems marketing, with OMRON in Computer Integrated Manufacturing, and with Nippon Telephone and Telegraph in value-added networks. IBM is not a jack-of-all-trades. It has not made huge fixed-cost investments. In the eyes of Japanese customers, however, it has become an all-around player. No wonder IBM has achieved a major "insider" position in the fiercely competitive Japanese market.

Sure, individual partners may not last. Every business arrangement has its useful life. But maintaining a presence in Japan by means of alliances *is* a permanent endeavor, an enduring part of IBM's strategy. And acting as if current arrangements are permanent helps them last longer. Just like marriage. If you start cheating on day two, the whole thing gets shaky fast.

Why does the cheating start? You're already pretty far down the slippery slope when you say to yourself, "I've just signed this deal with so-and-so to distribute my products. I don't need to worry about that anymore as long as they send me my check on time." You're not holding up your half of the relationship. You're not working at it. More important, you're not trying to learn from it—or through it. You're not trying to grow, to get better as a partner. You've become a check casher, a coupon clipper. You start to imagine all sorts of grievances. And your eye starts to wander.

One of Japan's most remarkable success stories is 7-Eleven. Its success, however, is not due to the efforts of its U.S. owner, Southland Corporation, but rather to the earnest acquisition of "know-how" by Ito-Yokado, the Japanese licensee. Faced with a takeover threat, Southland management collected something on the order of $5 billion through asset stripping and junk bond issues. The high-interest cost of the LBO caused the company to report a $6 million loss in 1987. Meanwhile, since the Japanese had completely absorbed the know-how for running 7-Eleven, the only thing Southland had left in Japan was its 7-Eleven brand.

When Southland's management asked Ito-Yokado to buy the 7-Eleven brand name for half a billion dollars, Ito-Yokado's counterproposal was to arrange an interest-free loan of ¥41 billion to Southland in exchange for the annual royalty payment of $25 million, with the brand name as collateral. Should something happen to Southland so that it cannot pay back the debt, it will lose the brand and its Japanese affiliation completely. Yes, Southland got as much as half a billion dollars out of Japan in exchange for mundane know-how, so they should be as happy as a Yukon River gold miner. On the other hand, the loss of business connections in Japan means that Southland is permanently out of one of the most lucrative retail markets in the world. That's not a marriage. It's just a one-night stand.

Another company, a U.S. media company, took 10% of the equity of a good ad agency in Japan. When the agency went public, the U.S. investor sold off 3% and made a lot of money over and above its original investment. It still had 7%. Then the stockholders started to complain. At Tokyo's crazy stock market prices, that 7% represented about $40 million that was just sitting in Japan without earning dividends. (The dividend payout ratio of Japanese companies is usually very low.) So the stockholders pushed management to sell off the rest and bring the money back to the United States, where they could get at least a money-market level of return. No growth, of course. No lasting position in the booming Japanese market. Just a onetime killing.

Much the same logic seems to lie behind the sale by several U.S.-based companies of their equity positions in Japanese joint ventures. McGraw-Hill (Nikkei-McGraw-Hill), General Electric (Toshiba), B.F. Goodrich (Yokohama Rubber), CBS (CBS-Sony), and Nabisco (Yamazaki-Nabisco), among others, have all realized handsome capital gains in this fashion. If they had not given up their participation in so lucrative a market as Japan, however, the value of their holdings would now be many times greater still. Of course, such funds have since found other opportunities for profitable investment, but they would have to do very well indeed to offset the loss of so valuable an asset base in Japan.

This kind of equity-based mind-set makes the eye wander. It sends the message that alliances are not a desirable—or effective—means of coping with the urgent and inescapable pressures of globalization or of becoming a genuine insider throughout the Triad market. It reinforces the short-term orientation of managers already hard-pressed by the uncertainties of a new global environment.

When a dispute occurs in a transnational joint venture, it often has overtones of nationalism, sometimes even racism. Stereotypes persist. "Americans just can't understand our market," complain some frustrated partners. "The Germans are too rigid," complain others. "Those mechanical Japanese may be smart at home, but they sure as hell are dumb around here." We've all heard the comments.

It does not take companies with radically different nationalities to have a "clash of cultures" in a joint venture. Most of the cross-border mergers that took place in Europe during the 1970s have resulted in divorce or in a takeover by one of the two partners. In Japan, mergers between Japanese companies—Dai-Ichi Kangyo Bank and Taiyo Kobe Bank, for example—have journalists gossiping about personal conflicts at the top between, say, ex-Kangyo and ex-Dai-Ichi factions lingering on for 10 years and more.

Good combinations—Ciba-Geigy and Nippon Steel (a combination of Yawata and Fuji), for example—are the exception, not the rule. Two corporate cultures rarely mesh well or smoothly. In the academic world, there is a discipline devoted to the study of interpersonal relationships. To my knowledge, however, there are few scholars who specialize in the study of *intercompany* relationships. This is a serious omission, given the importance of joint ventures and alliances in today's competitive global environment. We need to know much more than we do about what makes effective corporate relationships work.

Having been involved with many multicompany situations, I do not underestimate this task. Still, we must recognize and accept the inescapable subtleties and difficulties of intercompany relationships. That is the essential starting point. Then we must focus not on contractual or equity-related issues but on the quality of the people at the interface between organizations. Finally, we must understand that success requires frequent, rapport-building meetings at at least three organizational levels: top management, staff, and line management at the working level.

This is hard, motivation-testing work. No matter what they say, however, many companies don't really care about extending their global reach. All they want is a harvesting of the global market. They are not interested in the hard work of serving customers around the world. They are interested in next quarter's ROI. They are not concerned with getting back to strategy or delivering long-term value or forging entente. They want a quickie. They want to feel good today and not have to work too hard tomorrow. They are not serious about going global or about the painstaking work of building and maintaining the alliances a global market demands.

Yet the relentless challenges of globalization will not go away. And properly managed alliances are among the best mechanisms that companies have found to bring strategy to bear on these challenges. In today's uncertain world, it is best not to go it alone.

4

Forming Successful
Strategic Alliances in
High-Tech Businesses

Edward Krubasik and
Hartmut Lautenschlager

The past several years have witnessed a dramatic jump in the number of high-tech companies that have, for strategic reasons, turned to one or another form of alliance—cooperative arrangement, joint venture, whatever you want to call it. In some industries—electronics, pharmaceuticals, computers, and aerospace, for example—there has been as much as a fourfold annual increase. These linkages, moreover, are not the desperate acts of failing companies trying to keep a toehold in their industries. In many cases, they have become, instead, the strategies of choice of industry leaders such as IBM, Hewlett-Packard, and Texas Instruments.

IBM, for example, has used alliances in a variety of different areas and for a variety of different purposes. Marketing alliances have been established with networking companies, software houses, value-added retailers, Telenet, and so on. Research and development (R&D) alliances have been used in the memory business or as part of industry joint ventures like Sematech. There have been alliances in new business areas like data networks and communications, including cooperation with Siemens. The reason for this flurry of activity is simple: to experiment and expand by leveraging the skills of many participants in the industry—that is, to harness the capabilities and the dynamism of a wide spectrum of players in order to do things it would be hard to do alone.

A PASSING FASHION?

Some observers dismiss this flurry of activity as no more than a fashion or fad. There are chief executive officers (CEOs) who cannot hear the word "alliance" these days without regarding it as an excuse for managers not trying to repair their businesses themselves. We see things quite differently. In our view, alliances offer a clear economic game, in which short-, medium-, and even long-term economic benefit is at stake for both parties. This is not airy fashion. It is sound, hard-nosed business. As Exhibit 4.1 suggests, these potential benefits result either from the introduction of new products or from the more effective management of high-tech business facing the pressures of globalization and cost-based competition.

With new products, for example, the increasing development costs and shortening life-cycles in maturing industries often lead companies to

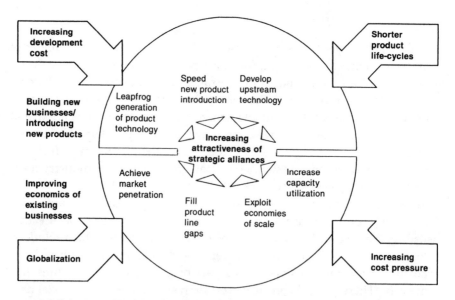

Exhibit 4.1 High-tech alliances are driven by economic factors.

think about alliances. This is especially so when they have missed a product generation and cannot leapfrog alone, when they cannot meet all by themselves the required deadline for the introduction of a new product generation, when upstream programs are too risky and too costly to be pursued alone, and when new or latent markets cannot be tapped by a single competitor but only by the cooperation of several parties. (This last was the case with data networks and office communications when Ethernet and other standards were introduced.)

Similarly, with upstream ceramic technologies for aircraft engines, development programs are too expensive for individual companies to fund. So cooperative activity makes sense. Software companies that take too long to develop products often go for a cooperative arrangement with people that have an architecture for the product ready to go. In much the same way, if you miss the entry window for, say, a new digital audio studio system, you buy a competitor, take a license, or find an alliance.

Economic motives can also favor or require alliances in an ongoing business. In the aerospace industry, for example, you may prefer to use your capacity for many projects in which you have 10% each instead of one in which you have 100%. That way, if one program fails or ends, you are not left with a massive profit impact and almost impossible lay-offs. Further, in those industries where scale effects alone cannot be exploited at the subsystems level, cooperative arrangements of some sort are economically preferable. Then, too, product-line economies can often be improved by sourcing "missing" products from competitors or joint venture partners and putting them through the same high fixed-cost logistics systems and sales forces. Finally, the challenge of entering Triad markets in Japan or the United States frequently demands such short reaction times that joint ventures offer a far cheaper mode of entry than building up a whole sales network from scratch.

Consider in a bit more detail the economics of new product introduction in the aircraft industry. Even for the largest player, Boeing, a new product requires more financial resources than the company's entire equity base. Few European companies can carry the risk of such a development effort. And if even one project goes wrong, it can mean financial ruin.

Similarly, in telecommunications, the scale of up-front R&D reinvestments makes joint ventures and alliances very attractive. To amortize the $1 billion to $2 billion investment in R&D needed for each new generation of switches, European manufacturers with only 2 to 3 million lines per year to sell will have to ask for prices of close to $200 per line. Competitors with 6 to 8 million lines per year to sell with be able to charge about half that amount. At an expected price level of $150 per line, break-even runs in the area of 3 to 4 million lines per year. That means a lot of competitors desperately need additional volume—and that, in turn, means looking for partners or acquisitions.

DESIGNING, NEGOTIATING, AND REALIZING THE ECONOMIC VALUE OF ALLIANCES

These benefits notwithstanding, the attitude of managers is, quite often, that alliances threaten a loss of needed independence and that cooperation is a handicap, not a potential source of bottom-line improvement. Yes, of course, mistakes can be made or wrong approaches taken. The strategic rationale may have too narrow a focus. Negotiations may be handled badly. Learning may not take place. Economic benefits may not be adequately captured. But all these are failures of execution and approach, not an indictment of the value of alliances.

From a range of examples that we have analyzed and from our direct experience with a wide variety of alliances, we know in general that they can work and, equally important, in which kinds of circumstances they *do* work. We know, for example, that alliances are more successful where they bring complementary skills together (64% success rate) than where they create a lot of overlaps in the business systems of the partners (47% success rate).

More specifically, we have taken a close retrospective look at these high-tech alliances to try to distill from them a series of practical lessons for managers.

Overall, we have found that, in designing, negotiating and implementing alliances, management could focus much more on the joint economic perspective of the two partners than is generally the case. In detail, we have found eight practical lessons. The first four call for more strategic design of alliances; lessons five and six, for a more outright economic focus in negotiations; and lessons seven and eight focus on faster realization of the economic value of alliances.

Why Not the Best?

In the strategic design of alliances, the first point is quite simple: If you are contemplating an alliance, focus on creating the best and strongest consortium possible. Do not play around trying to create something that will, at best, be only a marginal player. Unfortunately, all too often managers are pulled into negotiations with marginal players because these are the first to ask for help.

The criteria for a good consortium are much the same as for any strong competitor in an industry: a product line that covers major regions and customer segments, has a strong customer and/or installed equipment base, fits well with sales channels, and exploits synergies in components (like commonality among lot sizes).

Financially, the consortium should be able to make continued investment in R&D and manufacturing. Ideally, it should be able to help improve industry structure and economics by capturing scale benefits—for instance, the amortization of R&D among existing competitors. Strong joint forces with respect to these criteria should be negotiated; weak combinations (and secondary, one-sided criteria) should be avoided.

Not by Mergers and Acquisitions (M&A) Alone

As already noted, the motives for forming cooperative arrangements are quite varied. Many can be satisfied—even best satisfied—by options that fall short of traditional mergers or acquisitions. Everything—from licenses to technology sharing through OEM manufacturing or product exchange to development joint ventures, manufacturing joint ventures, sales joint ventures, and full business joint ventures—is possible. But many potentially attractive options get ignored (see Exhibit 4.2). The choice of vehicle is critically important.

The more resources involved, for example, the more impact a joint venture can have—but also the more independence is given up. Such tradeoffs need to be made carefully. A McKinsey study of some 50 cross-border partnerships showed that acquisitions make sense when there is little "complementarity"—that is, when there is a lot of direct overlap in functional skills and regional coverage. By contrast, minimal regional or functional overlap is usually a good precondition for alliances. Most successful alliances are found in this group of partnerships. But this tells only part of the story. Exhibit 4.3a and 4.3b, which compares the usage of alliances by IBM and GEC, shows that not only can the *form* of cooperative arrangement vary with differences in strategic need. So, too, can the *ends* to which those alliances are put. The need, of course, is for a customized solution, not a knee-jerk reliance on merger and acquisition (M&A).

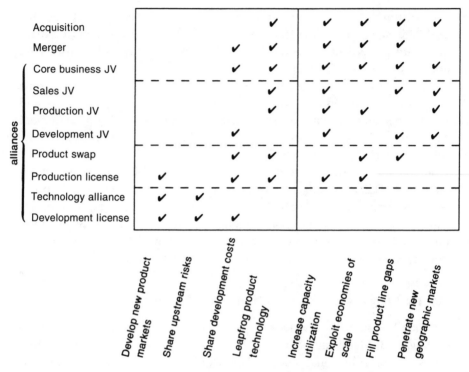

Exhibit 4.2　Many alliance options are available.

Does Money Count?

Yes, but much less than customers and know-how. All too often, cash-driven alliances end up in a downward spiral of failure: a lack of understanding of markets and technologies leads to an inflated price premium, which in turn leads to unrealistically high financial measures of performance, missed targets, insufficient ongoing investment, and even worse performance.

Experience suggests that it is preferable to exchange markets for technology and technology for markets than to try to buy your way into either. The Japanese, for example, very often do not sell technology. They only exchange it for markets. Europeans very often trade markets for technology or entry into one market for another.

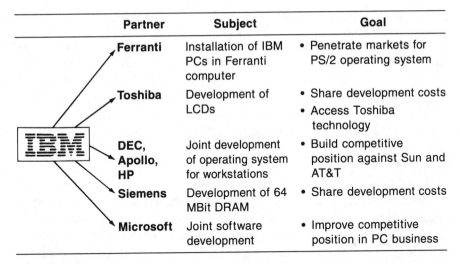

Partner	Subject	Goal
Ferranti	Installation of IBM PCs in Ferranti computer	• Penetrate markets for PS/2 operating system
Toshiba	Development of LCDs	• Share development costs • Access Toshiba technology
DEC, Apollo, HP	Joint development of operating system for workstations	• Build competitive position against Sun and AT&T
Siemens	Development of 64 MBit DRAM	• Share development costs
Microsoft	Joint software development	• Improve competitive position in PC business

Exhibit 4.3a IBM uses alliances to strengthen specific elements of its business system.

Partner	Subject	Goal
General Electric (USA)	Construction of gas turbine with GE know how	• Break up Rolls-Royce monopoly position
CGE	Merger of power generation and distribution divisions	• Build largest power plant manufacturer in Europe
Alsthom	Power plant installation	• Restructure industry
General Electric (USA)	Home appliances	• Restructure industry
Philips*	Medical technology	• Build strong competitive position against Siemens

GEC

30 major alliances between 1988–1990

* Negotiation termatinated.

Exhibit 4.3b GEC uses alliances as "strategic tools" to aggressively change the industry structure.

Is Cooperation a Strategy?

Put bluntly, no. It can, of course, be part of a strategy, but it is not a strategy in itself. If managers focus on it to the exclusion of all stand-alone possibilities, they become vulnerable to negotiations that drag on and never turn out well, deals that fail to materialize or that materialize late, delays in necessary cost cutting or development programs or market entry, and lost time and profits. Equally troubling, if an alliance-seeker has no other bets to place, competitors can drag out negotiations and allow the too-narrowly-focused company to drown.

In the aerospace, automotive, and machinery-tool industries, for example, we have seen participants try to build a consortium to achieve needed industry consolidation. In each case, more than a year of negotiations led to nothing, and each of the involved parties had to fall back on a stand-alone strategy. Only then did competitors come back to talk seriously. If any of them had stopped rationalization measures during that period, they would have incurred enormous losses.

The Partner's Point of View

Negotiating alliances, in our experience, could very often be much more oriented toward the economic benefits of both parties. Often, a management looking for support from a joint-venture partner is trapped into making this the sole objective of negotiations.

For alliances to work, the strategies on which they are based must not be one-sided. They must, instead, take into account the needs—and the abilities—of both sides. Say a company has had some bad times but has now mostly recovered—albeit with a gap at the high end of its product line. Say, too, that that gap creates problems in key countries like Germany, England, and Spain. If a second company has strengths in these problem areas, there is the basis for a deal—assuming, of course, the strengths of the first are also helpful to the second. Understanding the needs of the partner leads to interesting business proposals and avoids those proposals that sound like simple requests for help in solving one partner's own problems.

No Carpet Sweeping

In successful negotiations, problems do not get swept under the carpet, conflicts get addressed early, and balanced solutions get found. In the aircraft industry, for example, it makes no sense to discuss a new aircraft development project in isolation. Everybody knows that derivatives will have to be developed to make the whole concept viable. The product line overlaps that are created have to be openly talked about. If realizing economies of scale in a subsystem means closing one partner's manufacturing line, both have to discuss the payback for this closure. Exhibit 4.4 outlines some of the typical kinds of questions that must be addressed— early and explicitly—if alliances are to work well.

Overkill in Planning

Realizing the economic value is the most difficult task of all. Even if two parties have designed and negotiated a strategically viable alliance, they often grow disappointed after two or three years, looking in vain for the millions in profits that were promised during the negotiation phase. When implementing alliances, therefore, it is important to move quickly to realize the planned-for economic value. Quick implementation in turn depends on an overkill in planning. Most companies, however, seriously underestimate the level of planning effort needed.

Part of the problem is that conventional approaches to strategy formulation will not work. Usual modes of situation analysis are hampered by differences in company cultures and language; strategy development, by the lack of a common vision; and implementation, by the necessary focus of management on organizational and, especially, personnel questions. So long as people do not have a clear perspective about their own future, so long as they lack a cogent, shared vision of where the alliance is headed, even the best-laid plans will fail of execution.

A. Conflict questions	B. Routine questions
• Shutdown of plants	• Transfer prices
• Current or future product overlaps between partners	• Specifications of systems
• Multiple- versus single-brand strategy	• Commission paid to sales companies
• Readiness of partners to develop parts jointly and to exchange production	• Coordination of volumes and brand policy by country

Exhibit 4.4 Alliance issues need to be addressed early.

It is like Maslow's hierarchy of needs: Food and drink will come before more esoteric needs. "Will there be layoffs?" and "Will I have a job?" are more critical than "Which strategy will we follow?" Preplanning has to answer such people and power questions early on. Only then can progress be made on details of a business plan and implementation actions.

Clear Leadership

The evidence is unmistakable; alliances with strong partners are much more likely to be successful than alliances with one or two weak partners. As discussed in Chapter 2, 67% of alliances formed between two financially strong co-parties succeed, versus 39% for alliances involving weaker partners. Let strong leaders lead.

This is as true at the project level as at the top management level. Good coordinators and champions at the project manager level are essential. But there is also need for excellent top management contact between the two companies—in particular, for a champion able to fly "air cover" in case problems arise lower down and to legitimize quickly the decisions taken to resolve them. Giving clear leadership to the more experienced or skilled partner overall or in the respective functional area has turned out very beneficial for both sides, even in cases where they had a 50-50 equity alliance.

Strong leadership of this sort is the only path to a fast realization of the economic benefits of an alliance. Projects have to be sorted by urgency and impact and ease of realization. With some, it is critically important to go fast and implement quickly—development joint ventures, for example. With others, there are potential quick wins that can be used as motivators—for example, selling each other's products at certain key accounts. In addition, there will be some longer-term strategic projects that ought to be started early if benefits are to appear within the first 12 months.

SUMMING UP

Successful high-technology alliances need not be set in concrete. Nor need they last forever. Changes may well have to be made in their focus over time. And when they have fulfilled their initial task, it may be necessary to reposition or even dissolve them. We have seen many joint ventures that both partners deemed successful despite the fact that they had

Design	>	Negotiate	>	Implement
1 Form powerful competitive force, not marginal player		5 Develop strategy from partner's point of view		7 Overplan to realize full value
2 Exploit the range of options, not only M&A		6 Clarify conflicts early and secure balanced benefits		8 Institute clear leadership roles
3 Pay in kind for market and technology				
4 Pursue stand-alone strategy in parallel				

Exhibit 4.5 Developing successful strategic alliances.

brought it to an end—sometimes by acquisition, sometimes by simple dissolution. Permanence does not matter.

The important thing is to realize the intended economic and competitive benefits along the way and to focus all three phases of alliance development very clearly on this goal: Design the most powerful combination of partners in the market, maximize the economic value for both parties; tailor the economic value achievable from an alliance in detail in the negotiation phase; and realize the economic value fast and uncompromisingly after closure. Following the eight lessons in Exhibit 4.5 will make such realization more likely.

5

Rebuilding an Alliance

Varun Bery and Thomas A. Bowers

If an alliance is to survive and bring profits to both partners, it must be able to manage change and to accept change in itself. Effective rebuilding can strengthen an alliance's underlying business proposition as well as the relationship between the partners (see sidebar). We found this to be true in the case of the U.S. and Japanese transportation companies with which we worked for a period of two years. We also found that a commitment to rebuilding can help companies avoid the sustained period of stagnation or decline that many alliances suffer.

Managing the basic parameters of such a relationship must be a conscious, ongoing process. Keeping an alliance alive requires a flexible structure that permits continuous evolution of products, technology, scope, and ownership. In fact, although companies entering alliances often focus on developing the right contract, the hallmark of successful alliances is that the partners develop a strong cooperative spirit and rarely, if ever, need to refer to the contract.

THE PARTNERSHIP SOURS

A cross-border alliance is much more volatile than many executives realize. Given the increasing rate of change in the international business arena, an alliance designed to meet today's needs is unlikely to be appropriate for the medium to long term. A recent McKinsey study of 49 major alliances in the Triad (see Chapter 2)—the United States, Europe, and Japan—showed that more than 30 had problems in the first three years, 19 of which dealt with their problems by broadening their scope.

Volatility, of course, is a natural part of living with alliances. If it is ignored, however, it can create difficulties, as it did between the U.S. and Japanese partners noted here. The two companies had been working together for two years, and there was a growing mistrust and lack of commitment in the relationship. Both had misgivings, but these were not being adequately communicated because of flawed reporting structures and linkages.

Structural Flaws

The Japanese partner's misgivings stemmed from the fact that it was a subcontractor, not a true partner. It was compensated on a cost-plus basis for distribution in Japan. All revenues accrued to the U.S. partner. Ultimate authority for service design rested there as well. In order to centralize planning for a global product line, the U.S. company had been making many of the product and pricing decisions for the Japanese market. This approach had worked in other Asian markets, yet it was failing in sophisticated Japan.

Worse, the Japanese partner was faced with a conflict of interest. The distribution agreement dealt with a substitute for a significant existing service. Although the Japanese partner saw this substitution as an opportunity and as inevitable over time, the flaws in the agreement and in the relationship made them reluctant to lead the shift to the new service.

The U.S. company was increasingly frustrated with its Japanese partner's resistance to agreeing to product and pricing changes that had already been implemented in other markets. This frustration blossomed into mistrust when the results of the service agreement were poor and there were signs that the Japanese partner had reverted to promoting its existing services rather than the new service. As a result, the U.S. partner's level of commitment to the alliance started to tail off.

Communications Failures

The poor communications links between the companies exacerbated the problem. The alliance reported through the U.S. company's Far Eastern organization to the U.S. headquarters. Since much of the central product planning was done there, the Far Eastern organization had limited flexibility to accommodate the changes requested by the Japanese. Although some of these requests were passed on to headquarters, little action was taken against them, since there was no precedent for country-specific service offerings.

Managerial exchanges around these product line debates grew increasingly heated and were complicated by language barriers. The situation had deteriorated to the point at which the U.S. side began to view the Japanese as uncooperative, and the Japanese felt the U.S. company was inflexible and not fully in touch with conditions in Japan.

Restructuring Successes

There are a myriad of reasons why alliances reach a crisis. Once there, they can frequently be difficult to rebuild. However, a growing number have been successfully revitalized through the determined action of one or both parents and have then gone on to new levels of success.

One example is the 50-50 joint venture formed by Caterpillar and Mitsubishi Heavy Industries back in 1963 to serve as a distribution channel for Caterpillar bulldozers and wheel loaders in Japan. After an initial period of high growth, the alliance became ineffective because Mitsubishi's small specialty equipment group (including tunneling machines and excavators) had not been included in the alliance. An unexpected shift in demand away from bulldozers and toward hydraulic excavators eroded the joint venture's competitive position. Both Mitsubishi and the joint venture were losing out by selling incomplete product lines in the extremely competitive Japanese market.

Once management realized that the 20-year-old structure had become a major handicap, the joint venture was completely restructured in 1987. Mitsubishi's hydraulic excavator division was merged with the alliance, removing competitive conflicts and roughly doubling the alliance's size. It has since emerged as a much stronger competitor and is a key element in Caterpillar's global strategy to compete with Komatsu by applying pressure in its home market.

Another example, the restructuring of a 38-year-old alliance between Monsanto and Mitsubishi Kaisei, shows that finding focus is not a one-time event, but a continuing process. This alliance was originally set up to leverage the parents' technologies for various market opportunities. Over the course of its life, it entered a wide range of businesses, including gallium-arsenide chips, thermoplastic elastomers, rubber additives, engineering plastics, and even artificial turf.

In part because of its expansion, the alliance experienced increasing marketing and product conflicts with its parents. After a long-overdue review by a joint team, Monsanto and Mitsubishi Kaisei agreed to shrink the alliance to less than half its previous size and focus on engineering plastics, an area in which there are technology and skill synergies between the parents. The best of the remaining businesses were spun back to the parents.

Problems with alliances are often solved only when the situation has deteriorated into a crisis. In 1963, Hewlett Packard (HP) and Yokogawa Hokushin Electric set up Yokogawa-Hewlett Packard (YHP), a 49-51 joint venture, to sell scientific instruments in Japan. At the outset the objectives of the venture were unclear. HP's expectation was to grow at a gradual pace that would allow the venture to reach break-even quickly. HP assigned only one person to the venture and gave management control to Yokogawa, which they believed had the required skills to develop the venture. Yokogawa's primary goal was to build a market presence; profits were of secondary concern.

Problems arose when Yokogawa used its management autonomy to build its market position aggressively without adequate regard for profits. They assigned a large staff complement to the venture, set up a large new plant, and purchased substantial amounts of new equipment. Things came to a head when the venture incurred large losses in the first two years, falling far below HP's expectations and pushing the venture close to insolvency.

This provided the trigger for HP to renegotiate the venture and take control. They appointed a co-president and, under his guidance, transferred operating skills to the venture. At the same time they reduced the headcount and sold excess equipment. HP also created training programs for Yokogawa in order to fill gaps in management skills. On this new platform of superior expertise *and* management skills, YHP became profitable in a year and has been one of the most successful joint ventures to date.

TAKING STOCK

The souring of the alliance led the U.S. company, which clearly held the dominant position, to review its overall strategy for the Japanese market—and even its need for a partner (see Exhibit 5.1). This was the first strategic review of the Japanese market that the company had conducted since the original alliance had been set up. At that time, the U.S. company's objective had been to establish a foothold in Japan. Since then, aggressive initiatives by other leading foreign competitors had made the Japanese market a strategic priority in establishing a global business.

Evaluate alliance	Develop redesign options	Define new alliance
• Decide whether existing alliance is best vehicle to achieve objectives	• Gain agreement of partner to restructure alliance and jointly develop general nature and scope of new relationship	• Develop business objectives and plans for new alliance
• What internal or external changes are making the alliance ineffective? • What are your current objectives? • Is an alliance still necessary? • Is the current partner still the right partner? • Can the alliance be fixed?	• Does the partner want to restructure the alliance? • What is the ideal business proposition that combines the strengths of both parents and makes the alliance a viable standalone entity? • What changes are needed to rebuild trust?	• What are the objectives and strategy for the alliance? • What are the detailed plans including products, technology, organization, etc.? • What are the parent company contributions?
U.S. parent company decides to restructure alliance ➡	Nonbinding letter of intent signed by both parent companies ➡	Contracts signed to form new joint venture

Exhibit 5.1   Steps in rebuilding an alliance.

The review was conducted, with our assistance, by a team from the U.S. company consisting of managers representing key functions. It was led by a manager from the Far Eastern headquarters through which the alliance reported, but the rest of the staff were sent over from the United States. Although the Japanese company was not involved in the review process, the U.S. company had made them aware that it was going on and invited them to join in the assessment of the problems with the existing alliance.

The team's first task was to interview major customers and industry experts to assess their needs and to ascertain their perspectives on market evolution and on the service offerings of key providers in the market. We then helped them carry out an economic analysis to evaluate trade-offs among the U.S. company's build, buy, and alliance options.

The Build Option

The market analysis showed that the "go-it-alone" strategy would take too long to show real benefits in a rapidly evolving competitive situation. Breaking into the high-volume corporate segment of the market would require several years of building relationships and credibility among corporate buyers. Further, although the company had world-class operational skills, it had little experience in providing the high level of customer service required in the Japanese market. Until the company could build credibility, it would be difficult to hire and keep the high-quality Japanese talent needed to bring customer-service skills in-house. A further drawback of the build option was that real estate was an important element of the cost structure of the business. Any new entrant would be at a considerable disadvantage to established providers that had significantly lower-cost facilities.

The Buy Option

Buying a Japanese company was an expensive option and likely to be fraught with difficulty. The list of candidates consisted of larger companies: the only players of adequate size to have the required corporate relationships were generally part of larger conglomerates. For a foreign company to acquire a Japanese company of such size was unprecedented. A decision to buy would be expensive and difficult to execute because of the large portion of equity in friendly hands.

The Alliance Option

Although it was not the perfect solution, an alliance was still the best course to follow. However, the business proposition of the original alliance was seriously flawed. As already noted, the alliance covered a fledgling service that was an offshoot of a much larger existing service. To build credibility with customers and to ensure that the new service was successful, the alliance had to offer both the existing and the new services.

A review also indicated that the current partner was clearly the best choice—even under a revised business proposition. It had a dominant position in the local market for the new service, and a significant position in the cross-border market for the existing service. Given the right structure, the U.S. company and its current Japanese partner were well positioned to become the leading overall player in the business.

This objective view of the marketplace, coupled with a clearer understanding of each party's misgivings, rejuvenated both partners' desire to work together. As the true nature of the Japanese market and its specific requirements became apparent to the U.S. partner, they became willing to consider a product line tailored specifically for Japan-originated services.

Because this strategic review gained visibility at the highest levels of the two companies, both could see that defining the right business proposition was even more crucial in the new competitive environment. They also realized that, with the right structure, a more comprehensive alliance could not only win in the marketplace, but also be a vehicle for skill transfer between them.

REBUILDING BEGINS

The challenge that the two companies faced was how to redesign the alliance to capture the opportunities that had been identified and, at the same time, to rebuild mutual trust. Starting by renegotiating the contract did not make sense. Three years' worth of frustrations would get funneled into the negotiations. The chances that such an approach would lead to a broader, more equal structure were very low.

The alternative was for the companies to begin to work together as partners to define the best business proposition. Once a winning plan had been agreed to, they could then negotiate the specific terms of the new alliance and of the parent company contributions to it. By focusing from the outset on cooperation, rather than negotiation, the objective was to arrive at a solution that captured potential synergies and helped build the working relationship needed to make the alliance work.

Given the state of the relationship, trying to cooperate on a joint business plan without such a new demonstration of commitment would have been impossible. There were major complaints on both sides. As a prelude to actually rethinking the alliance, the partners needed an agreement that addressed and alleviated these complaints, thereby leaving managers free to sit down and discuss how they should work together.

A Basis for Commitment

The solution was a joint effort by the two companies to develop a "letter of intent" that addressed all major concerns. A key element for the letter of intent was that it should not be legally binding. This allowed the senior management of each side to demonstrate the commitment needed for the two sides to start working together, but it kept the alliance design process open-ended enough to allow for adjustment and restructuring as new ideas emerged.

A small working team of key managers from the two parent companies was charged with developing options for redesigning the relationship. The first few weeks of this effort became an exercise in venting frustration. Communications between the parents had been so inadequate that neither side understood the other's position. Even simple facts about the business, such as historical volumes, were hotly disputed.

Once through this initial phase, in which understanding was strengthened and trust established, the working team began to brainstorm possible options for tapping the strengths of both parents. Although this process was difficult at first, the new focus of a common objective gradually led to ideas for significantly broadening the scope of the relationship. Options emerged, for example, for cooperation in totally unrelated geographic areas, such as Europe. By focusing on "win-win" business propositions, the team was gradually freed from the "tit-for-tat" negotiating mode that had hitherto characterized the relationship. This was the breakthrough that allowed the two companies to begin working together to capture the potential synergies in the alliance.

Top-Level Option Generation

The next critical step used a series of discussions at the chief executive officer (CEO) level. Options developed by the working team were taken separately to the steering committees of the two parent companies. The senior management of each could react to the ideas on the basis of their perceived business merit, without having to commit to a particular mode of participation. Clearly unacceptable options were eliminated and feedback on the remaining possibilities was communicated to the other side. These went back to the working team for further development. This mechanism allowed the two CEOs to work out a meeting of the minds on the long-term positioning of the alliance without having to take adversary positions often required in a direct negotiation process.

This whole process took six months and resulted in a simple, four-page letter of intent to create a totally new alliance. For the Japanese company, it promised that the new alliance would be a 50-50 joint venture in which they would become a completely equal partner. For the U.S. company, it promised that conflicts of interest would be eliminated by having the Japanese partner fold their competitive business into the alliance.

Beyond this, the letter of intent included few details. The specifics of new alliance structure, parent company contribution, product offerings, and marketing strategies were all to be worked out during the next six months. Joint venture contracts were to be signed only after the CEOs of both parent companies had agreed that the business proposition of the new alliance was "optimal."

A NEW BUSINESS PLAN

Following the success of the effort to draft a letter of intent, a new working team was established to develop the optimal business plan and work out the details of the scope and structure of the alliance. This team reported to two steering committees: one for the U.S. parent company (consisting of the chairman, the head of international, and the head of sales and marketing), and the other for the Japanese parent (consisting of the chairman, the president, and the head of international).

The role of this team was to generate ideas and plans for the new alliance, which would then be taken to the respective parent company steering committees for reaction and further direction. This team became, in effect, the advocate for the new business. It was structured with marketing, sales, and operations subteams to sharpen the focus on the key business issues that needed to be resolved.

Motivating for Success

Several factors contributed to make this phase of the process work, even given the history of mistrust that existed between the two companies. First, the managers selected to lead the joint team were destined to be—and became—the top managers of the new alliance. They were put on the project full-time and knew that their futures depended on properly structuring the alliance. Most other team members were also selected because they were ultimately to become employees of the new company. As a result, the team gradually became much more concerned with developing a viable business than, for example, with whether the U.S. or Japanese parent was going to pay for the software development of key information systems.

Second, although the senior managers of each parent company were closely involved in directing the formation of the alliance, they did not negotiate face-to-face with their counterparts in the other. This allowed them to react directly to the joint team's ideas and plans and to concentrate on arriving at practical business solutions, rather than having to respond to positions adopted by the other side. The integrated business plans, by definition, incorporated both costs and benefits for each parent company, which put a premium on all team members taking a business, rather than a transaction, perspective on their work.

As in developing the letter of intent, the alliance redesign process was smoothed by having a neutral third party act as facilitator at both the steering committee and joint working team levels. The key issues of geographic scope and parent company business contributions were resolved by iterative indirect discussions between the steering committees, which focused on how best to build the business. At each stage, ideas from the working team were reviewed by each steering committee. This senior-level feedback was communicated to the other company and to the working team, which then began its next iteration. An indication of the success of this process is that both companies agreed to expand the business significantly beyond what had been agreed to in the letter of intent.

Resolving Detailed Arrangements

Both steering committees felt that the parents' contributions should be balanced, yet they were convinced that building the best business was more important than the initial financial arrangements. To ensure coordination with alliance scope and business plans, the joint working team became the vehicle for resolving issues of parent company contribution and transfer price. These were the final difficulties that needed to be resolved before contracts could be signed to launch the new alliance.

For these discussions, senior finance managers from each parent company temporarily joined the team. A conscious decision was made not to set up a separate negotiation process for these issues. We wanted to ensure that the spirit of cooperation would not be replaced by one of negotiation.

Although resolving the financial arrangements added two extra months to the original six-month schedule, the cooperative nature of the effort was maintained. As a result, the joint venture contract captured both the business and the financial agreements and required very little final negotiation. All major issues had been resolved through the joint working team process.

THE ALLIANCE REBUILT

The process used to revitalize the alliance succeeded in creating a more equal and viable entity and in helping to repair a damaged relationship. The new 50-50 joint venture made the Japanese company a full partner in the business. It also created an integrated product line—consisting of current, new, and hybrid services—that was unmatched by any existing competitor.

By combining American and Japanese sales forces, gaining broader access to the parents' customer bases, and developing a more integrated business with better economics, this approach created a solid base for new growth. At the same time, management teams and organizations had been developed in the United States and Japan that were able to launch the restructured business two months after the contracts—and less than a year after the letter of intent—were signed.

Looking back, there were several keys to the successful restructuring of this alliance:

- The entire process was designed to develop and maintain a spirit of cooperation and equality. The focus was on idea generation and building a better business, rather than on negotiation.
- The top management of both parent companies recognized that the overall business proposition was compelling. They were committed to building a strong long-term alliance and were not overly focused on the short-term balance between the two sides.
- Joint working team members were very committed to the alliance because of their personal stakes in its future.
- The process was kept focused and moving by having a neutral third party as a facilitator and communications link at both the senior management and the working-team levels.
- There was a recognition from the outset that time and patience would be required to develop the business plan, structure the deal, and do a large part of the initial implementation before the contracts were signed. Thus, both partners were prepared to maintain their enthusiasm throughout the 14 months it took to restructure the alliance.

Although this process may not work for all alliances facing difficulty, there are many situations in which a cooperative restructuring process can be effective. The experience reported here indicates that companies need to think creatively about means as well as ends as they try to tap the full benefits of their relationships with other current or potential partners.

6

Succeeding at Cross-Border Mergers and Acquisitions

Joel Bleeke, David Ernst,
James A. Isono, and Douglas D. Weinberg

Achieving growth, access to markets, and access to technology has led companies in all parts of the Triad to pursue cross-border mergers and acquisitions (M&A) as a tool to meet the challenges of global competition. As these challenges intensify, it will become increasingly critical for managers to understand how and when to acquire abroad. To determine the key success factors for such activities, we examined the foreign acquisition patterns of leading companies from each leg of the Triad.

Our examination revealed, surprisingly, that cross-border M&A for the largest companies has a relatively high success rate compared with other forms of corporate expansion. The main reason is that cross-border acquirers buy companies in familiar businesses to which they can add value, rather than simply "high-return" targets. In cross-border M&A, the basic principles of domestic M&A still apply. Some of these principles—buying targets where value can be added, for example—have been fully described elsewhere, so we will not elaborate on them here. Less often discussed, however, are the following characteristics of successful cross-border acquirers:

- They buy targets in their core business.
- They seek strong local performers.
- They focus resources on a few critical elements of the target's business system, especially those that are global.
- They do significant "skills transfer" both to and from the acquired company.
- They integrate critical systems by "patching" them together initially, resisting the urge to spend heavily.
- They execute multiple acquisitions, not one-off deals.

Many of these principles apply to domestic M&A as well. But this article highlights success factors that apply particularly to cross-border activity.

FOCUS ON CORE BUSINESS

The overall success rate of cross-border purchases was 57%, much higher than we had anticipated. Compared with other methods of expansions, this rate is quite high. For example, in a study McKinsey conducted several years ago of *Fortune* "200" companies, the success rate for domestic diversification was only 25%, less than half the rate for cross-border M&A.

As noted earlier, the main reason for this level of cross-border performance is that *a successful cross-border acquirer buys targets in its core business*—in other words, the same business it is already in. In core businessess, the acquirer can often add value both to itself and to the target by making operational improvements and by increasing economies of scale.

In our study, 14 of the 16 successful programs were in the core acquirer's business (see Exhibit 6.1). By contrast, four of the six noncore programs failed. One leading U.S. financial services company's foreign acquisition failed largely because the acquirer was unfamiliar with the retail banking business.

Similarly, a European telecommunications service company was unable to succeed when it bought a telephone equipment manufacturing company. Buying in a core business does not guarantee success, but it is a prerequisite for succeeding in most of the cases we investigated.

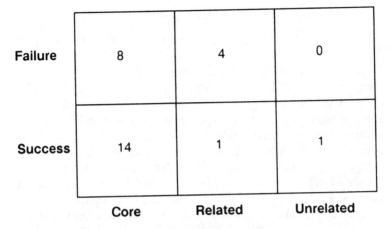

Exhibit 6.1 Acquisition programs in core business have high success rate (numbers represent number of acquisition programs).

Percentage/number of acquisition programs

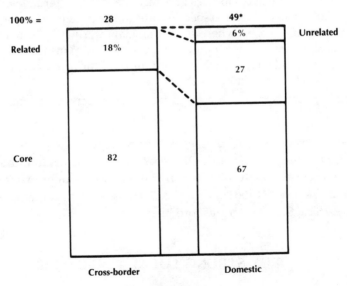

* One company did not make any domestic acquisitions.

Exhibit 6.2 Top 50 U.S. companies focus more on core business when buying abroad.

--------------------------- **Methodology** ---------------------------

We reviewed the foreign acquisition programs of the top 50
companies, ranked by market value, in each of the legs of the
Triad (Japan, Europe, and the United States). Looking at those
companies that did more than $100 million in foreign deals be-
tween 1981 and 1987 (to provide sufficient time to evaluate performance), we screened out programs whose results were too
recent to judge or about which there was insufficient information to evaluate success. In all, we looked at 28 programs, representing 319 deals valued at over $68 billion. The programs
reviewed represent a diversity of industries and regions, including 8 U.S., 9 Japanese, and 11 European companies.

The success of a program was determined by several criteria.
For programs whose acquisitions totaled more than 20% of the
acquirer's market value, we looked for maintenance or improvement in the acquirer's performance, judged mainly by returns
on equity and assets. We considered smaller programs to have
been successful if returns from their acquisitions met or exceeded the acquirer's cost of capital, using public and proprietary information to make an assessment. We should note that
these success criteria are distinctly American. Most Japanese
and European companies generally have longer term, less financially constrained perspectives for judging their purchases.

In some cases, where such financial information was unavailable, interviews with industry experts or McKinsey consultants
revealed clearly the success or failure of the acquisitions, based
on such factors as market access.

The focus on core businesses is considerably higher in cross-border acquisitions than in domestic. Of the 49 U.S. companies in our sample that
acquired domestically, only two thirds—67%— bought primarily in core
businesses (see Exhibit 6.2). Of the 28 cross-border programs of U.S. companies, 82% focused on the core business.

BUY STRONG LOCAL PERFORMERS

*Good acquirers tend to buy well-performing, strong local players: they do not
overestimate their ability to turn around foreign targets.* The complexity of
operating in a foreign environment, created by such factors as differing

labor laws and local distribution arrangements, often makes changes that are relatively straightforward at home difficult to execute in another country. In our sample, we found that companies buying performers with strong return or equity and assets succeeded in five out of six cases. On the other hand, acquirers of poorly performing targets failed in four out of seven cases. While acquirers bought strong performers, they did not pay premiums beyond what they could recoup.

In addition to buying companies with strong financial performance, good cross-border acquirers also seek targets that have strong local presence—that is, are top-tier industry performers. Eight (shaded boxes) of the nine purchases of companies with strong local presence succeeded, but 7 (shaded boxes) of the 10 purchases of targets with poor or medium market presence failed to repay the acquirer's cost of capital (see Exhibit 6.3).

Number of acquisitions

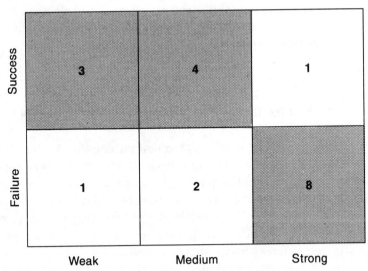

Target's local market presence*

*Nine programs were excluded because they could not be classified for their strength of market presence.

Exhibit 6.3 Successful acquirers buy targets with strong local market presence (numbers represent number of acquisition programs).

Several Japanese financial institutions have incurred major losses after failing to assess adequately the bad-debt risk on the books of their U.S. targets. Another Japanese company was unable to surmount the weak distribution capabilities of an acquired electronics company. In both these cases, the target was weak in a local function—credit analysis and distribution and sales—and the acquirer lacked the market knowledge to turn the situation around. Acquirers buying weak companies are among the least likely to succeed. Many of the failures we reviewed supported the notion that diversifying abroad while trying to turn around a target is extremely difficult to accomplish.

One exception to this rule is when a purchaser is seeking only technology or skills. In cases where successful acquirers bought targets with only a medium local presence, technology transfer contributed significantly to their success. For example, a U.S. automaker bought part of a foreign company that was weak in the United States and second tier at home. However, the U.S. company's gains in productivity methods and auto design made the acquisition successful. Similarly, a Japanese computer company bought a medium-strength U.S. player, whose excellent product development skills and technologies made the acquisition successful for the Japanese buyer, which contributed high-quality, low-cost manufacturing capability.

FOCUS ON CRITICAL—ESPECIALLY GLOBAL—BUSINESS SYSTEM ELEMENTS

Once the target has been selected and purchased, the next step is adding value to it (or obtaining value from it). In almost every successful program, we found that acquirers did not try to get everything right initially. Instead, *they focused resources on the critical elements of their business systems that provided sustainable competitive advantage*. A European food company focused on improving the distribution, marketing, and sales of its targets, increasing its share of shelf space and improving their marketing. A U.K. pharmaceutical company focused on marketing and sales in its purchase of an over the counter pharmaceuticals company, capturing synergies quickly by having sales forces sell both companies' products, for example.

The critical elements in the business system are often *company-specific* rather than *industry-specific*. In many cases a company develops a "tweak" in its business system that gives it competitive advantage and that is essential for the company to create in its acquisition. One financial services company going abroad focused mainly on the functions central to building customer relationships, such as sales and customer service. Areas that were not critical to its formula for success, such as new product development, received much less attention.

Furthermore, *successful acquirers typically concentrate first on the global functions of their businesses, where they often derived the most value.* Global functions are those in which worldwide scale or coordination leads to significant competitive advantages; local functions are those in which advantages are primarily felt at a country level. In a pharmaceutical company, for example, R&D may be global, but distribution and sales are probably local. This was clearly illustrated by a foreign acquisition of a U.S. pharmaceutical company, which had performed abysmally due to weak marketing— until the acquirer was able to introduce two new drugs based on its global strength in R&D.

Local functions require case-by-case evaluation and are often best tackled later in the post-acquisition integration process. A retail bank, for example, introduced into its European acquisition "global" products, such as NOW accounts and point-of-sale equipment financing, but left many of the local systems in place. A transportation company moved quickly to plug local "feeder" acquisitions into its global operations, initially leaving local operation systems intact.

TRANSFER SKILLS TO CAPTURE VALUE

Acquirers use a variety of methods to add value. Among the most common is what we call "skills transfer." By "skills," we mean those things that the institution as a whole, rather than individual employees, does well.

Of the 14 successful acquisition programs we reviewed, 11 (shaded box) involved a high degree of skills transfer either to or from the target (see Exhibit 6.4). In all 10 (shaded box) failed programs, skills transfer was insignificant. *In most of the successful cases, skills and systems transfers had a greater impact than pure scale increases.* The skills transferred initially were usually those in the acquirer's critical business system elements. For a number of consumer product companies, for example, that meant product management or sales and distribution. For a U.S. bank, it meant operations, marketing, and product development.

Skills transfer is often achieved by moving just a few senior managers in key positions, who identify and direct operational improvements. This is fortunate

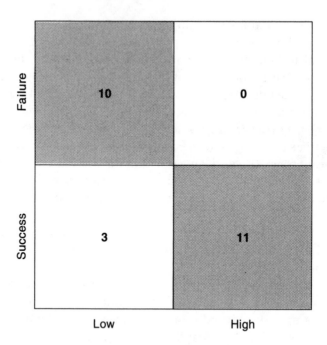

Extent of skills transfer*

* Four programs were excluded because they could not be classified for their extent of skills transfer.

Exhibit 6.4   Skills transfer is key for cross-border success (numbers represent number of acquisition programs).

for the pocketbooks of foreign acquirers; the cost of supporting an expatriate, according to a European chemical company, is three times that of using indigenous managers. In most of the companies we reviewed, this transfer is temporary, the ultimate goal being to train a local managerial cadre. To get extra managerial talent, some acquirers recruited heavily from local institutions.

Not all skills are transferred from acquirer to target. In some cases skills transfer was reversed. Take the case of a European chemical company that tried to build a U.S. presence by piecing together several small U.S. acquisitions. The attempt met with limited success because the acquirer lacked the managerial capability to integrate its purchases. The acquirer then changed strategy, buying a company with skilled management. The purchaser replaced most of its U.S. management with managers from the acquired company and created a successful U.S. operation.

A similar reverse transfer occurred with a European pharmaceutical company. It acquired a U.S. company with excellent management skills and moved the U.S. company's senior managers into seven of the nine key functional positions at the new company. The resulting firm performed better than either of its predecessors.

It is important to be careful about transferring expatriates into culturally-sensitive positions. We ran into a number of cases where expats lacking local market experience got into trouble. One, a bank's computer manager, who was transferred from Argentina to a Spanish acquisition, focused inappropriately on rapid deposit clearance due to his background in a high-inflation market. Consequently, he designed a system that over-performed and cost the company significant profits.

PATCH TOGETHER KEY SYSTEMS

Another key lever for adding value, related to skills transfer, is systems transfer. Integration of large systems can be extraordinarily complex, especially over large distances and when adaptation to national differences is required. *Successful acquirers tend to limit their transfers to the few critical systems that need to be operational, "patching" them together initially and resisting the impulse to spend heavily.*

Many systems can be left in place and changed over time. A U.S. bank, for which systems are critical, waited five years before significantly altering its systems in a European country. In the meantime, it was able to introduce new products and patch existing systems to keep them running. People working with information technology often propose initial investments in a much more elaborate system than a company currently has, arguing that a new system will provide much greater capability. But making changes too early risks losing the opportunity to incorporate early lessons learned about operating in a new market.

As with skills, systems changes should be aimed at key systems. The critical systems of an international packaged express company were its billing and tracking systems. To adapt to differences between its headquarters and local companies computer tracking numbers for goods, it initially used a translation table between its domestic system and the others, enabling it to monitor goods-in-process and follow through on billings using two or more country-based computer systems. The company plans to implement an integrated system after the systems in place have run separately for a while.

A consumer products company rapidly patched together its sales order entry system with that of its acquisition but resisted an initial temptation to centralize R&D systems in order to avoid stifling local flexibility and creativity. Many functions continue to run on separate systems, even several years after the acquisition.

PUT BUYING PROGRAMS IN PLACE

Cross-border experience increases the chances of success. In our sample, successful companies had nearly twice the average and median number of purchases as unsuccessful companies (see Exhibit 6.5). Through initial acquisitions, the acquirer refines its M&A skills and becomes more comfortable with—and proficient at—using M&A for international expansion. In an early acquisition, a pharmaceutical company focused on integrity products while neglecting the importance of encouraging product managers and other key employees to stay with the company. In subsequent acquisitions, the company identified valuable employees and gave them big incentives to remain with the company.

Many successful acquirers pursue a phased program. One consumer goods company, for example, made an "anchor" acquisition of a leading brand, then used its distribution clout to push several brands that were subsequently acquired. A financial services company leveraged a small team of operations and product development specialists in a series of acquisitions abroad—many of which have followed similar strategies.

Number of deals per program

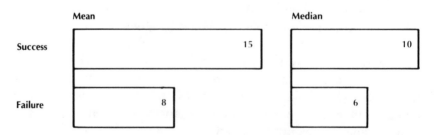

Exhibit 6.5 Successful cross-border acquirers have more experience.

Cross-border M&A is a very effective tactic that has been used by a wide variety of companies to achieve growth, market access, technology access, and other objectives. While leveraging the basics learned from domestic M&A programs, companies also need to understand the unique characteristics of successful cross-border M&A programs, which reflect the added complexity of global competition and multicultural environments.

7

The New Shape of Cross-Border Mergers and Acquisitions

Joel Bleeke, David Ernst, James A. Isono, and Douglas D. Weinberg

Companies in each part of the Triad confront a unique set of incentives and constraints when they contemplate cross-border activity. Structural variations create dramatically different, and sometimes surprising, patterns of activity across the Triad. Japanese companies spend three times as much on cross-border mergers and acquisitions (M&A) as on domestic deals. European companies, spurred by the single-market directives and the opening of Eastern Europe, do more cross-border than domestic activity, with more than half of total cross-border volume targeted at non-European Community (EC) countries. And U.S. companies continue to be the largest net sellers on the global cross-border M&A balance sheet. But it is the Europeans, not the Japanese, who are the big buyers.

This chapter is based on extensive revisions of "The Shape of Cross-Border M&A," by Joel Bleeke, David Ernst, James Isono, and Douglas Weinberg, which appeared in the *McKinsey Quarterly* (Spring 1990).

This chapter looks at trends in cross-border M&A and at its effects on the global position of the U.S., European, and Japanese companies.

CROSS-BORDER MERGERS AND ACQUISITIONS
AT HIGH LEVELS, AFTER BOOM AND BUST

Cross-border M&A grew explosively during the late 1980s. Across the Triad, the number of deals more than tripled between 1984 and 1989, while the value of deals increased ninefold as more and more megamergers took place. The 1989 total, $102 billion, was greater than the gross domestic products of 5 of the 12 EC countries (Denmark, Greece, Ireland, Luxembourg, and Portugal). And this figure even understates the actual value of cross-border M&A because it includes only those deals whose value has been disclosed (typically fewer than half of all deals).

Since 1989, the volume of cross-border M&A in the European Community, United States, and Japan has declined sharply, to about $41 billion in 1991. The number of deals also declined, although not as steeply (Exhibit 7.1). This decline was caused by several factors, some of which are permanent, while others are likely to be temporary: a global turndown, the bursting of the Japanese "bubble," problems with the high-yield bond market, and the need for many aggressive acquirers to pause to integrate their earlier targets.

Even after the decline, cross-border M&A continues to be critically important as a strategy vehicle. It is still running at a historically high level, with twice the number of deals and four times the volume compared with the mid-1980s.

Many industries have been reshaped by leading companies that, by aggressively acquiring abroad, forced competitors to follow suit—or exit the business. During the past 10 years, Electrolux has built a leading position in a number of globalizing product markets by making over 100 acquisitions, many of which were cross-border. By standardizing product components to achieve manufacturing scale and transferring skills across borders, it gained a substantial cost advantage over competitors, which must now catch up in building their global positions. A similar example is BSN, which built a dominant position in several European food categories through foreign acquisitions. And ASEA, merging with Brown Boveri, reshaped the world power generation equipment industry by being able to offer a broad range of products in virtually every major market.

NUMBER OF DEALS

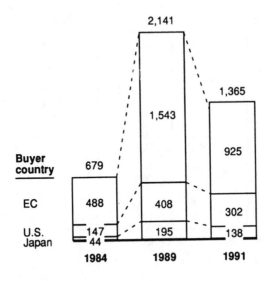

VALUE OF DEALS
$ Billion

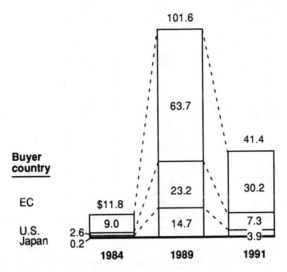

Exhibit 7.1 Cross-border M&A peaked in 1989. *Source:* KPMG Dealwatch; Daiwa; Yamaichi; Euromoney; EC; Mergerstat; Acquisition Monthly; McKinsey analysis; majority acquisitions for 1989, 1991; majority and minority acquisitions used for 1984 where majority data unavailable.

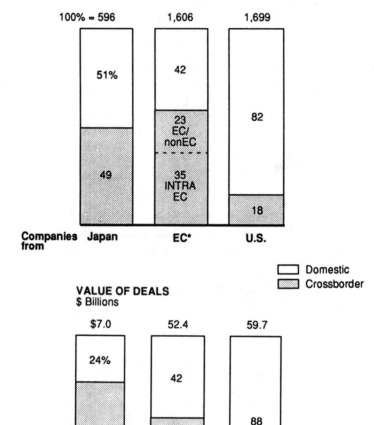

Exhibit 7.2 Cross-border M&A as a percentage of total merger and acquisitions, 1991. *Source:* KPMG Dealwatch; Yamaichi; EC; Mergerstat; McKinsey analysis; majority acquisitions for EC, U.S.; majority and minority acquisitions for Japan.

The degree to which a region's total M&A is aimed abroad varies widely across the Triad, but cross-border M&A activity is very important in Japan and the EC. Nearly 60% of all acquisitions of EC companies are cross-border; 23% of transactions and 32% of the total value of deals involve an EC and non-EC company. In Japan, about half of the total transactions and three quarters of the volume are directed abroad. In the United States, by contrast, cross-border acquisitions represent only 18% of total purchases and 12% of acquisition value (Exhibit 7.2).

THE UNITED STATES: NET SELLERS

The huge and continuing imbalance in cross-border transactions involving U.S. companies is striking. Companies in the United States are the most active sellers but only infrequent buyers abroad. Foreign companies' acquisitions of majority ownership of U.S. companies totaled $68

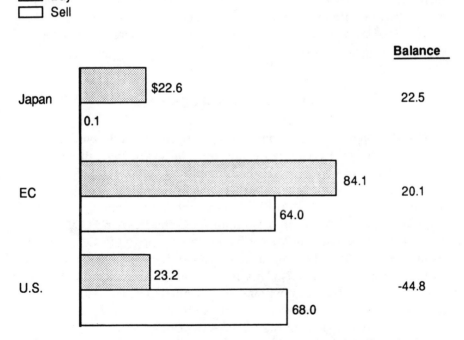

Exhibit 7.3 Cross-border M&A balance, 1990–1991 ($ billions). *Source:* KPMG Dealwatch; majority acquisitions only.

billion in 1990 and 1991—nearly three times the value of U.S. acquisitions abroad (Exhibit 7.3). U.S. firms conduct only about 300 foreign acquisitions each year.

The imbalance in purchases and sales is especially clear in the largest transactions. Of the 21 largest cross-border M&A deals announced in 1991 that involved a U.S. company (Exhibit 7.4), 15 were acquisitions by foreign companies of U.S. companies (three were acquisitions of the European subsidiaries of U.S. companies). Regional-specific factors, such as the persistently weak U.S. dollar, the need to recycle dollars accumulating offshore because of the U.S. trade deficit, and limited restrictions on foreign ownership, continue to make U.S. companies attractive to foreign acquirers.

The recent sale of U.S. companies to non-U.S. purchasers is in sharp contrast with the historical position of U.S. companies as major investors in Europe. Based on market values estimated using current earnings (rather than historical book values, which ignore inflation and are highly dependent on the date of the original investment), the U.S. foreign direct investment position in Europe is almost five times that of the European direct investment position in the United States (Exhibit 7.5). U.S. companies, therefore, often choose to invest in their existing foreign operations by making capital improvements, while European companies are more likely to look for U.S. acquisitions to build position and increase their base of skilled management in the United States.

EUROPE: AGGRESSIVE BUYERS

As already noted, EC-based companies are the largest cross-border acquirers. Their purchases accounted for over $30 billion in 1991, three fourths of total Triad cross-border M&A and more than half of total global M&A activity. Driven by the single-market directives and deregulation, there has been a sustained shift in EC M&A activity away from national M&A and toward cross-border M&A. Both intra-EC and EC–non-EC M&A have grown faster than national M&A (Exhibit 7.6). Surprisingly, EC companies spent as much ($13.5 billion) on cross-border acquisitions in the U.S. as within Europe (Exhibit 7.7). This is true because of a handful of large deals; the top seven EC acquisitions in the United States in 1991 amounted to nearly $6 billion. However, EC companies conducted twice as many cross-border acquisitions in the EC as in the United States.

Among European countries, though, patterns of cross-border M&A differ greatly (Exhibit 7.8). France has been the biggest net buyer

Buyer	Buyer country	Seller	Seller country	Price offered/ paid ($ millions)
Groupe Schneider	France	Square D Co.	U.S.	$2,015
Viag AG	Germany	Peter Kiewit Sons Inc. (Continental Can Europe)	U.S.	1,000
Groupe Axa S.A.	France	Equitable Life Assurance Society	U.S.	1,000
Roche Holding Ltd.	Switzerland	Sara Lee Corp. (European Consumer Medicine Business)	U.S.	821
Kohlberg, Kravis Roberts & Co.	U.S.	The News Corp. Ltd. (Murdoch Magazine Group)	Australia	650
Alcatel N.V.	Netherlands	Rockwell International Corp. (Network Transmission System Div.)	U.S.	625
Whirlpool Corp.	U.S.	Philips Electronic N.V. (Whirlpool International B.V.)	Netherlands	610
Broken Hill Pty. Co. Ltd.	Australia	Hamilton Oil Corp.	U.S.	525
Heinz (H.J.) Co.	U.S.	John Labatt Ltd. (JL Foods)	Canada	500
Pacific Gas & Electric Co.	U.S.	British Petroleum Co. plc (TEX/CON Oil & Gas)	U.K.	400
TransCanada Pipelines Ltd.	Canada	Pacific Gas Transmission Co.	U.S.	350
Sony Corp.	Japan	General Electric Co. (RCA/Columbia Home Video)	U.S.	300
Roche Holding Ltd.	Switzerland	Cetus Corp. (GeneAmp Technology)	U.S.	300
Banco Ambrosiano Veneto	Italy	Citibank Italia S.p.A.	U.S.	273
Central & South West Corp.	U.S.	British Petroleum Co. plc (Gas, Transmission Business)	U.K.	250
Molson Cos. Ltd.	Canada	Chemed Corp. (Dubois Chemicals Unit)	U.S.	243
American Express Company	U.S.	Signet Ltd.	U.K.	235
Banco de Santander S.A. de Credita	Spain	First Fidelity Bancorporation	U.S.	221
Brambles Industries Ltd.	Australia	Environmental Systems Co.	U.S.	203
Roquette Freres	France	H.J. Heinz Co. (Hubinger Co.)	U.S.	200
Private Group	Japan	Monsanto Co. (Animal Feed Ingredients Operation)	U.S.	200

Exhibit 7.4 Twenty-one largest M&A deals announced involving a U.S. company, 1991. *Source:* Mergerstat; includes uncompleted transactions; majority and minority acquisitions.

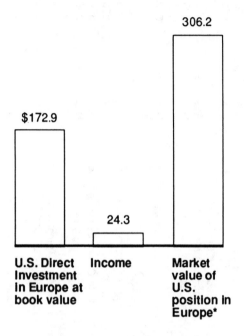

* Market value of U.S. position in Europe calculated based on weighted average 1989 P/E for Belgium, Denmark, France, Germany, Italy, Netherlands, Spain, and United Kingdom.

Exhibit 7.5 Foreign direct investment positions, United States versus Europe, 1991 (estimate). *Source:* U.S. Department of Commerce; GT Guide to World Equity Markets; McKinsey analysis.

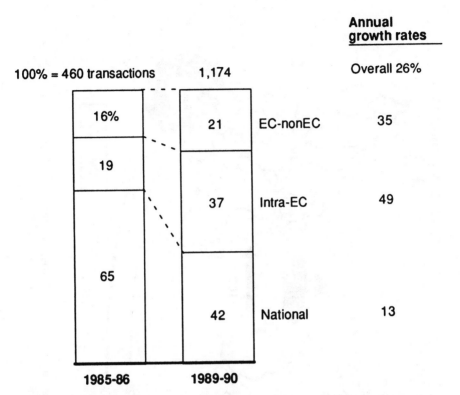

Exhibit 7.6 Cross-border M&A is growing rapidly relative to domestic activity in European Community. *Source:* EC Commission on Competition. Includes majority and minority stakes; survey limited to approximately 1,500 companies.

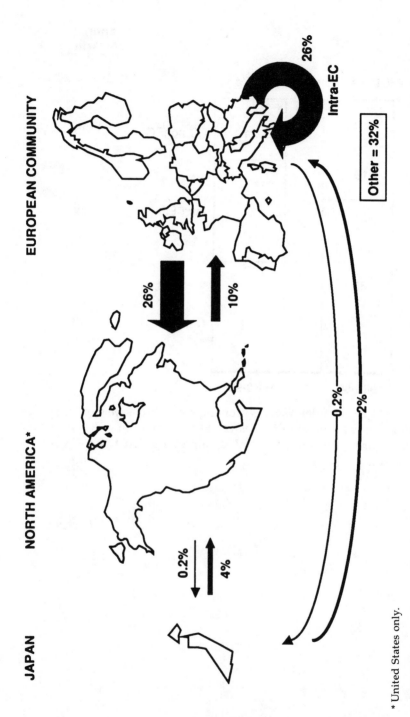

JAPAN   NORTH AMERICA*   EUROPEAN COMMUNITY

26%

Intra-EC

26%

10%

Other = 32%

0.2%

2%

0.2%

4%

* United States only.

Exhibit 7.7 European Community companies are largest buyers—Cross-border M&A Flows, 1991 (100% = $51.7 billion). *Source:* Dealwatch; McKinsey analysis; majority acquisitions only.

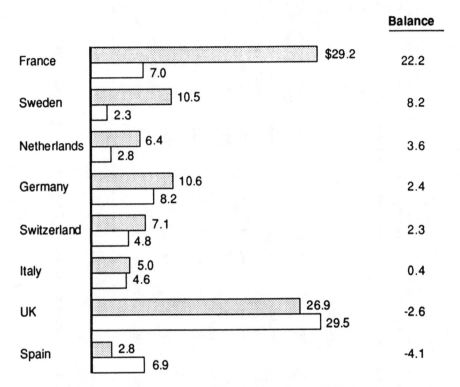

Exhibit 7.8 Cross-border M&A balance of selected European countries 1990–1991 ($ billions). *Source:* Dealwatch; McKinsey analysis; majority acquisitions only.

recently, with a balance of plus $22 billion in 1990–1991. Swedish and Swiss companies, continuing previous patterns, were net acquirers as well, as were Germany and the Netherlands. The relatively accessible U.K. market showed the greatest amount of activity overall, while Spain was an attractive target.

The opening of Eastern Europe has had a significant effect on the shape of European cross-border activity, although many of these deals are still pending, or take alternative forms such as joint ventures (and thus do not appear in the cross-border M&A data). However, the value of planned investments is quite substantial. European investors account

Investor	Country	Partner/target	Industry	Country	$ Million	Comment
VW	Germany	Skoda automotive BAZ	Autos	Czechoslovakia	$6,500	Initial 31% stake to be upgraded to majority; 10-year investment plan
Fiat	Italy	FSM	Autos	Poland	475*	51% stake (pending)
John Brown	U.K.	Gasprom	Chemicals	Russia	500	JV to develop ethylene and polyethylene plant in Siberia
Suzuki	Japan	Consortium	Vehicles	Hungary	400	40% stake; $50 million share capital; 10-year investment plan
GM	U.S.	Bakony Raba	Vehicles	Hungary	415**	67% stake; share capital $115 million
Philips	Netherlands	Polam Pila	Lighting	Poland	300***	51% stake; 7-year investment
Siemens	Germany	Skoda machinery (two divisions)	Industrial equipment	CSFR	285	57% and 51% stakes (pending)
Mercedes Benz	Germany	LIAZ AVIA	Vehicles	CSFR	280	31% initial stake to be upgraded; 6-year investment plan (pending)
GE	U.S.	Tungsram	Lighting	Hungary	250	50 (+1)% stake; $150 million acquisition price
Electrolux	Sweden	Lehel	Refrigerators	Hungary	250	100% stake; $70 million acquisition price

*Initial $75 million plus additional $400 million
**Level of investment reported varies from $250–415 million
***Level of investment reported varies from $35–300 million

Exhibit 7.9 Large foreign investments in Eastern Europe (estimates). *Source:* Eastern European Press, national agencies; includes pending deals.

for 7 of the 10 largest deals announced in Eastern Europe. These would amount to more than $8 billion, nearly 30% of EC cross-border M&A spending in 1991. The most popular targets are Czechoslovakia, Poland, Hungary, and the former Soviet Union (Exhibit 7.9).

By contrast, the German unification has had more impact on domestic M&A in Germany than on European cross-border M&A. As of December 1991, the Treuhandanstalt had announced the sale of more than 5,200 companies, of which nearly 5,000 were purchased by German buyers. German buyers had pledged $42 billion in new investments, while non-German buyers had pledged $7 billion.

JAPAN: SMALL ROLE IN GLOBAL M&A PATTERNS

Japanese cross-border acquisitions grew rapidly from a small base in the latter half of the 1980s, marked by a number of highly publicized deals. However, since 1989, Japanese cross-border acquisitions have fallen sharply to under $4 billion in 1991. There are a number of reasons for the decline. Most obvious is the bursting of the "bubble economy." As Japan's stock and real estate markets declined sharply, Japanese banks and companies have pulled back sharply. After exporting nearly $600 billion in capital (for M&A, securities, real estate, and other investments) during 1985–1990, Japan repatriated $37 billion in 1991. Another reason for the decline in Japanese cross-border acquisitions is that many Japanese companies are now favoring alliances after encountering difficulties in their cross-border acquisitions.

It is not clear when Japanese cross-border acquisitions will pick up momentum again. However, when they do, Europe is likely to be the primary target. Between 1985 and 1991, the proportion of Japanese acquisitions in Europe had already increased dramatically relative to other regions. And a survey by McKinsey & Company of international executives of leading Japanese companies shows clearly that Japanese companies have shifted their sights from the United States to Europe (Exhibit 7.10).

As yet, few cross-border acquisitions are directed *into* Japan; nor is there any sign that an increase in inbound acquisitions is underway. Between 1985 and 1991, Yamaichi Securities reported a range of 15 to 26 inbound acquisitions each year, with a slight downward trend. And the total value of foreign acquisitions in Japan has remained under $1 billion each year. Because of cross-shareholdings and strong informal relationships between suppliers, manufacturers, and distributors,

Number of acquisitions by Japanese companies

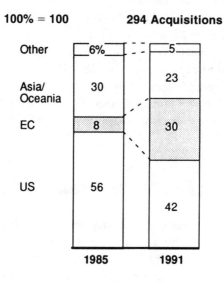

Main focus for expansion by 25 leading Japanese companies

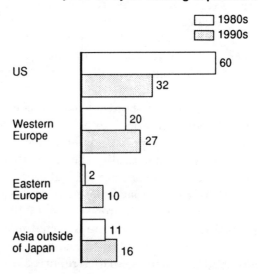

Exhibit 7.10 Japanese cross-border acquisitions shifted to Europe in late 1980s, and this focus is expected to continue in 1990s. *Source:* Yamaichi Securities; McKinsey survey of 90 executives from 25 Japanese companies; includes majority and minority acquisitions.

foreign companies often find that joint ventures are a better way into Japan.

The downturn in Europe and the United States, together with some tough lessons learned during the M&A frenzy of the late 1980s, have combined to sharply reduce cross-border M&A. This does not mean that cross-border acquisitions are unimportant or unattractive. However, it does put a premium on knowing when and how to use cross-border acquisitions. (In Chapter 6, we looked closely at the overall success rate of cross-border M&A and identified the common characteristics of firms that emerge as winners.)

PART
TWO

THE REGIONS:
JAPAN, UNITED STATES, EUROPE

In Part One, we walked through the strategic issues that face global managers in mergers, acquisitions, and alliances. We generalized across industries, countries, and cultures, marrying strategic goals, macroeconomics, and business problems into a new collaborative mind-set.

But this is only half the story. Remember, cross-border strategy is an arbitrage of skills, capital, and access to customers. And arbitrage works because markets are not all the same. Differences are the engine of arbitrage, and it is differences between regions—due to culture, consumer preference, economic history, or government policy—that will be taken up in Part Two. We've organized this portion of the book into three subparts, corresponding to the regions of the Triad.

Some observers view the differences among the regions of the Triad as constraining and rail against them. The carping is familiar: Japanese shut foreigners out of their distribution networks; clubby European capital markets stifle the struggle for corporate control. The U.S. market is so large and competitive it is all but impossible for outsiders to gain a profitable foothold. The complaints go on and on. But they all miss the point. *Differences do not constrain strategy. They define it.*

The key is to understand how durable and deep the differences are. If the differences do not endure, then the deal based on them will collapse. Long, mutually profitable collaborations rest on persistent differences between markets and competitors; partnerships thrive only so long as partners offer each other something that is otherwise unobtainable.

Determining the durability of differences across the Triad is particularly difficult. Consumer preferences, technology, and environmental regulations are indeed rapidly becoming more similar around the Triad. Capital markets are converging. But at a closer level of detail, things are far more complex.

For example, the often discussed converging global consumer market may be converging geographically, but at the same time, it is diverging into niche customer segments around the world. There is no single large global market for automobiles. Automobiles have fragmented into a global luxury market, a market for off-road vehicles and trucks, a market for family vans, and so on. Similarly, the converging clothing market is simultaneously fragmenting with companies as different as Hermes, Ferragamo, Benetton, and the Gap each claiming their segment. The fragmentation of customers, made possible by global scale, continuously creates new opportunities for focused cross-border alliances and acquisitions. Blockbuster Video's joint venture to enter the video rental business in Japan, for example, highlights the importance of increasing customer segmentation as a basis for emerging global alliances.

The balance between convergence of geographic markets and divergence of customer segments coupled with the differences across countries among skills, capital, and access to customers provides the basis for global arbitrage. Part Two offers insights on how to tailor strategies to the specific challenges of each region. In each case, the ultimate goal needs to be to reach the right mix between global scale and becoming an insider in local markets.

JAPAN

The ability to collaborate is absolutely necessary for developing an insider position in Japan. Go-it-alone strategies in Japan require a lot of money. Relatively few acquisitions of attractive Japanese companies take place, and more than half of all foreign entries into Japan have been accomplished through alliances.

An essential part of developing a local position in Japan is dealing with the *existing* collaborations or "soft integration" between suppliers, manufacturers, and distributors. Even when there is no real cross-ownership, companies may swap personnel and have overlapping quality control, product development, and just-in-time inventory systems. The net effect is that price alone does not provide market share. Getting inside these relationships often requires a very long time, if not an entirely new approach to distribution such as the recent opening of a superstore Toys 'R' Us, or the door-to-door sales of cosmetics by Avon.

Maintaining a fair arbitrage between Western and Japanese partners is difficult, especially given the longevity of alliances in Japan. Alliances in Japan tend to last for 15 to 20 years, twice as long as average elsewhere. Even if both partners aren't satisfied, the costs of breaking the relationship are high, and it is often difficult to find replacement local partners. Historically, Western companies have offered innovative products or technology in return for access to the Japanese market. But over time, the Japanese partners learn these technologies themselves. A "mid-life crisis" often ensues because the Western partner is no longer contributing a fair share. Once this happens, the Japanese partner is well-positioned to buy out the venture. Not surprisingly, Japanese companies have been the acquirers in approximately 70% of the terminating ventures in Japan.

Because the Japanese market is so different, alliances are often necessary to open a window on the strategies of top competitors—"Strategic Learning." Even where an alliance is directed at production or marketing, it usually also involves an extensive transfer of knowledge about production and marketing processes. To compete in Japan, several U.S. companies have modified and accelerated their product development approach based on learning from their Japanese competitors. This type of knowledge cannot be learned through observation at a distance; only through close contact with a partner on a day-to-day basis.

THE UNITED STATES

As discussed in Chapter 10, Japanese companies face tough challenges in the United States. Outside the auto and consumer electronics business, Japanese companies have consistently had relatively poor performance in the United States. This is particularly true for Japanese acquisitions. In comparison with the better than 50% success rate for their U.S. and

European counterparts, the largest Japanese companies have only about a 30% success rate in their cross-border acquisition programs based on both financial and strategic objectives. Several reasons for this are discussed in this subpart, including that many acquisitions in the United States have been done on a "hands off" basis. This has prevented the collaboration necessary for skills transfer to the acquired company or two-way learning, and has also minimized the opportunity for capturing value through consolidation. Japanese alliances in the United States, in contrast to acquisitions, have been more successful, often providing the sharing of skills and the development of a collaborative mind-set.

Although foreign-based managers sometimes view the U.S. as a single market, developing a "local" position in the United States really means serving a series of markets, each of which can be as large as many European countries. As discussed in Chapter 11, by Magnus Nicolin and Bart Robinson, the United States is a diverse and expensive market. Entering the United States often requires extensive tailoring of marketing and distribution strategies on a local basis. Since the United States has 10 major consumer markets with a population over 2 million (Japan only has two), this is complex and costly. American companies spend about 2.5% of total U.S. gross national product on advertising, about twice the level of smaller markets like Sweden.

The large size of the United States means that acquisitions on a national scale are difficult and expensive. And foreign acquirers tend to pay dearly. Between 1976 and 1988, the average premium paid by non-U.S. companies for acquisitions in America was 49% above market value, versus a 35% premium paid by U.S. companies. Other costs, such as product liability claims or insurance premiums, compensation for top local managers, and professional services, are also higher than in Europe or Japan.

Although European companies have built impressive strategic positions in the United States, the costs of serving the U.S. market and its competitive intensity have often led to disappointing operating returns. There is obviously no single answer to succeeding in the United States. However, an assessment of the experience of 11 leading Scandinavian companies (see Chapter 11) suggests several lessons.

EUROPE

Managers trying to fashion cross-border strategies for Europe face unique challenges as well. The single-market directives, deregulation, and the opening of the Eastern bloc have made Europe the focus of global acquisitions and alliances (roughly half of global linkages involve a European company as acquiror or alliance partner). To date, many large European companies have competed primarily within their home markets. The future of these companies hinges on their ability to collaborate with foreign partners in order to improve skills, increase scale, or gain access to new markets. For these companies, developing appropriate cross-border alliance and acquisition strategies is crucial, given the pace and irreversibility of industry restructuring.

Before deciding to pursue acquisitions or alliances rather than outright sale, though, managers need to understand the extent to which their current position is bolstered by formal or informal protections, and how it compares with benchmarks set by global competitors who may not yet have entered home markets. Japanese players in particular, with relatively little presence in Europe prior to 1990, see Europe 1992 as much more of an opportunity than a threat and are using the full arsenal of cross-border strategies. Nissan has built its own assembly capacity in the United Kingdom and other Japanese automakers are following; Fujitsu has acquired ICL to expand its stake in computers.

Chapter 13 discusses alliance and acquisition options available in Europe to different groups of competitors. For example, in already concentrated global businesses such as autos and electronics, mergers between European players may not offer enough benefit to offset the problems of postmerger integration. The real challenge is to design alliances to trade access to home markets in return for access to critical skills—before home market profitability vanishes due to deregulation and the expanded presence of new competitors. Alliances with Japanese companies, such as Rover/Honda and Volkswagen/Suzuki, offer opportunities to improve manufacturing skills in return for access to the U.K. and German markets.

All European alliances require great sensitivity to local requirements. This is particularly true in the negotiation phase, where a U.S.-style "predatory" approach will usually be rejected out of hand by friendly stakeholders or supportive national governments. (In Germany, France, Italy, and Spain, for example, most acquisitions have relied on a preexisting stake or a private purchase of stock.) To acquire attractive companies and to leverage management skills across Europe, companies such as Electrolux are even pursuing "reverse takeovers"—where power is transferred *to* the management of acquired companies.

THE ROLE OF GOVERNMENTS

Differences between countries and companies define the terms of the collaboration and arbitrage that is involved in cross-border alliances and acquisitions. Many of these differences—especially access to markets—are themselves driven by government policies. Japanese regulation makes access to its market a very valuable bargaining chip for Japanese companies. Germany's proximity to Eastern Europe will give German companies greater and greater bargaining power as these new markets mature. The open markets and university research clusters such as Silicon Valley or Cambridge, Massachusetts, in the United States give U.S. companies a strong bargaining position in high tech, pharmaceuticals, and computers.

But the government's role is often negative as well. In pursuing short-term increases in trade, or protecting home markets, policy makers can inadvertently cripple their nation's companies' ability to bargain effectively. They can unwittingly rob entire industries of the potential to win in the global marketplace. For example, at various times, the U.S. government's focus on the trade deficit has led to a weak dollar. This may be good for trade numbers, but it has also tipped the table against U.S. companies in the arbitrage that is transnational strategy: U.S. assets and skills have been bought on the cheap by overseas companies; conversely, U.S. companies must spend more to build or invest overseas. At the same time, the "bubble" in the Japanese economy in the late 1980s—partly due to government policies affecting land and capital markets—provided highly valued assets that could be used to make foreign acquisitions, thus increasing the global arbitrage power of Japanese companies.

Domestic policy also constrains cross-border collaboration and arbitrage in subtle ways. U.S. antitrust policy and European industrial policy, for instance, give too little weight to how global an industry is. For businesses with a regional character, such as supermarkets or department stores, antitrust and industrial policy does a good job of protecting the consumer from the price gouging and low product and service quality that would come from monopolies. Yet it inappropriately prohibits consolidation in truly global industries, such as autos, electronics, and aircraft. To make an extreme case, it is hard to see the harm to consumers in letting General Motors or Ford buy Chrysler or Mercedes buy BMW—assuming GM, Ford, or Mercedes-Benz had the cash and the desire to do so. Yet such a deal would probably be prohibited on anticompetitive grounds. In fact, the U.S. and German auto markets, the world's market for that matter, are extremely competitive due to the presence of

Japanese players and would be no less so with two U.S. automakers or two German automakers instead of three. It is these government policies, however, that provide much of the basis for global arbitrage of markets and simultaneously create opportunities and destroy opportunities for global competitors.

MEASURING SUCCESS

One final "regional twist." Managers in different regions of the Triad bring very different expectations and ways of judging the success or failure of collaboration. Business is not business. U.S. managers often focus on profits, market share, and specific financial benefits of cross-border acquisitions and alliances. Japanese players are more often seeking to build strategic position or improve skills, and are willing to forego profits for years to develop position. And European players may be seeking to balance market position, profitability, *and* social considerations such as avoiding layoffs or preserving a national position in specific industries. Recognizing and reflecting these differences is necessary for successful collaboration.

8

Japan: Allying for Advantage

Kevin K. Jones and Walter E. Shill

Alliances are a vital issue for Western companies determined to do business in and with Japan. Indeed, the majority of foreign companies enter Japan through some form of alliance, usually a joint venture. Even so, many non-Japanese participants continue to find alliances distinctly uncomfortable. As one manager concluded, "Alliances are like Winston Churchill's comment about democracy: the worst form of strategy except for all the alternatives." The usual problem: growing discontent between the partners as they discover how differently they view the world, how hard it is to keep their relationship in balance, and how easy it is—especially for the Western company—to forget what it has learned about making alliances work.

Early alliances in Japan were aimed primarily at gaining access to the Japanese market, one of the largest country markets in the world, in return for the foreign company's know-how or concepts. Elsewhere, the best way in might have been through merger or acquisition. In Japan, however, acquisitions are extremely difficult to execute and to manage (see sidebar, "Acquisitions"). And that has often made alliances the entry vehicle of choice.

—————————————————— **Acquisitions** ——————————————————

Acquisition, typically a major route for international expansion, is of minor significance for foreign companies entering Japan. Acquisitions in Japan have totalled around 250 a year, slow by international standards, but growing steadily. The problem for most foreign-affiliated companies (FACs) is that it is difficult to acquire a company in Japan—and doubly difficult to make something of it. In a study we did of 170 acquisitions between 1985 and 1990, 40% of the target companies fitted the classic "distress" image—they were in either financial or strategic trouble. Just under 10%, however, were on the receiving end of aggressive or hostile moves. This may be an underestimate, since some aggressive acquisitions are dressed up in public to appear friendly.

The bulk of the aggressive moves have come from the so-called *Kaishime* or green-mailers. Trafalgar-Glenn, a small U.K./U.S. partnership, established one route for doing this in 1984 when it bought up Minebea's convertible bearer bonds in Switzerland and then showed up in Tokyo with the equivalent of 25% of Minebea's equity. The attack failed—Minebea issued shares to a friendly company, which diluted Trafalgar-Glenn's holding and gave Minebea a safe shareholder base—but the method was clear.

M&A by acquiree situation

Percent   **100% = 170 cases**

Others

Target of aggressive move

Strategically troubled

7%

7%

FAC pullout

8%

25%

Diverting non-core business

12%

16%

Financially troubled

Dependent on related company

12%

13%

Joint growth opportunities

Source: Press statements; McKinsey analysis

Another route has been to build shareholdings through nominees. Ironically, Minebea has used this approach itself to acquire several companies. Since insider rumors abound in Tokyo, this method of assemblying shareholdings takes a lot of skill. Typically, the *Kaishime*—such as Azabu Jidosha, the Videosellers Group, and Nippon Tochi—have proved themselves adept at this, gaining 50% of Fujiya, the confectionery company, before the company realized what was happening. Aggressive takeovers have, therefore, become feasible. Because such moves are unexpected, relatively few companies in Japan have established effective defenses against them. When Shuwa Corporation built up a shareholding in two small supermarket chains, the companies attempted the standard defense, used by Minebea, of issuing equity to a friendly company. Shuwa challenged in court their right to dilute shareholders' equity in this way—and won, a landmark decision.

This may seem to bode well for acquisitions by foreign companies. To this day, however, all acquisitions by foreign companies fall into the "friendly" category. When Merck took control of Banyu in 1983, the Japanese company no longer had the product pipeline to remain independent and turned voluntarily to its joint venture partner of 30 years. Similarly, when the BOC group became the leading shareholder* in Osaka Sanso, it did so through negotiations with the retiring chief shareholder, who thought the company needed a strong international partner to provide technology.

The reason for staying on the friendly path was made clear by the recent Boone Pickens/Koito struggle, in which—despite much sound and fury—Boone Pickens leading shareholding of 26% did not gain him any control of the company. Recently, in private discussions, the chairmen of 10 of the largest foreign companies in Japan were unanimous in saying that they did not have the management resources to control a Japanese company gained through an aggressive move, though they might be able to play the role of a white knight.

This presents a foreign company with a dilemma. If it acquires a company that is already under pressure (much as several pharmaceutical companies have acquired small, generic manufacturers), it may gain in scale but will get few managerial skills, little technology and, often, a very old-style Japanese company—hard to handle for foreign managers. If it dreams of acquiring a larger company, it probably has to begin with an alliance, but with no guarantees that a later acquisition will ever be possible. These difficulties underscore the attractiveness of alliances.

---

*This is usually given as an example of an acquisition. In fact, BOC at the time of writing owned only 25% of Osaka Sanso's equity, up from 21% when it bought it in 1983, and had convertible bonds and options to carry it to just below 50%. BOC was the de facto parent—a position achieved through the cooperation of the other (Japanese) shareholders.

However, the goals and structures of alliances in Japan have changed radically during the past 10 or 15 years.* During the 1980s, as many foreign companies lost the position of technological or concept leadership that had been their contribution to earlier alliances, the approach to building such partnerships changed. Goals and methods became more diverse. Access often still was the foreign company's goal—but it was often achieved in return for, say, access to distribution channels in Europe or the United States (see Exhibit 8.1). Recently, still another type of access has become even more important for Western firms: practical, close-up exposure to what competitors are doing in Japan, as well as to how they intend to apply their skills elsewhere. We call this "strategic learning."

One form of strategic learning is, of course, operational: How, for example, do the leading Japanese firms develop a new product or manage production with affiliates? Another is strategic: What are our competitors likely to do next outside Japan and how might we anticipate it? Neither kind of learning can be gained as a distant observer. Both require immediate, daily contact with the intricacies of Japanese operations and markets. Once again, alliances can provide an invaluable way in.

These new partnerships, however, often do not have the structural simplicity of the earlier joint venture. As the organizational forms in which they are embodied grow ever more subtle, multinational, and multielement, Western managers can be forgiven a twinge of nostalgia for the familiar problems of simple, discrete, old-fashioned joint ventures.

Though the goals of partnerships aimed at learning may be clear, they often rely on linkages that are relatively informal. They are structures

---

* We have used the word alliance to cover relationships between companies to provide reciprocal access to resources or skills for which there is, typically, no natural market. Historically, a joint venture company was often used as the vehicle for such relationships.

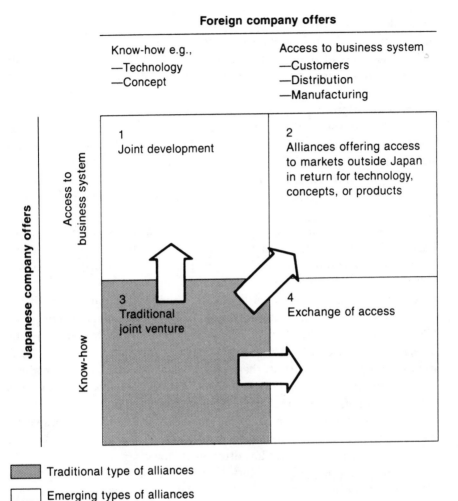

Exhibit 8.1   Basic alliance goals in Japan.

without structure—networks of focused relationships without the familiar touchstone of simple, single-company responsibilities. They are more fragile, readily prone to wear-and-tear, less difficult to exit if things go poorly, but more difficult to steer in one piece through periods of stress.

Managing them effectively toward where they should be in 10 or 15 years' time takes a far higher level of skill than was the case with earlier generations of ventures in Japan. It also takes a willingness to make deep changes in the organizational processes of parent companies. At best, this is uncomfortable work. The understandable impulse is to walk away. But given the strategic importance and potential of these alliances, walking away is not, for many companies, a viable option.

Such feelings of discomfort are both real and legitimate. Making alliances work is hard and is becoming harder. And alliances *do* break up, sometimes quite rapidly. Sometimes quite bitterly. It does happen. But not all that often.

The truth of the matter is that when alliances go bad, they usually do not fall apart in some dramatic fashion. Headline-grabbing collapses are not common. Precipitate breakup is not the fate of most failed alliances. What happens, instead, is that they gradually turn sour and, bit by bit, wear down the interest and enthusiasm of even those managers most dedicated to making them work.

Frustration and misunderstanding—if allowed to fester—blossom into nagging discontent and that, in turn, into a chronic feeling of malaise about the whole undertaking, especially on the part of the non-Japanese partner. When alliances fail, they go not with a bang but a whimper.

This kind of disillusionment is always a risk with alliances, but it is a particular danger in the relationships of Western with Japanese companies. Given the marked—and disturbingly unfamiliar—differences in their philosophy, managerial approach, and structures, lack of mutual understanding can flourish and, with it, the feeling of malaise that can undermine a partnership. Indeed, most of the alliances with Japanese companies that go wrong do not officially break up. They just fall into disuse.

Hence, the dilemma—and the challenge: Alliances with Japanese companies are more important than ever to their Western partners, but the experience of those partners has often been one of great discomfort. As a result, the skills needed to reduce this discomfort and build successful alliances are becoming in themselves a source of competitive advantage in many global industries. But few companies have as yet given the task of building those skills the explicit attention they deserve.

WHERE HAVE ALL THE BREAK UPS GONE?

The managerial folklore is wrong: the survival record of alliances is pretty good. We have made a study of some 200 cases in which foreign companies either discontinued their alliances in Japan or sold down their shareholdings to below 10%. Several interesting facts emerge. Most last longer than is often imagined—20 years on average (see Exhibit 8.2)—longer, in fact, than they do in the United States. Of the half that do not survive until their 20th

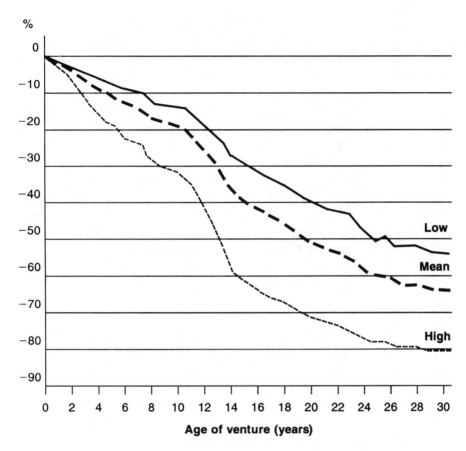

Exhibit 8.2 Cumulative attrition of ventures.

birthday, just over half fall apart because the business relationship has failed. Nothing to be proud of, perhaps, yet far from the catastrophe that some observers claim.

Equally important, these breakups are, in many cases, not an evidence of failure: the companies involved have achieved their ends and decide to move on. In the pharmaceutical industry, for example, both Sandoz and Bayer used joint venture-based alliances (with Sankyo and Takeda, respectively) to help build independent businesses. Having now exited the ventures, the companies rank number 9 and 12 in the Japanese pharmaceutical industry. In other cases, the foreign partners sold out for substantial sums of money (McGraw-Hill to Nikkei, for example, or Southland's 7-Eleven franchise to Itoh-Yokado).

The folklore, though it may be misleading on longevity, is not always wrong. Unpleasant things do happen. When the Meiji-Borden joint venture in ice cream and margarine broke up, for example, each party publicly criticized the other for acting in bad faith. Scathing articles in the U.S. press accused Meiji of perfidy. And when Borden decided that it did after all need a partner and approached Morinaga, equally scathing articles in the Japanese press accused Morinaga of selling out Japanese industry to a badly behaved foreigner.

Hurt feelings aside, however, the actual performance of this joint venture had been unusually strong: growth to over a 10% share of the margarine market in an industry otherwise marked by stagnant shares, coupled with a leadership position in premium ice cream. As in many such cases, the real problem had less to do with objective levels of performance than with a painful sense of mutual disillusionment and missed opportunities.

Joint Venture Successes

Perhaps the most direct way to assess alliance performance is to examine what has happened to joint ventures. This is so, in part, because until the early 1980s virtually all alliances took the joint venture form, and also because the clear, legal nature of a joint venture makes it easy to track. These ventures account for some of the largest and most prominent foreign-affiliated company (FAC) positions in Japan, representing, for example, 64 out of the 100 largest foreign companies there. Of these 64, some six are share-holdings in Japanese businesses that already existed. The remaining 58 were built from scratch. And all but 10 of the remaining 36 independent entities are part of corporations that have joint ventures and alliances as well as their independent ventures.

Of the six largest sectors in which FACs are active in Japan, joint ventures are among the leaders in each. FACs represent around one third of the oil industry, almost totally through joint ventures. In electronics, there are some notable independent players, such as IBM and DEC, but there are also Fuji-Xerox, probably the most famous joint venture in Japan, and Yokogawa Hewlett-Packard, which covers Hewlett-Packard's range of products.

In chemicals, 8 of the 10 largest foreign companies are joint ventures. The same is true of the 3 largest foreign engineering companies. Eight of the top 10 pharmaceutical FACs have developed their businesses through joint ventures. The largest consumer packaged-goods company, Procter & Gamble, entered as a joint venture, from which it eventually built its own independent business.

Number of companies, 1990

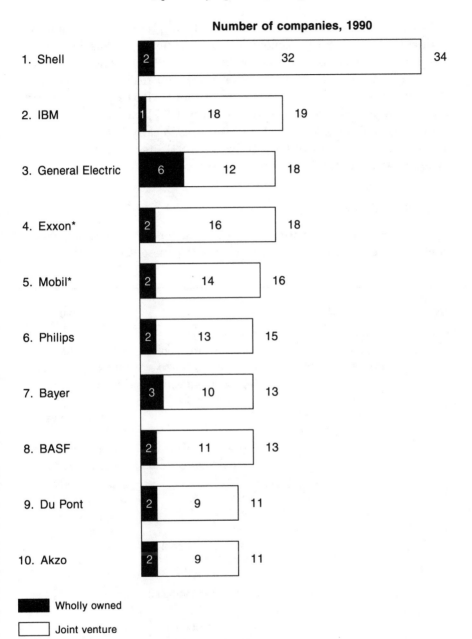

| | Wholly owned |
| | Joint venture |

*Nine companies are jointly held by Exxon and Mobil.

Exhibit 8.3 Top ten FAC affiliate groups in Japan. Technical support, service, real estate, and regional sales companies have been excluded. *Source:* McKinsey FAC Database; McKinsey estimates.

What is more, the largest FACs are nearly all present through multiple entities (see Exhibit 8.3). General Electric, for example, has 12 of its 18 companies in Japan as ventures. In 1989, the 20 largest FACs averaged 7 joint ventures each (excluding sales, service, and real estate companies), not counting other kinds of alliances. Although IBM's presence is best known through its wholly owned subsidiary, IBM Japan, with over 20,000 employees, it also had nearly 20 joint ventures in early 1990, most of them added after 1985 (see Exhibit 8.4). By mid-1991, its number of alliances, including joint ventures, was reported to exceed 35.

The Discontented Middle

If the evidence to date on alliances is reasonably positive, why do so many joint venture partners, both foreign and Japanese, declare themselves

Before 1980	1980–1984	1985–1989	1990
1937: IBM Japan (100%)*	1982: Nippon Office Systems (35%)	1985: Japan Information Engineering (35%)	MSI Co. Ltd. (49%)
	1983: Advanced Systems Technology (39%)	Nippon Information and Communications (50%)	RIOS Systems Co. Ltd. (50%)
	Computer Systems Leasing (51%)	1987: S&I Co. (38%)	Chiyoda Life Information Systems (35%)
		A&I Systems Co. Ltd. (35%)	Tohoku Information Systems (35%)
		Nissan Systems Development (35%)	Japan Logistics Development (40%)
		1988: NI&C International (39%)	Ryoyu System Business (35%)
		1989: Display Technologies (50%)	
		Japan Distribution Service Systems (35%)	

*Shareholding held by IBM or its representative.

Exhibit 8.4 IBM companies in Japan.

dissatisfied and frustrated? Complaints vary. The venture has much potential but is failing to achieve it. The partner is stealing technology. The partner is not providing adequate technology. The Japanese company knows nothing of marketing, product profitability, or distribution. The Western company cannot seem to apply itself to the hard work of getting a product to market.

With so much frustration in the air, why hang on? Why not just get out? The main reason is the practical difficulty of exiting. As a rule, Japanese companies do not exit a business and lay off employees unless the whole corporation is endangered. Even then, they take extraordinary care to find a new home for employees and cushion the blow to distributors. Much the same is true for FACs, but they are far more likely to see their reputation tarnished and their other businesses damaged.

A reputation for "not being reliable" is hard to overcome. So is the perception that FACs cannot be counted on "to do the right thing" or "to behave the right way" in a difficult situation. As a result, there is strong reason either to stay involved or to hand over the problems to their Japanese partners. Of ventures that failed, only 26% were liquidated, 67% saw the Western stake sold out to the Japanese partner. In just 7% of the cases was the venture acquired by the foreign partner (see Exhibit 8.5).

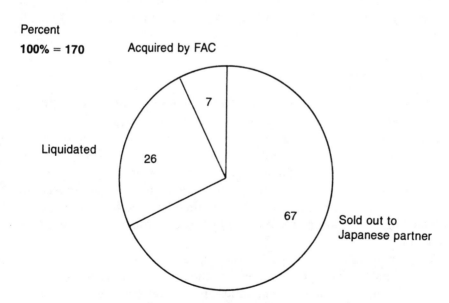

Percent

100% = 170   Acquired by FAC

Liquidated

26

7

67   Sold out to Japanese partner

Exhibit 8.5   Method of exit for FAC.

Even where no change in structure or ownership takes place, the verdict on many alliances has a disturbing familiarity: so little done, so much to do. And the lower the achievement, the faster the growth of distrust. The cause, as we might read in New York, is that Japanese companies are Machiavellian and deceitful. In Tokyo, the more common interpretation is that foreign companies fail to make a genuine commitment to the Japanese market.

Undoubtedly, there are legitimate examples of both. But most of the time, the real reasons that alliances do not live up to their potential lies elsewhere. There is a dogged, consistent pattern to the difficulties that undermine alliances, that start to eat away at their foundations from day one.

THE FORCES THAT CORRUPT

How is it that one company can create 15 or more alliances in Japan over a period of 25 years and not see one failure, while another is on its third partner in the same business in 15 years? One simple explanation is that companies often make bad initial choices. Yet many of these same companies have had quite successful experiences with alliances and business tie-ups elsewhere in the world. Why do they make mistakes in Japan? Why do they fail to anticipate where their alliances might lead or what kinds of problems they are likely to encounter or what scale of effort it will take to keep an alliance productive?

Different Dreams

There is an old Chinese saying: one bed, different dreams. Foreign managers often find Japanese dreams to be incomprehensibly "different," even heretical. The dream of a Japanese company, for example, is almost never purely financial. Rather, it is to be a leader in those businesses in which it participates and/or to build a basis for the future by entering new sectors.

An alliance is one way to gain the skills needed to do either. Indeed, in one Japanese company we analyzed, more than half the 40 or so major restructuring changes during the past 30 years have come from alliances of some sort.

To see how Japanese companies have used alliances to enter new sectors, it is instructive to look at some of the most frequent users of joint ventures. The 10 Japanese companies in our database with the most ventures average 13 "reported" joint ventures apiece (see Exhibit 8.6).

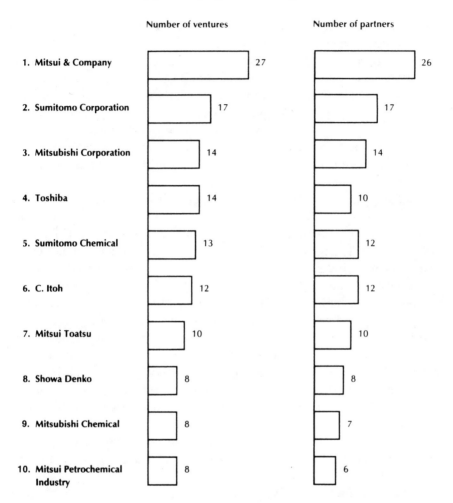

Number of ventures   Number of partners

1. Mitsui & Company	27	26
2. Sumitomo Corporation	17	17
3. Mitsubishi Corporation	14	14
4. Toshiba	14	10
5. Sumitomo Chemical	13	12
6. C. Itoh	12	12
7. Mitsui Toatsu	10	10
8. Showa Denko	8	8
9. Mitsubishi Chemical	8	7
10. Mitsui Petrochemical Industry	8	6

Exhibit 8.6   Joint venture counts for Japanese companies, 1990.

According to data published for 1990, Mitsui & Co., the trading company, participates in 27 joint ventures with 26 different partners. Its one major involvement is a 33% share in the Unisys affiliate, Nippon Unisys, which dates back to the 1950s. Apart from this, the ventures have some 60 employees apiece and are mainly in the growth sectors of fashion/leisure goods and telecommunications.

Although it entered almost no ventures between 1965 and 1979, Mitsui undertook 10 during the 1980s in these two areas, which helped it to diversify away from its core trading business. The second and third companies on the list, Sumitomo Corporation and Mitsubishi Corporation, also trading companies, show similar patterns.

The next, Toshiba, has typically concentrated on ventures related to achieving leadership in its core electronics businesses—for example, a 50/50 arrangement with Motorola in semiconductor manufacturing and technology, 30% of Prime Computer's Japanese subsidiary, Nihon Prime Computers, and 20% of Olivetti Corporation of Japan. The few moves into related areas include Toshiba EMI, an alliance with Thorn EMI, to build a recorded music business based initially on Thorn's catalogue of records and artists, including the Beatles.

Similarly Sumitomo Chemical has concentrated on alliances related to its core businesses. Of the 12 identified, four are with pharmaceutical companies formed before Sumitomo Pharmaceutical was established as a separate company. The roster of its other partners reads like a roll call of the world chemical industry: Akzo, Bayer, Dow, Hercules, Imperial Chemical Industries (ICI), Rohm & Haas.

The heart of many of these alliances is skill building, and Japanese companies work hard to learn and digest the skills of their partners. As one Japanese executive commented, "We are ashamed that we have to go outside for help. This is, however, necessary at times. So it is our duty to master these skills as fast as possible." Although often maligned as "Machiavellian," this is often a key, explicit goal of an alliance. (Foreign companies are no exception—witness their rush to learn technologies from Japan.)

The issue here is not one of moral rectitude, but of clearly recognizing the alliance's objective in the first place—and of designing and managing it to that end. All too often, however, the foreign company's dream is of financial returns, preferably quick and risk free.

Take the case of one consumer goods company, which projected its sales and profits in Japan over a five-year period under two scenarios: going it alone and establishing a joint venture. The latter was, by far, the more financially attractive alternative. Going it alone never received serious consideration: After five years, the company would still be building a sales force. The real choice, therefore, was among possible joint venture partners.

Not surprisingly, the best financial case was presented by a company that was already in the industry. What the analysis missed, of course, is that this company would also be a likely future competitor. The problem with relying purely on financial criteria, however, is that they systematically lead FACs to choose the wrong partner for building a business long term.

Measured by these different dreams, many joint ventures do fulfill their original objectives. The foreign company makes good money (through selling out if not through dividends), and the Japanese company learns new skills. As one Japanese manager pointed out, "Our foreign partner came in looking for a return. They got it. Now they complain that they didn't build a business. But that isn't what they set out to create."

Contribution and Dependence

Different dreams start to undermine an alliance from day one. After all, alliances happen only because both parties believe they will further their business interests. There is nothing necessarily fixed or permanent about them. As Lord Palmerston said long ago about Britain's relations with other nations, "We have no eternal allies and we have no perpetual enemies. Our interests are eternal and perpetual, and these interests it is our duty to follow." At the outset, both parties contribute to an alliance in some balanced fashion, and each depends on the other for the furtherance of its own interests. But, over time, that economic raison d'être can disappear. The balance of contribution and dependence can go wrong.

In the past, Western companies often entered Japan through alliances in which they provided technology in return for access to Japanese distribution channels. Initially, both partners saw value in such an arrangement. Each made a contribution; each depended on the other. In practice, however, the foreign partner often remained dependent on the Japanese partner for distribution while making less and less of a technical contribution. By contrast, the Japanese partner built up its technological skills and became less dependent. As the balance of contribution and dependence decayed, so did the justification for the alliance—and the joint commitment to its success.

The value of each partner's contribution is relative, not absolute. It is a reflection of the other partner's options and capabilities. It also has a finite span of life. This may range from the few years during which a new technology enjoys a clear position of leadership to the decades offered by the near monopoly of a raw material. Rarely, however, are these lifespans the same. Thus, if an alliance is to survive for a long time, the mix of contribution and dependence needs to be reviewed and renewed. Otherwise, the basis for the relationship will gradually slip away, leaving the partners ever more frustrated and disillusioned.

The harsh reality of decaying balance introduces a difficult compromise between short- and long-term interests. The most attractive partner in the short run is likely to be a company that is already established and competent in the business, but with a need to master, say, some new technological skills. The best long-term partner, however, is likely to be a less competent player or even one from outside the industry. The reason is simple: the latter case offers much greater opportunity to maintain a healthy balance of contribution and dependency.

This logic helps explain the success of Fuji-Xerox, an alliance between Fuji Photo Film and Rank Xerox. Similarly, Taito-Pfizer, a 1950s venture between Japan's leading sugar producer and a U.S.- based pharmaceuticals company, helped Pfizer build the foundation to become one of the largest foreign pharmaceutical companies in Japan. In fact, of the 30 still-extant joint ventures in Japan founded before 1950 that we have on record, only three have major Japanese partners in the same or a related industry. The remainder are with individuals, small companies, trading companies, or banks—partners unlikely to threaten the balance. Similarly, of the 20 or so electronics industry ventures that have lasted more than 25 years, only two are with major Japanese companies.

Frictional Losses

In an engine, "frictional losses" reduce the desired output, measured against potential, and produce unwanted heat. Similarly, in an alliance, such losses—the problems caused by differences in management philosophy, expectations, and approaches within an alliance—can significantly reduce performance and produce a lot of organizational heat. When companies try to collaborate but dream different dreams, employ different problem-solving processes, and subscribe to different beliefs about what good business practice is, they create friction.

These differences are not simply linguistic. What one company sees as natural, the other sees as unprofessional, even stupid. Inevitably, performance suffers. These differences affect nearly all functions and processes—from sales force time allocation and call patterns to corporate strategy and planning. With capital investments, for example, a foreign manager noted, "Our partner just wanted to go ahead and invest, without considering whether there would be a return or not." According to his Japanese counterpart, however, "the foreign partner took so long to decide on obvious points that we were always too slow."

This is not an isolated case. "There was no understanding of marketing, and no sales plan. We had to insist and insist and insist to get one done," says the foreign manager. "We spend all our time planning and none doing," says the Japanese counterpart. The first responds, "This group of *kachos* [Japanese term meaning middle managers, literally "section heads"] came in and put up lots of figures about the market, spent hours discussing irrelevances, and then came to no conclusions." To which the Japanese manager answers, "We simply don't know how to convince our foreign partner."

In many joint efforts, such differences as these lead to endless, energy- and time-consuming debates—futile talk that produces a lot of heat and prevents the company making the decisions it has to. Opportunity drifts away. After a while, many foreign managers just throw up their hands in despair and essentially abdicate responsibility for the venture. "Why not leave everything to the Japanese partner? They know what they're doing." This may provide temporary relief, but it is no solution.

When an alliance has to draw on—or convince—the parents, disagreements only grow more intense. Misunderstandings are no longer confined to managers within the venture, who have some concrete feel for the issues at hand. They overflow to managers back at headquarters, who have much less direct experience, especially in the case of the foreign partner. Because the Japanese company stays in close touch with the staff it puts into the venture, it usually understands (in detail) what is going on, though it may not approve. And because, like most children, the venture will be most influenced by the parent it can talk to, the foreign parent, which keeps its distance, grows ever more confused, troubled, and frustrated.

As differences mount, the slow rate of progress undermines the venture's success. Both partners become disillusioned and less committed, which intensifies the vicious cycle of decline. "We've given them two years," says the visiting divisional manager, "and still no sales and marketing plan. This time we tell them we quit."

Corporate Amnesia

Western companies often face such difficulties because they doggedly insist on forgetting anything useful learned in Japan. This corporate amnesia is so pronounced that, at times, it seems to be a deliberate policy. Determined to boost short-term financial returns, these companies regularly minimize the number of people they put into a Japanese venture. Moreover, since joint ventures are so wearing on management, they move the few people who do remain after two or three years. Superficially, this appears to reduce frictional losses. As a result, however, little or no corporate memory is built up of how to compete in Japan or of the venture's history and practices. Indeed, the original objectives are forgotten as new waves of managers seek to make their mark.

It is easy to underestimate how seriously this kind of amnesia undermines a foreign company's ability to develop a venture, understand its trials and tribulations, and build the know-how to create a more successful alliance next time. Not surprisingly, it reinforces a "keep your head down" attitude among senior Japanese managers in foreign companies. They learn that there is no point in educating the current wave of expatriates. They do not really care. Even if they do, they will only be replaced as soon as they learn anything. There are exceptions, of course, mainly among German and Swiss companies, which tend to keep alliance managers in place for eight years or more. But they are rare.

A group of senior managers from the U.S. parent of one of the financially most successful alliances in Japan came in to discuss with us why their partner was turning down a new alliance proposal. We asked each of them how well they knew the managers of their partner. "Not very well," they told us. "We see them once a year for a good dinner." Who knew them longest? "Well, no one has had more than two years in Japan, and I'm new in the job," said the Asia-Pacific head. Wasn't there a handover? "No, our policy is that handovers get in the way. We like a clear responsibility from day one." Was there someone elsewhere in the corporation who knew the partner's managers well? "No." No wonder the company made no progress with its new alliance proposal. It did not understand its partner well enough to know where the roadblocks were, and the partner did not trust it well enough to tell it.

In another case, a senior FAC manager visited his counterpart in the company's Japanese partner to propose an expansion of the relationship. "You know," said the Japanese manager, "I think we should give this the same earnest consideration we did the last time you presented the idea to us 10 years ago. On that occasion, I believe, we were willing to go ahead, but you became less enthusiastic for some reason. I hope this time the affair may progress better." The foreign manager, red-faced, muttered his excuses and withdrew to ransack the files and to seek out someone who might remember.

The usual kind of situation in which corporate amnesia develops is when too few people are directly involved in a Japanese alliance for too short a time, and then move on to unrelated tasks. Contrast this with the explicit policy of a German chemical company: "We aim to put in half the management team, say 15 people. That way, we are party to the daily decisions that really affect the development of the venture. Also, because our network into the venture is as good as our Japanese partner's, we can pick up rumors or peculiarities before they become problems—or before they become problems for us. Most of our management team is Japanese and will probably spend the rest of their working lives in the venture. The non-Japanese members are there for five years or so."

Ignorance and lack of experience are often at the root of alliance failures. As a rule, it is not the larger, well-established FACs that experience regular breakups of their alliances, but the companies with little presence in Japan. Fully 60% of the venture breakups we have studied had less than 100 total employees (see Exhibit 8.7). In fact, 90% of the failed ventures in our database were the only representation the foreign company had in Japan.

Lack of experience—and of memory—also manifests itself in the attention paid by foreign managers to establishing a 51% shareholding position. With little real knowledge of the Japanese environment, they all too easily believe that the Holy Grail of 51% will give them the ability to

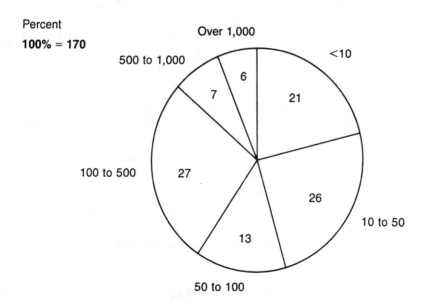

Exhibit 8.7 Distribution by headcount of venture breakup. *Source:* Press reports; McKinsey estimates.

control. Legal control, of course, can be useful. As can the implicit status of holding 51% in a venture with a leading Japanese company. But if managers have neither a deep understanding of the alliance nor the skills needed to manage it, the literal fact of control is irrelevant.

"Every five years," said the chief executive officer (CEO) of a FAC with many successful ventures in Japan, "a venture reaches a strategic fork in the road. At this point, unless you have built up a deep understanding of the venture, you will have three problems. The first is that you probably don't know you're at a fork, although your partner may. The second is that, even if you do, you won't know enough to make a wise choice. And the third is that, even if you make the wise choice, you won't know enough to put your choice into action."

Corporate amnesia stunts the growth of an alliance and can also leave a company worse off at the end of a venture than at the beginning, as well as ill-prepared for any further alliances. One consumer goods company that had established a presence in Japan decided to put its activities into an alliance with a Japanese company in the same industry. The Japanese partner took over nearly all the business operations while the foreign company reduced its staff from around 70, who were closely involved with the business, to a handful involved just with coordination. Fifteen years later, when the alliance broke up, the foreign company had no one left who understood the market.

As these problems illustrate, the classic desire to find a partner and leave everything to it is likely to have a short, though perhaps a profitable, life. It virtually guarantees that the only partner to remain in the business long term will be the Japanese partner. The management structure that best capitalizes on existing know-how and keeps costs down in the short term is, inevitably, supplied by the Japanese partner. The inattentive foreign company never learns.

Alliances with Japanese companies are usually inherently unstable. They require constant adjustment if the foreign company is to achieve more than a few years of returns. And corporate amnesia leaves the FAC incapable of making the necessary adjustments. No wonder discontent takes hold—even more so, when the alliance in question is not a traditional joint venture, but one of the newer, multielement arrangements.

STRUCTURE WITHOUT STRUCTURE

As previously noted, the basic building block of most alliance thinking in the past has been the joint venture. The joint venture was comfortable.

It played, for the most part, a single role in a single country. It had a single, coherent management team. Its performance could be readily identified and assessed.

By contrast, the more recent forms of alliance rely on informal kinds of linkages that break the organizational shackles of the classic joint venture. These linkages are often scattered across the globe, with no single theme or focus. They represent not one relationship, but a series of discrete international ties of varying sorts between the two parent companies. And the forms they take are not usually rooted in familiar, concrete organizational structures.

These new forms of alliance, however, are just as vulnerable as the old to the problems of different dreams, unstable balance, frictional losses, and corporate amnesia. But their greater complexity and organizational subtlety have significantly raised the level of skill and experience needed to manage them.

Beyond the Joint Venture

Nontraditional forms of alliance have grown rapidly in number since the early 1980s. In earlier years, the vehicle used for any major independent business established as part of an alliance in Japan was a joint venture. Its various activities were tied together, as needed, by a small coordinating unit—especially so, if the foreign company's business presence in Japan was fairly modest. In this way, the business piggybacked on the existing relationship between the parent companies. Something designed and manufactured in Europe, say, would be shipped to Japan to be distributed, sold, and serviced by the local partner (see Exhibit 8.8). Alternatively, the link might be just through licensing. In either case, the foreign company's presence in Japan was slight and its interests protected by a small coordinating unit.

An example of this approach is Meiji-McVitie, the alliance between a U.K. biscuit manufacturer and a Japanese confectionery company. Here, the production and sales systems depend on Meiji, so that only a small, representative presence was established by McVitie to coordinate activities.

Further along the spectrum of involvement is the situation where there is a substantially independent business, all the pieces of which are typically put into a joint venture. The Fuji-Xerox business system, for example, was created by the partners from scratch and embedded in a 50-50 joint venture in Japan. Today, it is largely independent, although it still relies to some extent on its parents' business systems—in particular, on the research and high-end products of Xerox. Much the same is true of Shin

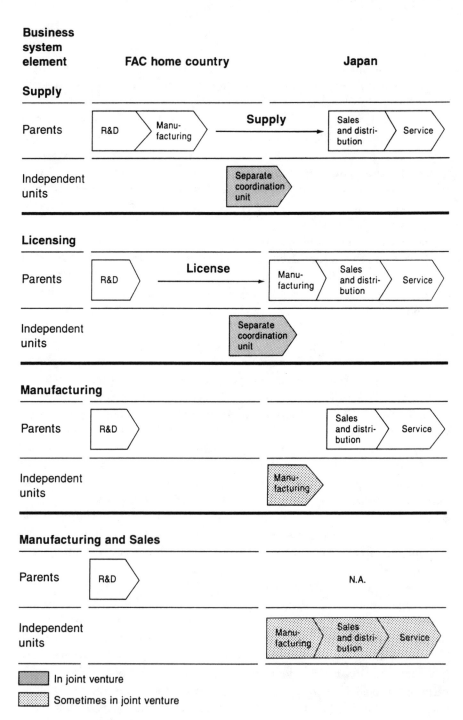

Exhibit 8.8 Traditional structures (illustrative).

Caterpillar-Mitsubishi—the joint venture between Caterpillar and Mitsubishi Heavy Industries. Today, this is a substantial company in its own right, although it still depends on Caterpillar both for research and for some products.

By contrast, some of the newer alliances are forsaking the joint venture apparatus, with its various coordinating mechanisms, for a different approach entirely—a nonstructure structure based not on some legal entity but on a far more intense set of relationships. Philip Morris, for instance, arranged its alliance business system in a very different way. Sales and distribution are carried out through companies especially created for this purpose by two of the trading companies. Marketing and sales strategy are in a wholly owned subsidiary of Philip Morris. Because integration is achieved through day-to-day processes, not ownership, company boundaries fade away. Kellogg has followed a similar approach in its arrangements with Ajinomoto.

On research and development (R&D) collaborations, setting up a joint venture laboratory, as IBM and Toshiba have done for their work on liquid crystal displays, is only one of several possible approaches. Other companies have chosen to exchange personnel and ideas, without establishing formal structures—American Telephone & Telegraph, for example, with NEC in their joint Integrated Circuit research and again, more recently, with Mitsubishi Electric.

International Linkages

The other notable dimension of these new "structure without structure" arrangements is the growing number of alliances in which the quid pro quos lead to a series of ties in various international businesses, often in quite unrelated areas. These relationships might be embodied in existing companies, joint ventures, minority shareholdings, or even the type of amorphous piggybacking described earlier.

An early example was the set of back-to-back joint pharmaceutical ventures (in the United States and Japan) between SmithKline (now SmithKline Beecham) and Fujisawa. Other examples include the series of product exchange agreements between AT&T and Ricoh and the technology and product supply agreements between Olivetti and Toshiba, which are the obverse of Toshiba's 20% holding in Olivetti Japan.

Within these more complex, less structurally rooted alliances, maintaining the balance of contribution and dependence becomes far trickier to handle than in traditional joint ventures. Contributions that are interdependent when being negotiated often become independent when separated into individual businesses. Consider, for example, a situation where a Japanese and a U.S. company agree to piggyback on their existing businesses. The Japanese company provides access in Japan for the U.S.-based company's products, and the latter does the same for its Japanese partner in the United States and parts of Europe. Each sales force would sell the other's products.

At the negotiation stage all seems clear. Unfortunately, neither sales force has any interest in actually doing this. Both can always find a thousand reasons not to spend time or effort on the partner's products. Will the Japanese company directly penalize the U.S. company's business in Japan as a tit-for-tat for problems elsewhere? In the short term, that is probably unlikely. Will the partners be happy with one another and take extra effort to make the alliance a success? No.

In another case, two chemical companies established back-to-back joint ventures in Japan and overseas. In the latter, the Japanese company was interested in building volume and competence at the expense of profit. The foreign partner had no interest in this. It wanted high-potential, high-margin products and refused all the Japanese partner's suggestions. In Japan, the reciprocal venture fared well in the short term but found support for its efforts dwindling as the overseas venture's relationship became more and more troubled.

To date, companies have tried two approaches to resolving this kind of problem. The first is to ensure that each alliance is attractive in its own right—that is, to ensure that its balance of contribution and dependence makes sense and then to let it operate independently. The second is to place all the activities of an alliance under an umbrella structure in which both partners have an interest. That way, both sides want to see everything succeed. This structure can take the form of a single company or a set of interlinked companies, in which the foreign partners might hold, for example, 49% of the Japanese entity and 51% of the U.S. or European.

These emerging forms of alliance are, in one sense, more structured than traditional joint ventures since they are typically made up of multiple focused relationships. At the same time, however, they are less structured. The challenge to renew and recreate them is far greater. In the past, the company identities of joint ventures acted as a barrier to exit, an incentive to go back and try again. With more informal relationships, there are fewer barriers. So holding the relationships together and keeping them fresh demands a much greater level of managerial skills.

ALLIANCE LEARNING

Alliances with Japanese companies are—and will remain—a major part of the strategic panoply of many Western companies. "We are turning increasingly to alliances," said the CEO of one FAC, "because we do not have the leadership or, to be frank, the patience to build our own business positions from scratch. They allow us to do things we could not do on our own—and to gain a competitive advantage from doing so." According to another, "Japan is the second largest country market in the world for our product. We have to be here to spread our costs. At the same time, we get to see our competitors and have access to the latest technologies. But we could not have done it alone, so we turned to an alliance." Or as another said, "By combining worldwide with our Japanese partner, we have become a viable number two player in a global industry."

Building successful alliances requires developing, nurturing, and extending the skills needed to manage them. Experience shows, however, that few foreign companies understood or anticipated the problems they would have to face, possessed genuine commitment to maintaining the momentum for success, or prepared themselves to redirect or exit the venture at the appropriate time. The pattern is all too familiar: Many of these companies did not truly see alliances as part of their corporate strategy of development in Japan, but rather as a legal vehicle that allowed them to abdicate managerial responsibility and repatriate profits.

The lesson is simple: Building successful alliances means developing—and sustaining—the relevant skills, accumulating relevant experience, and deploying both junior as well as senior management. Properly applied, such experience can have great value in the up-front work of designing alliances, giving a company the ability to look before it leaps. But it is doubly valuable in giving it the ability to guide an alliance through the immensely difficult process of renewal.

Look Before You Leap

Our work indicates that the companies that have been successful with alliances have tried from the beginning to look where they were going and how they might get there—not just where they might start. The designs toward which they worked pay close attention to realizing the desired goals over a 10- or 15-year period, not just to ensuring quick financial returns.

To be effective, designs of this sort require more clarity about a company's strategic aspirations than can be gained by running the numbers on five years of projected sales. But these goals are, in our experience, rarely considered. As the head of planning in an experienced FAC told us, "It's hard enough demonstrating that an alliance can meet our basic business needs and make money in three to five years. We have no energy for trying to look further."

Developing this long-term perspective begins, of course, with the task of getting a company's aspirations in sharp focus. It matters if the aspiration over, say, a 15-year period is to create a viable business, a leading position in Japan, or a major pillar of a global strategy. After all, the level of aspiration, when compared with what a company can achieve on its own, helps clarify what an alliance is expected to contribute. "Clarity" here is not a synonym for the usual, woolly "we need to achieve critical mass," but a clear definition of specific needs.

Next comes the challenge of thinking through how different types and forms of partnership structure would be likely to endure during that 10- to 15-year period. The challenge is also to judge how well each of these different forms would survive the problems they would inevitably face. This process of thinking through alliance options is inevitably iterative. Each scenario of the future provokes questions that suggest modifications to the starting assumptions and aspirations. Indeed, the most beneficial output of this process is often that its forced discipline helps bring a degree of realism to the whole effort. The key questions:

1. What is needed to reach our aspirations?

The range of viable alliance options is directly related to the specificity of the needs: the more specific the needs, the wider the range. At first glance, for example, the selection by Toys 'R' Us of McDonald's Japan as its partner may seem strange. Yet what Toys 'R' Us needed was McDonald's know-how in site selection, logistics, recruiting, and dealing with Japanese legislation.

Sandoz improved its sales force management by borrowing sales managers from its former joint venture partner, Sanyo, in return for the cross-licensing of two products. In both cases, by concentrating on filling a specific gap, rather than on meeting a blanket insistence that "we need a partner," the companies have been able to create successful, innovative alliances.

2. What role might an alliance play?

There are, in our experience, three main roles an alliance can play in helping a foreign company toward its longer-term goals. The first is the often ill-defined wish just to have eternal friendship with a long-term partner. "You know," runs the common explanation, "we've not really thought where we might be in 10 years. We just assumed the arrangement would continue." So-called "marriages" of this sort rarely last as long as the foreign partner hoped. In most cases, the only way for two companies to avoid—or to steer through—the shifts in the balance of contribution and dependence is for them to "burn their boats" and commit all their joint interest to the alliance, as Fuji-Photo Film and Fuji-Xerox did. The main field for creating this type of alliance today seems to be in restructuring a globalizing industry.

The second role is to help build up the foreign company's business system in Japan during a period of, say, 10 to 20 years. In such cases, the most effective alliances build the potential for evolution into the initial structure and agreement. Thus, Hoechst's joint venture with Mitsubishi Kasei in dyestuffs began its life selling nearly all its products through the Mitsubishi sales force, but with the right to sell through the nascent Hoechst sales effort. By the late 1980s, more than half the sales volume went through Hoechst's own sales force (part of Hoechst Japan). Later still, the two companies combined their sales forces and put them into the venture itself.

The third role is to complete a specific task. Witness, for example, many of Boeing's relationships, which are limited to specific subtasks in airframe construction. For these purposes, the alliance need not always be embodied in an independent company structure, but only in a set of agreements and management processes. Sometimes, of course, a joint venture structure may add focus. In their liquid crystal display (LCD) development, for example, Toshiba and IBM created a joint company, Display Technologies, to act as a separate focal point for the effort on LCD screens. Many alliances effectively fall into this last group, where the specific task is only to sell a product, yet they imagine they are in one of the other two.

3. With whom should we work?

Partnership discussions usually focus on short-term benefits, risks, and quid pro quos. All of this is necessary. The crucial element, however, is to focus on where the alliance is likely to lead. After all, the partner chosen will have a major effect on the likely shifts in the balance of contribution and dependence—and on the likely frictional losses.

4. How should we structure the alliance?

Much too often, managers concentrate on the legal vehicle, the joint venture, not on the crucial underlying network of business elements and relationships. But, as the familiar caution goes, structure follows strategy. Successful alliances usually work out which business arrangements make sense before reaching a decision on which vehicle to use.

Managing technology contribution, for example, is often a particularly tricky issue. An alliance between German and Japanese suppliers of semiconductor equipment illustrates this point. Both recognize that they need to stay on top of the latest technologies if they are to catch the industry leader. Yet each is concerned about technology leakage. So they have decided on an isolated laboratory with access given to only a limited list of people and with official "gatekeepers" supervising which technology is made available to whom. This is, perhaps, a little clumsy but fairly effective.

The choice of alliance partners and structures is, like politics, an exercise in the art of the possible. One of the most successful joint ventures in Japan is heartily disliked by both its parents. Answering the four preceding questions leads to an iterative process of testing the chosen alliance concept. Is its structure competitive? How is it likely to evolve? What risks is management prepared to take? How willing is it to make the necessary financial and manpower commitments? From this process typically flows a recalibration of aspirations and abilities. At the same time, the soul-searching helps define what the foreign company will have to do to manage the instabilities.

Building Renewal Skills

There is no point creating an alliance so complex that the foreign partner lacks the skills needed to manage it. Putting someone who cannot drive into a Ferrari F40 will just lead to a bigger crash. Yet mastering these skills—overcoming amnesia—demands a major investment in corporate learning. Even if the goal is no more than to license out a product, it is usually worth considering whether to invest heavily in having people learn how to work in Japan and with Japanese allies—in preparation for the next alliance. Moreover, even if a company makes good initial choices, it will soon face what some call the "unk-unks"— the unknown unknowns—that inevitably appear. Guiding an alliance through such upsets requires a good relationship between the partners and a deep, inside understanding of the problems.

One U.S. company, for example, that has substantial experience in creating and managing alliances keeps much of its know-how in a team in Japan. As a result, the on-site team assessing a proposed new alliance has been through it all before at least 10 different times. The manager making the final call has had much the same experience. If the new proposal is accepted, some of these people will go on to be part of the alliance. The learning cycle continues.

Skill building is also a necessary part of the preparation for evolving within and beyond an alliance. Few companies can realistically hope that an individual alliance will last forever. It is—or should be seen as—a step on a staircase. However, when companies new to Japan have tried to use their initial alliances as a way to build up their own business systems in Japan, they have often been shaken at how ill-equipped they were to stand alone.

They find that the management team both inside and outside the country was not equipped to judge the situation. Their muscles are weaker than they thought. The needed skills, experience, and judgment not only take a long time to develop but also a concerted organizational effort if they are not to be frittered away. In frustration, many of these companies make things worse by throwing up their hands in despair and turning over de facto control to their Japanese partners. The better course would be to focus on building skills for the future.

The growing importance and the increasingly unstructured nature of today's alliances are placing increasing emphasis on having these skills available globally, not just in Japan. They are needed to maintain the close, top-level links with the Japanese partner, which can provide a kind of continuity that structure alone no longer offers and can accommodate the types of changes inherent in unstructured business relationships.

One Western company that has built such links claims that the trust and understanding between top management teams make it much easier to launch new ventures and to display patience with problems in individual alliances. This approach is not an unalloyed benefit, since the company now worries about the potential constraints and risks that such close links to one main partner may bring.

Doing business through alliances with Japanese companies is undoubtedly hard. But for many companies, it is a competitive necessity. The emphasis in most discussions is on selecting and negotiating an alliance to meet immediate needs. This is less than half right. The crucial issue is to build the management experience and skills to understand how alliances develop and change and to deploy these skills effectively over time. Only then will a company be able to use its alliances as a tool to achieve and sustain competitive advantage.

The skills in question come only from genuine, cumulative strategic learning. Today's best practitioners are those that have already created several alliances. To develop these skills. Western companies must reverse their common, if inadvertent, drift toward corporate amnesia and develop, instead, a team of senior people, knowledgeable about and probably located in Japan, who are a trusted part of the global top-management team. This will inevitably prove unsettling for the home-country-dominated senior management approach still followed by most foreign companies. But it is *the* critical ingredient if those companies are to ally for advantage in Japan.

9

The Dilemma of Foreign Affiliated Companies: Surviving Middle Age in Japan

Kevin K. Jones

"Our biggest challenge to succeeding in Japan is the changes we have to make outside Japan in order to compete here," said the Japan head of a European pharmaceutical company. Historically, the successes in Japan of foreign affiliated companies (FACs) have predominantly been based on the transfer into the country of technologies and concepts well ahead of those available domestically. As recently as 1960, Japan's gross national product (GNP) per capita was where that of the United States was, in real terms, in the mid-1880s. So the opportunities were abundant. Indeed, notwithstanding the trade barriers of the time, 80 of the 100 largest FACs entered Japan before 1975.

Today, however, FACs are confronted with a serious form of mid-life crises: They have to reinvigorate, even reinvent themselves because the sources of their early advantage are much harder to find and to sustain. With no real technological or concept "edge" to fall back on, FACs now

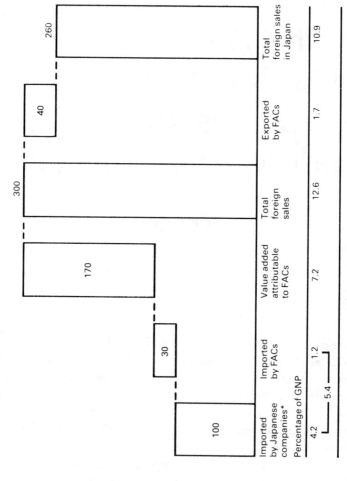

Foreign sales in Japan
($ billions rounded to nearest $5 billion)

	Imported by Japanese companies*	Imported by FACs	Value added attributable to FACs	Total foreign sales	Exported by FACs	Total foreign sales in Japan
	100	30	170	300	40	260
Percentage of GNP	4.2	1.2	7.2	12.6	1.7	10.9
	5.4					

* Not adjusted for the equity participation of Japanese companies overseas.
Note: At $1 = ¥142; GNP $2,387 billion in 1987.

Exhibit 9.1 Foreign industrial presence in Japan, 1987. *Source:* Estimates based on: Economic Planning Agency; Ministry of Finance; McKinsey FAC Database.

Exhibit 9.1 *(continued)*

Foreign equity-weighted sales in Japan
($ billions rounded to nearest $5 billion)

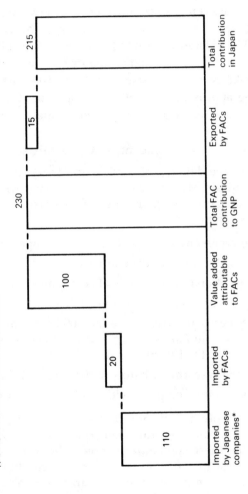

have to be exceptionally fleet of foot within the Japanese market itself. This puts an immense strain on their local capabilities. Perhaps more troubling, it often requires significant changes in the parent company's activities outside Japan—especially in operations at headquarters—at a time when getting global organizations to work effectively is already a complex challenge.

These problems matter so much because FACs represent a considerable body of economic activity. In 1987, foreign industrial presence in Japan, most of it U.S.-related, amounted to roughly $300 billion, or about 13% of GNP—or $230 billion after adjustments for the proportion of FAC equity actually held by non-Japanese companies (see our estimates in Exhibit 9.1). Of the approximately 450,000 people employed by FACs in Japan, some three quarters work for U.S. companies, which in turn represent

---

Leading FACs Database

Most of the data in this article are drawn from a database we have built in McKinsey's Tokyo office to track the leading foreign companies in Japan. This database covers some 1,320 companies composed of:

- The representatives of the *Fortune* companies:

  U.S. 500 industrial companies

  International 500 industrial companies

  Top 50 U.S. and top 50 non-U.S. banks

- The representatives of the top 500 European industrial companies from *Europe's 15,000 Largest Companies,* the annual review by ELC International.

- All the investment banks registered in Tokyo.

- Any foreign company with over 300 employees.

A single foreign corporation may have many FAC representatives in Japan. General Electric has around 25, for example. Tracking these companies is not without its difficulties, since the closest to a performance figure consistently published is headcount. Only half the FACs in the database regularly report sales: fewer still report profits. Furthermore, based on our client experience, we know the profit figures have often suffered so many adjustments for fiscal purposes as to be next to useless. As a result, sales have had to be estimated from a wide range of sources, but most typically press statements.

FAC equity-weighted position

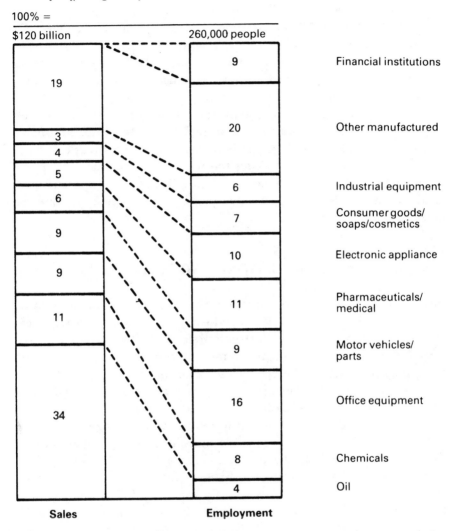

Note: At $1 = ¥142.

Exhibit 9.2 Concentration of FAC activity in Japan, 1987. *Source:* National accounts; McKinsey FAC Database.

about two thirds of the U.S. *Fortune* "500." (The comparable ratio for Europe is about one third.) This activity is also fairly concentrated. Some 80% of FAC sales and 70% of FAC employment in Japan are accounted for by seven industries, including financial services, as Exhibit 9.2 shows. In four—oil, chemicals, pharmaceuticals and medical equipment, and office equipment—FACs have achieved industry penetration greater than 10%.

How FACs resolve the dilemma created by their mid-life crisis will do much to shape the Japanese economy of the twenty-first century as well as Japan's economic relationships with the rest of the world. And make no mistake about it, the dilemma is real. Traditional sources of advantage no longer work, and making the necessary adjustments requires carrying out substantial changes, not just in an FAC's operations in Japan, but also at its parent's headquarters. Such change does not come quickly or painlessly.

THE TRADITIONAL ADVANTAGE

In the office equipment sector, the competitive position of the leading FACs was established in the 1960s and early 1970s when they were several years ahead in critical electronics-related technologies. Much the same is true for pharmaceutical and medical equipment companies. And true again for FACs in the chemicals sector. In each case, the basis of effective entry into the Japanese market was technology. Indeed, more than 60 of the top 100 FACs established and consolidated their initial positions on a foundation of clear-cut technological advantage.

In sectors where FAC presence is unusually strong—pharmaceuticals, say, where the FAC share of sales comes to 45% (just over half of which comes from licensing)—technology leadership, as represented by the drug portfolios of Swiss, West German, and U.S. companies, was the overwhelming basis for entry. Similarly, in chemicals, where FACs account for about 20% of sales, the original source of advantage lay primarily in West German mastery of pigments and dyestuffs. More recently, that source of advantage has shifted to leadership in areas like engineering plastics by companies such as General Electric and Hoechst-Celanese. In electronics, Texas Instruments entered in the mid-1960s based on its integrated circuit (IC) leadership. Both Hewlett-Packard and Honeywell were able to build significant sales based on their instrument technology. Philips built its Philips-Matsushita joint venture on electrical appliance technology.

The remaining 40 of the top 100 FACs, however, got in by a different route. Most established themselves by bringing a completely new product or a new business concept to Japan (see Exhibit 9.3). This was not easy work. In nearly every case, especially the most successful ones, building this kind of nontechnology-based position in Japan would not have been possible without the determined, at times pigheaded, stubbornness of the original entrepreneurs.

The managers often had to face down strong local resistance and refuse to listen to an ever-louder chorus of naysayers who continually urged them to give in and follow the conventional risk-averse Japanese wisdom about what was needed for success. And to do so for a long period of time—until their approach proved its value. Moreover, because they doggedly persisted in building their advantage, when the tide did turn, they were ready and able to move with great speed to capitalize on the opportunities now available.

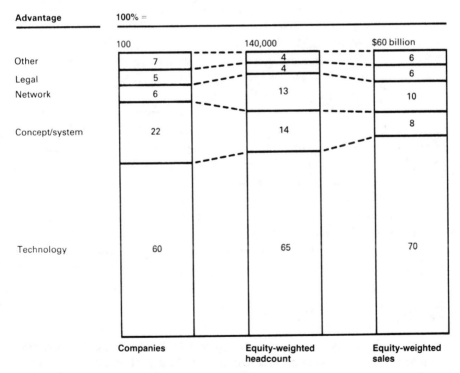

Exhibit 9.3 The top 100 FACs by main advantage. *Source:* McKinsey FAC Database; McKinsey analysis.

New Products

With fast foods, for example, like hamburgers and chicken, and with coffee, the key was to transfer a product/service concept from elsewhere, usually the United States, to Japan before the local market had begun. Naturally the products had to be modified to suit local tastes, but who (before McDonald's) would have thought that hamburgers could become a boom product in Japan? The companies that created the business in Japan, preempting local competition, built a strong and defensible business before local companies could react.

Nestlé formed its Japan subsidiary in 1933 but was in the country long before that. Apparently, it moved its headquarters to what had been its Kobe branch after the previous one was destroyed in the Great Kanto Earthquake of 1923. When, after many years of advertising, the coffee market finally took off in the 1960s, Nestlé had the dominant position in a market that it had largely created itself. To this advantage, it later added more breathing space through the complex technology needed to create dried coffee. Today, even after significant competitors have emerged— such as General Foods, both before and during its joint venture with Ajinomoto—Nestlé still holds about two thirds of the coffee market.

Many Japanese consumers view McDonald's as a Japanese company. The Japanese entrepreneur, Den Fujita, approached McDonald's in the early 1970s and offered to establish the franchise in Japan. He modified the burger and bun and set up his outlets in town centers rather than residential areas. By traveling extensively to identify the best sites and launch a large number of establishments before local competitors could react, he gave McDonald's a big enough lead to make it difficult to catch. Kentucky Fried Chicken followed an approach similar to that of McDonald's but linked up with an established company, Mitsubishi Corporation. Like Den Fujita, Loy Weston and Shin Ohkawara, the chief executives, have been entrepreneurs. In this case, Mitsubishi Corporation's real estate connections helped both build a network of restaurants quickly and preempt competitors.

New Business Systems

Importing new ways of doing business has also helped create profitable companies in Japan, particularly when combined with good new product ideas. The Coca-Cola Corporation had been supplying U.S. forces in Japan since the war when, at the beginning of the 1960s, the Japanese market itself became open. Coca-Cola seized the opportunity by end-running the established distribution system and rapidly signing up top-quality bottlers. It then spent five years training the bottlers, despite their strong opposition, in Coca-Cola's route sales approach.

The bottlers would have preferred to follow traditional Japanese distribution methods and advised Coca-Cola that its foreign ways would not work in Japan. But the company did not listen to their advice. It doggedly insisted on its route sales approach and reportedly sent more than a hundred people to Japan to help train the bottlers. The result: a subsidiary that has probably the most efficient distribution system in Japan and that is more profitable than the one in the United States.

In cosmetics, Avon brought its door-to-door sales approach to Japan in the early 1970s, together with its systems for managing Avon Ladies and for producing a new catalog every few weeks. Although the basic principles stayed in force, Avon heavily modified its approach from the geographically defined "cold-call" method used in the West to a system based on selling to friends and relations. Avon is among the largest FACs measured by headcount, and is very profitable despite holding only 3% to 4% of the market.

Or take another example: Amway, which does not rank among the top 100 FACs only because its salesforce do not count as employees. If they did, the company would be in the top 25. It has, however achieved reported sales of ¥75 billion (around $500 million) up from ¥5 billion in 1983, by using a direct sales approach that, in the Avon fashion, bypasses the high costs of the Japanese distribution system.

In all these cases, the company introduced a concept new to Japan and modified it to meet local market needs. In hindsight, this appears simple and obvious. Not so. How many companies would invest in building a hamburger chain when all the available market research said that no one in the target market eats hamburgers? It is easy to say, with the shoe salesman of legend, that a new country is a rotten prospect: "No market, no one wears shoes." It is far harder to say "Great market, no one wears shoes"—and to back it up with the necessary dollars and people and time and imagination.

Other Advantages

Three other sources of advantage—legal, network, resources—are responsible for the success of about 12 of the top 100 FACs. They are often hard to separate. Many financial institutions entered Japan on the basis of their network strengths but also exploited legal barriers. Citicorp, for example, among the largest foreign banks in Japan with a total of 1,500 employees, offered so-called "impact loans," dollar-based loans, when Japanese banks were forbidden to do so. Thus, it was well positioned to provide financing to the expanding Japanese trading community in the 1970s. It could also exploit its network to provide trade financing.

Other examples here include AIU, the Japanese subsidiary of American International Group (AIG), which offered travel insurance to Japanese businessmen before Japanese institutions could do so. Through an introduction by the Ministry of Finance, AIU reached an agreement with the Japan Travel Bureau, the country's dominant travel company, so that almost every Japanese traveler was recommended to take out AIU insurance. AIU had its network and the law on its side. Then, too, there are the Hong Kong trading companies, which have established a position in Japan based on their network and on their ability to source products from all over the world. Even the Ford, General Motors, and Chrysler automotive shareholdings arose mainly because of their network ability to distribute cars outside Japan—an early version of some of today's distribution-based alliances.

Resource-based advantages have proved difficult to exploit despite the strength of the oil industry, where success rests more on refining technology than on control of resources. Little headway has been made in industries such as forestry products, iron ore, or food. Progress for resource-based companies seems to depend on two other circumstances: that there also be technology leadership or that there not be a free market in the resources.

THE ROUTES IN

The dominant route into Japan for many years was the joint venture. Until the early 1970s, direct entry into Japan was legally constrained so joint ventures were the preferred alternative. When restrictions eased in the mid-1970s, joint ventures fell off sharply (see Exhibit 9.4). Soon after that, however, joint venture percentages by industry returned to previous levels, with the exception of financial institutions (see Exhibit 9.5). Although joint ventures had never been prominent among financial institutions, their sharp and permanent decline was mainly driven by the entry of 100% owned operations of securities companies and investment management companies in the mid-1980s. These accounted for almost 40% of all corporate entries after 1985. Thus, the shape of the total share of joint ventures

Percentage of joint ventures; 1988 status; by year of investment

Exhibit 9.4   The joint venture route into Japan.

shows: (1) a real drop immediately following the change in the law: (2) a recovery in the early 1980s as ratios climbed back to their earlier levels; and (3) a drop in the late 1980s because of the flood of financial institution entries.

The startling fact here is that some two thirds of industrial companies entering Japan still do so as joint ventures—despite the significant organizational problems that they almost always create. Why? Our analysis indicates three reasons: (1) access to channel and customers, particularly when an investment in capacity is required; (2) access to good people, management, or work force; and (3) a preference for short-tem results. In other countries, these needs could be met through acquisitions. In general, this approach is not open in Japan because of extensive cross-shareholdings.

1. To Gain Channel Access

Some industries in Japan exhibit "soft integration." Even when there is no real cross-ownership, companies act as if they were integrated. This soft

Percentage of joint ventures; consolidated

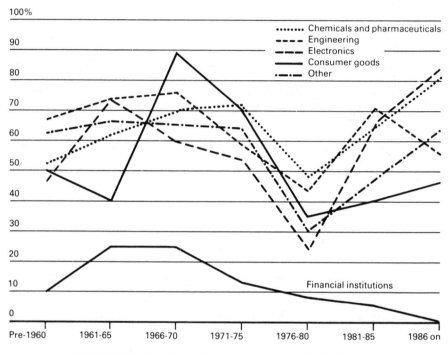

Exhibit 9.5 Joint venture percentages by industry.

integration may include overlapping quality control, product development, and just-in-time systems, as well as exchange of management. The net effect in affected industries is that price alone will not gain share. So a FAC has to learn how to meet a whole host of other requirements.

The natural answer to this challenge is to find a partner. The only exceptions come when the technology being offered is so far ahead that potential customers cannot afford to neglect it. But, as we shall see later, it is usually only a matter of time before the lead declines and the FAC has to come to grips with the unavoidable realities of soft integration.

2. To Gain Good People

Top-quality people in Japan—as well as people who "really understand" the country and its markets—tend to go to the leading corporations and to stay there. As a result, hiring good mid-career managers is extremely difficult for a new company. Moreover, FACs and their parents were reluctant to divert the attention of top managers back at headquarters to the microlevel problems of operating in Japan. As one finance director explained, "We wanted to find someone to understand Japan for us. We didn't have—or weren't prepared to spare—the top management resources to do it ourselves." Thus, if a FAC wants to establish, say a chemicals business, building the necessary management team can be extremely difficult. Again, the most natural answer is to seek a partner.

3. Preference for Short-Term Results

For the reasons just discussed, a go-it-alone approach will not show results in less than, at a minimum, five years. So when the top managers of a foreign corporation see a clear prospect of sales and profits during the next five years through the joint venture route and only a murky prospect of deferred returns by going it alone, they will—most of the time—choose immediate revenues. And that means a joint venture.

MID-LIFE CRISIS

Even those FACs that have started out well and that have found effective routes into Japan have often met a crisis as the initial window of advantage closes. Some technology-based advantages have lasted over 20 years; some less. And their duration is getting shorter all the time. When these advantages finally begin to lapse, FACs find themselves attacked by local competitors that have matched them on technology and can outwit them on market and channel knowledge.

Fuji-Xerox, for example, showed extraordinary returns until the mid-1970s, when it came under pressure from emerging Japanese competitors that were able to capitalize on small copiers and out-execute it in the market. Similarly, Procter & Gamble (P&G) created the disposable diapers market in Japan, but its share of almost 100% in 1979 tumbled to less than 10% as Uni-charm and Kao first met and then surpassed it on technology—and outwitted it in channel management. Since then, P&G has completely changed its trade strategy.

A senior Japanese executive of a FAC chemicals company, now in his fifties, recalls how "Twenty years ago I spent every night at the best restaurants in Tokyo, being entertained by the chief executives of major Japanese companies, who wanted to gain access to our technology through joint venture or licensing. And you must remember how junior I was then.

We thought we were kings. Today, Mitsubishi Chemical has technology to equal ours. Sumitomo Chemical has surpassed us in some aspects; and no one asks me out to dinner any more. We were like the tortoise and the hare. We slept, and they passed us."

In a similar vein, the head of a pharmaceutical company commented, "We created the market for X. A Japanese company came up with a variant that, according to our people, had no technical merit. Today, they have 60% of the market. I could never persuade our development laboratory to take the issue seriously."

Stages of Development

For those FACs that do not entirely disappear off the map, this plunge into a mid-life crises usually precipitates a major internal review. The conclusion, quite predictably, is that, "We need to become more of an insider." And this, in turn, leads to a decision to move from a *Gaijin* (foreigner, or non-Japanese) era in the FAC's management to a Japanese era (see Exhibit 9.6). Since it is difficult to attract suitable, top-level Japanese managers from outside the company, the internal managers are moved up rapidly. For the moment, at least, this development leads to an improvement in results because, indeed, profound knowledge of local practices can gain ground.

The next phase in the FAC's evolution, however, is usually that management at headquarters finds that it cannot really understand what the FAC's managers are doing—or why. At first, headquarters is likely to accept the local company's activities, reasoning that responsibility has been delegated and should not be undercut. But this "I trust you" approach usually erodes over time as mistakes get made and as distrust and frustration grow at headquarters. The result is often a swing back toward "foreign" management—most visibly, by the outright removal of the FAC's top Japanese managers or by shunting them sideways. This puts the FAC back where it was before—only this time competition is tougher and the need for local knowledge greater.

Moving the Mountain

A better alternative is to modify headquarters, not the FAC itself. A number of companies have actually shifted the relevant parts of their headquarters operation out to Japan in order to force top corporate management to understand Japan from close up. Johnson & Johnson asked a retiring

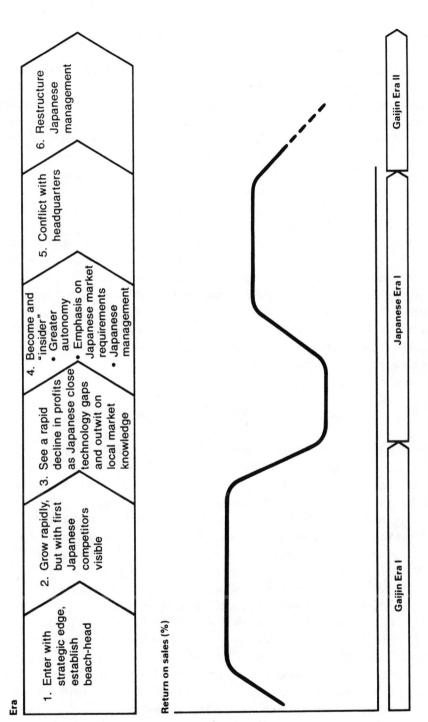

Exhibit 9.6   The FAC mid-life crisis.

Era

1. Enter with strategic edge, establish beach-head
2. Grow rapidly, but with first Japanese competitors visible
3. See a rapid decline in profits as Japanese close technology gaps and outwit on local market knowledge
4. Become and "insider"
   • Greater autonomy
   • Emphasis on Japanese market requirements
   • Japanese management
5. Conflict with headquarters
6. Restructure Japanese management

Return on sales (%)

Gaijin Era I

Japanese Era I

Gaijin Era II

159

member of its Executive Committee, Frank di Angeli, to head the area and based him in Japan. On the spot, he could take a corporate perspective on issues and, thus, speed decision making. Du Pont and ICI have taken their former Japan"heads" and put them in charge of the whole Asia-Pacific region (still based in Japan) with a new Japan head below them. Several European companies have followed a different route and substantially expanded their planning staffs to improve the quality and speed of their headquarters response to developments in Japan.

All of these changes highlight what is becoming a core challenge for FACs and their parents; harnessing global strength to compete effectively in Japan means changing the organization both outside and inside Japan. Success in a global competitive environment requires companies to "decompose" their global headquarters. There is often great resistance to doing so. Why, managers wonder, change comfortable arrangements many thousands of miles away when the problems are local in Japan? This, of course, is the heart of the FAC dilemma. Local solutions, by themselves, are not enough. In today's increasingly competitive environment, local problems demand global solutions.

NEW CHALLENGES, NEW SKILLS

As FACs in long-established sectors like electronics, engineering, and chemicals are fighting a mid-life crisis, new winners have emerged focused mainly on consumer markets. Some of these are exploiting the classic route of FAC entry by introducing a new concept to Japan. Thus, Kellogg is changing the Japanese idea of breakfast. But many of them are following a different route: not looking for the large, "structural" edge but, instead, taking a smaller advantage and capitalizing on it quickly.

With its launch of *Timotei* shampoo, Unilever relied on its ability to do "theoretical" market research—that is, its ability to develop, test, and refine a product concept without actually putting a physical product on the shelf. With *Timotei*, Unilever pushed this "theoretical" skill to the limit and identified a positioning and concept that no Japanese competitor had found. To minimize the potential for competitor response, the company decided to do one, and only one, test market. This gave disappointing results, but based on its judgment of the reasons for this, and what it saw as the potential, the management decided to go ahead.

The roll-out went national rapidly with the sampling of between 25 and 30 million households (about three quarters of the total and the largest sampling campaign ever conducted in Japan); and second, a major television launch coupled with sales-force efforts to have the product visible in outlets accounting for over three quarters of shampoo sales. This preemptive strike helped create an immediate hit product, which captured a (leading) 15% brand share within two years.

Unilever also indulged in a burst of product-range proliferation that any Japanese company would envy. The purpose: to occupy, as far as possible, all niches for variants on the original theme. Not surprisingly, imitators came. Four years later, 40% of the category was occupied by brands launched since *Timotei,* although *Timotei* still had a strong share.

Maintaining this position will clearly be a major challenge, but the progress so far illustrates the importance of their differential skill advantage in market analysis; of outstanding competence in making judgment calls on the market research and the final launch; and of the capability to define and execute a preemptive strategy. Not all FACs will face precisely these challenges, of course, but they will need to develop much the same kinds of competence and capability.

Competence

By competence, I mean the "brain" of the organization—the ability to decide rapidly and accurately on opportunities and threats in Japan. Unfortunately, many companies have become slower, rather than faster. Before Japan became as important as it now is to global organizations, many corporate managers left Japan to local country managers who, once they had been in the country for some years, could make decision on the spot. But as the Executive Committees of these companies became increasingly concerned about Japan, they have called for the most crucial decisions to be brought to them. As the head of one FAC put it, "We take the most crucial and complex decisions about Japan and give them to a group whose knowledge about doing business here amounts to an annual visit to the Okura Hotel."

Many Executive Committees recognize this problem and are unhappy with making decisions on Japan without exhaustive backup. In the case of one electronics company, this stretched-out decision cycle often amounts to a year and sometimes two. Given that technology-based competition is often neck-and-neck, this is a crippling blow to any hopes of success. Improving the quality of the local management will not solve the problem. Nor will decentralizing responsibility.

Few FACs have sufficient capabilities in Japan to battle head-to-head on their own with their Japanese counterparts. They have to harness global resources—but not when those resources and those who control them sit far removed from the day-to-day details of doing business in Japan.

Thus the pressure is on to move in the direction in which IBM moved in the early 1980s when it shifted the full set of headquarters functions for the Asia-Pacific region to Tokyo. Once there, the group would have no choice but to come to grips, daily, with the realities of the Japanese business environment. There have been several adjustments to the organization since then, but the basic principle still remains true: The Asia-Pacific leadership group has had to come to terms with Japan.

Capability

The ability to execute—effectively and rapidly—in Japan depends, in large measure, on the training and development of personnel. Few FACs recruit the quality of staff that enter their Japanese competitors, yet many still leave recruiting and training to their personnel departments, much as if they had too many rising stars, not too few. They do not seem to realize, as they might in a more familiar cultural environment, just how big the quality differential is. Whatever the reason, responsibility for the development of a capable organization is often delegated, whereas it should in many cases be a FAC's number one priority.

Effective execution and harnessing of global resources also depend on the transplanting of resources to Japan, despite the high costs of doing so. Nearly all the industrial companies among the top 100 FACs have, for example, now established R&D laboratories in Japan. Although tapping Japanese technology is valuable in itself, the predominant reason for establishing these facilities is to get new technologies to Japan early so that they can be developed with a Japanese flavor. In the electronics industry, for example, this codevelopment approach is often crucial if customers are to accept the final product. Arriving with a finished product developed elsewhere is often a recipe for failure because customers wanted something slightly different.

The demands of doing business successfully in Japan, however, go far beyond hiring practices and the transplantation of R&D laboratories. As the head of a chemicals company commented, "You cannot get the depths of the organization at home to understand what it takes to succeed here. We represent only 10% of their output. The other European markets represent 60%. We suffer in times of shortage. We suffer from other people's poor quality. We suffer irregular delivery times. We suffer. There are so many minor decisions that lead to this that I don't believe we will ever overcome these problems until we have a factory in Japan. Yet when they hear the land costs and the labor rates, our Executive Committee rejects the matter immediately."

The issue here, of course, is not just where a factory gets sited. In the Japanese environment, the management competence and the executional capability to capitalize rapidly on small advantages depends critically on the presence in Japan of relevant functional activities. But that is only half—perhaps even less than half-of the story. For these functions to get established and for them to perform as they must, there has to be a huge increase in a parent's skill in funneling quickly into Japan the best ideas and approaches and technologies from elsewhere in the world.

Local success depends on far more than local competences and capability. It depends on the distinctive global strength of the parental network in which each FAC sits—and, in particular, on the company's ability to harness that strength to support rapid execution in Japan. If the challenge is to do well in Japan, the primary question that has to be answered is how drastically must a parent reorganize and redeploy its global resources to support that goal. To boost local performance, what's needed is global skill. And that's the dilemma that FACs now face as they approach middle age in Japan.

10

Creating the "Hyphenated" Corporation: Japanese Multinational Corporations in the United States

Henry DeNero

For a decade and more, much has been said and written about the success of the large Japanese multinational corporation (MNC). With few exceptions, the view of U.S. managers, the business press, and the public at large is that these MNCs are superbly managed. The technological prowess, engineering brilliance, manufacturing know-how, and marketing skill of the leading Japanese players in industries like automotive, electronics, and financial services are legendary. And behind these companies, or so goes the story, lie distinctive—and hard to replicate—national development policies, government subsidies, loose antitrust laws, protection against corporate takeovers, cheap and abundant capital, well-educated workers, strong labor-management collaboration, close supplier-manufacturer alliances, and a shared culture that stresses hard work and personal sacrifice for the good of the collective whole.

Many of these factors have, in fact, supported the rapid development of Japanese MNCs. Yet most of these MNCs do not perform nearly as well in the United States or Europe as they do in Japan. Their financial performance, which is often not high by U.S. standards anyway, is disproportionately weighted toward the domestic Japanese market. Financial statistics on the U.S. performance of Japanese MNCs are quite limited. Only a few companies—Kyocera, Sumitomo Corporation, Haseko Corporation, and Toyo Saison, for example—report their U.S. or North American profits. In each of these cases, however, U.S. profitability, as measured by U.S. return on sales (ROS), averaged about 4% during the late 1980s, compared with a figure of nearly 17% in Japan.

To some extent, lower U.S. performance is due to the yen-dollar revaluation of the mid-1980s, which reduced the profitability of export-dependent Japanese MNCs. In many cases, however, lower U.S. profits are the result of a genuinely weaker competitive position in the United States than in the Japanese market, as embodied in lower margins and fixed cost coverage or in a higher cost of doing business.

Much the same is true in terms of market share. Contrary to conventional wisdom, in many of the U.S. markets in which the Japanese participate, they are not the market leaders: American and sometimes European companies are. Exhibit 10.1 profiles the results of a McKinsey-sponsored

Relative position of Japanese MNCs	Industry segment	Leading competitors		
		Japanese	U.S.	European/Other
High One or more Japanese MNCs are the leading competitors in the U.S. market	• Consumer electronics (TV, VCR, CD, HiFi/ Stereo)	• Matsushita (JVC, Panasonic, Quasar) • Sony • Sanyo • Mitsubishi • Several others	• Zenith • Bose • Harman	• Thomson (GE, RCA)* • Philips
	• Cameras	• Canon • Nikon • Minolta • Asahi (Pentax)	• Kodak • Polaroid	

*U.S. position increased through acquisition.

Exhibit 10.1 Leaders in selected U.S. markets.

Exhibit 10.1 *(continued)*

Relative position of Japanese MNCs	Industry segment	Leading competitors		
		Japanese	**U.S.**	**European/Other**
High (*cont.*)	• Semiconductor memories	• Toshiba • NEC • Hitachi	• Texas Instruments • Motorola	
	• Semiconductor manufacturing equipment	• Canon • Nikon	• Applied Materials • Varian	
Medium Japanese MNCs share strong position with U.S. and/or European companies	• Automobiles and light trucks	• Toyota • Honda • Nissan • Several others	• GM • Ford • Chrysler	• Daimler-Benz • BMW • Volvo • VW/Audi • Several others
	• Medium-class trucks	• Isuzu • Nissan • Hino	• GM • Ford • Navistar	• Daimler-Benz • Volvo
	• Farm and construction equipment	• Kubota • Komatsu/ Dresser	• Deere • Ford • Allied • Caterpillar • Tenneco (Case) • Harnischfeger	• Kloeckner-Humboldt Deutz • Fiat-Allis
	• Machine tools	• Fanuc • Yamatake-Honeywell • Komatsu • Okuma	• Litton • Cross & Trecker • Cincinnati Milacron • Ingersoll-Rand	• Asea Brown Boveri • Thyssen (Hueller/Hille) • Coman
	• Telecommunications equipment (consumer and industrial)	• NEC • Toshiba • Matsushita	• Rockwell • AT&T	• Northern Telecom • Siemens • Ericsson
	• Plain paper copiers	• Canon • Several others	• Xerox • Kodak	
Low Japanese MNCs not among leaders in U.S. market	• Mainframe computers	• Fujitsu/ Amdahl* • Hitachi/EDS	• IBM • Unisys	• Bull HN (Groupe Bull, NEC, Honeywell)*
	• Personal computers	• Toshiba (laptop only) • NEC (laptop only)	• IBM • Apple • Compaq	

Exhibit 10.1 *(continued)*

Relative position of Japanese MNCs	Industry segment	Leading competitors		
		Japanese	U.S.	European/Other
Low *(cont.)*	• Micro-processors and related ICs	• Hitachi • NEC	• Intel • Motorola • Texas Instruments • AMD	
	• Large home appliances	• Mitsubishi	• GE • Maytag • Whirlpool	• Electrolux/White*
	• Small home appliances	• Matsushita (microwave only) • Sharp (microwave only)	• Allegheny (Oster, Sunbeam) • Hamilton Beach • Black & Decker • NAACO (Procter-Silex) • Gillette (Braun)	• Krups • Samsung • Lucky-Goldstar
	• Automotive components and supplies	• Nippondenso • Bridgestone/Firestone*	• TRW • Rockwell • Eaton • Bendix • Goodyear	• Bosch • Michelin/Uniroyal-Goodrich* • ITT Teves • Pirelli
	• Steel	• NKK/National*	• USX • Bethlehem • LTV • Inland • Armco	
	• Scientific/analytic instruments	• Hitachi • Shimadzu	• Tektronix • Perkin-Elmer • Hewlett-Packard • Varian • Millipore (Waters)	• Siemens • SmithKline Beecham (Beckman Instruments)
	• Electrical equipment and general machinery	• Toshiba • Hitachi	• GE • Westinghouse • Emerson • Ingersoll-Rand • Reliance	• Asea Brown Boveri • Siemens
	• Medical imaging equipment	• Toshiba	• GE	• Siemens • Philips

analysis of the 20 largest U.S. consumer and industrial product categories in which Japanese MNCs compete. In total, these 20 industry segments represent approximately 80% of the total value of Japanese imports and virtually all of Japan's transplant production in the United States. This accounts for the vast majority of Japanese industrial activity in the United States (not including services or direct investments in real estate, resorts, and the like).

Of these 20 industry segments, Japanese MNCs are the clear leaders in only four. In another six, they are among the leaders. But in the remaining 10, Japanese MNCs are clearly not in a leadership or even a coleadership role.

Still another indicator of Japanese MNC's performance in the United States is the relationship between their U.S. and non-U.S. revenue. Of the 25 largest Japanese industrial corporations participating in the U.S. market in 1988, in only six cases were U.S. revenues more than 25% of total revenue. Four of the companies (Nissan, Honda, Mazda, and Suzuki) were automobile and/or motorcycle manufacturers. This is not surprising, given the huge size of the U.S. market (relative to Japan) and the MNCs' lack of a significant European presence. The results of another company (Bridgestone) reflect a major U.S. acquisition (Firestone). In fact only one nonautomotive company in this group of industrial giants—Sony—has achieved the proportion of its total corporate revenue in the U.S. market that one would expect of a leading global company.

Why haven't more of these world-class MNCs been more successful in the U.S. market? The principal reason is that—despite their massive investments in U.S. sales and marketing, manufacturing, and even research and development (R&D) facilities—few of these companies possess the full range of *institutional skills needed for globalization*. The necessary approaches to planning, measuring, rewarding, communicating, and day-to-day decision making all fly in the face of the centralized, functionally driven style of most Japanese MNCs.

The need to develop global management skills is not limited to Japanese MNCs. Most North American and European MNCs face important challenges operating outside their home environments. By understanding the common issues surrounding globalization—as well as those that are unique to the Japanese MNCs—managers in all three spheres of the global economy can more effectively address their performance needs.

"Globalization" does not simply mean having revenues and profits distributed among many countries. Nor is it merely the deployment of people, capital, and capacity outside of one's home market. Rather, it is the institutional ability to act local while being global. As simple as it sounds, this behavior represents a tremendous challenge for most—and, especially, most Japanese—organizations.

Perhaps most challenging for Japanese MNCs is the need to evolve away from the strong cultural influence of being "Japanese." They must create a new, multicultural form of organization—what I call the "hyphenated" corporation. Neither Japanese nor American, but Japanese-American, the hyphenated corporation will retain the best characteristics of a Japanese company, while adopting the local characteristics needed to compete effectively in North America. The same will be true for Europe.

COMMON PERFORMANCE GAPS

During my 17 years with McKinsey, I have been fortunate enough to work with several major Japanese MNCs. These have included "brand name" companies in automobiles, automotive components, personal computers, home appliances, sporting goods, and food products. In every case, the company has been—and still is—among the worldwide leaders in its industry, as measured by share of global market, brand image, product quality and performance, and overall reputation. But with only one or two exceptions, each of these companies is a second-tier competitor in the U.S. market.

My personal experience is multiplied by that of 20 to 30 of my partners in other parts of North America and Europe who, together, have served more than half of Japan's 100 leading multinationals on a wide range of strategy and operating issues. (Of course, our partners in Japan have served most of these companies in Japan as well.) In most cases, their experiences parallel my own.

We are all intensely aware of the ability of Japanese MNCs to design and manufacture the highest quality products at significantly lower costs than can most of their U.S. and European competitors. In many industries—automobiles, consumer electronics, cameras, electronic components (semiconductors and computers among them)—the product design and manufacturing know-how of these MNCs is well documented. So, too, is their outstanding ability to innovate. Witness, for example, the "high-design" motorcycle (Honda), "personal" consumer electronics (the Sony Walkman and its relatives), the "ergonomic" 35mm camera (the Kyocera Samurai), and the "nostalgia" car (the Mazda Miata, which was actually conceived and designed by

Mazda-USA to be produced in Japan for the U.S. market—as a genuinely hyphenated corporation should be able to do).

In fact, many of these companies, which do have real competitive advantages in terms of product quality and cost, succeed *despite* performance gaps in other areas. They are world-class in their ability to design and manufacture—the skills of the traditional Japanese exporter. But they are not world-class along a variety of other performance dimensions. Our experience identifies six such "gaps" that represent significant opportunities for Japanese MNCs operating in the United States to strengthen their local performance: American and European MNCs have similar opportunities to improve performance outside their home markets.

Stronger Sales, Marketing, and Intermediary Management

There are numerous examples of Japanese MNCs undermarketing or mismarketing a superb product. These companies generally have weak or underresourced sales and marketing organizations in the United States and often sell their products through "second-class" distributors and dealers.

In the mid-1980s one large consumer goods manufacturer (Number 3 worldwide in its product category and Number 1 in Japan with a 50% market share) was desperately trying to increase its 5% share of the U.S. market. Its sales force, however, was only one third the size needed to service its dealers adequately; it had a U.S. marketing staff of only 15; and it spent perhaps only 20% to 25% of the dollars needed to strengthen its brand awareness and image with U.S. consumers. Further, the company's pricing structure so favored its largest retailers that they were wholesaling to smaller dealers, which created an unwanted "two-tier" distribution system.

The company makes a consumer durable product that has been well-researched in the U.S. market. Approximately 40% of end-user purchases are determined by the retail salesperson because the consumer has little or no brand preference. Another 40% of purchases are influenced by a moderate end-user brand preference, and half of these end users get switched by the retailer. Only 20% of the market goes to consumers with a strong prepurchase brand preference who are seldom influenced by the retailer. Equally important, 90% of all purchases take place within 5 miles of the consumer's home. These facts all add up to a very simple equation: To succeed, you must have high brand awareness, a favorable brand image, and a large retail network that is motivated to sell your product, not the other guy's.

This company's product was—and is—among the finest in the world, and it was competitively priced. But because of the company's misdirected and underresourced sales, marketing, distribution, and dealer price structure, the product remains one of the best kept secrets in the U.S. market.

Greater Marketing Differentiation

At the same time that Japanese MNCs are underresourcing their overall sales and marketing efforts, many also fail to differentiate their approach on a segment-by-segment basis. Again, this is the case with both consumer and industrial products. An MNC thinks it has a product to offer to the U.S. consumer. So it establishes distribution in all key markets (that is, in the top 100 metropolitan areas). Then it establishes marketing "policies" (pricing, promotion, dealer/retailer incentives and support levels, advertising program, warranty programs, and so on) for the U.S. market as a whole. Varying these policies by geographic market or by end-user segment is often considered "too complicated."

Invariably, while the Japanese MNC is treating the entire United States as one market, the best U.S. competitors are tailoring their marketing approaches and even their products to match the needs of regional and end-user segments. During the 1980s, as direct marketing and even neighborhood marketing emerged as major forces, the "differentiation gap" between the Japanese MNCs and their leading U.S. competitors actually widened. And this gap is not limited to midsize, unsophisticated companies. I know one Japanese MNC with over $1 billion in U.S. revenues that is only now beginning to take advantage of target marketing techniques.

Better Fine-Tuning of Products

One of the "Big Three" Japanese automotive companies recently introduced a really terrific car designed especially for the U.S. market. The car is of the highest quality, is very attractive, accelerates and handles near the top of its class, and has a solid price/value ratio. The car is doing very well. Yet small and subtle features (or the lack thereof) detract from the ownership experience. The interior is a bit too spartan for American taste, and one or two of the colors seem just a little "off" to the American eye. Thinking it in bad taste, another car manufacturer did not put the little red blinking light on the door handle of an expensive model. The designer failed to realize that U.S. consumers want this light—a warning to would-be car thieves that the alarm is activated.

These minor misses are not isolated examples. Nor do they reflect a failure to make extensive use of market research. Nor are they isolated to consumer goods. They occur because headquarters personnel often give too much attention to global scale economies and, in so doing, accept products that represent the best "average" result for several markets rather than push to meet each distinctive set of local customer needs. It is impossible for a company to develop the fine points of a product or service through research unless it has already "internalized" local customer tastes, wants, and needs.

When asked by one of my Japanese clients why this is so, I answer with a question. "Could I plan, arrange, and give a party in the home of one of my long-time friends in Japan without appearing—at best—awkward?" The answer, of course, is no. You've got to be an insider in order to think like one and to understand the subtleties of local tastes and values.

More Efficient U.S. Operations

One Japanese industrial products manufacturer operates a $200 million U.S. parts and service department with a decade-old warehousing and distribution system. Another spends 20% to 25% more than it needs to on product liability and warranty costs. One of the world's leading consumer electronics manufacturers recently spent three years turning around its principal U.S. factory. These examples run counter to the public's perception. The fact is that most Japanese MNCs are far less efficient in managing their operations in the United States than they are in Japan. In fact, many are far less efficient than their leading U.S. competitors.

When the vast majority of these MNCs' value-added was generated by operations in Japan, it did not really matter if their U.S. subsidiaries were inefficient. It matters a lot now that manufacturing, sourcing, logistics, and R&D are increasingly being performed here. We have already seen several instances where a superior cost position, which was created by low-cost design and manufacturing in Japan, has been wiped out by the inefficiency of an MNC's operations in the United States.

In truth, most Japanese MNCs have done a remarkably good job of transferring their manufacturing technology and know-how to the United States. Bridgestone's near tripling of productivity in Firestone Tire & Rubber's truck tire factory in the early 1980s is a classic example. The green-field factories in the United States of Japanese automobile and electronics companies are world-class operations. But the rest of the U.S. business system of most MNCs is not, due to weak functional and cross-functional management.

Faster, More Responsive Decision Making

Many Japanese MNCs in the U.S. market do not possess the speed, flexibility, or responsiveness of their leading U.S. competitors. It often takes them too long to make a decision. This is partly due to the Japanese cultural emphasis on consensus building. Poor internal communications and overly centralized decision making are also contributing factors.

Again, this weakness runs counter to a major Japanese MNC strength. Although many Japanese companies are at the forefront of accelerating product development times, they give up some of their speed advantage by slower-than-average "feedback changes" and by unresponsive handling of customer problems.

In product design, for example, the car company that got its new model "almost right" was slow to make the minor changes needed to make it "just right." In manufacturing, many Japanese MNCs have been slow to adjust their production schedules to reflect known changes in U.S. market demand, resulting in spot shortages of some products and excess inventories of others that shouldn't have been produced. In sales and service, major customers are often left waiting to see how their Japanese suppliers will handle a complaint or solve a problem with the company's product. Most frustrating, they cannot find the person who can actually make the decision to resolve a complaint—often because no such person exists.

Smarter Investment Decisions

Many Japanese MNCs have recently acquired U.S. companies as a means of diversifying or of expanding their core businesses. Many of these acquisitions have been made at a substantial premium over the acquired company's market value—despite an often limited ability of the Japanese company to improve U.S. performance of the acquired company.

And, as with many acquisitions by large corporations, the public may never know how many of these investments actually pay off. Our research indicates that in many cases, the Japanese MNCs are often either not buying what they think they are or are paying far too much. Moreover, these MNCs are not doing as good a job as they need to in managing the sensitive and difficult postacquisition process. This will inevitably result in lower performance of the acquired companies and may dash the hopes of synergy or market access on which these acquisitions were originally based.

Any one or two of these performance gaps can largely be overshadowed by the quality and cost advantages of Japanese MNCs in the world market. Collectively, however, they can keep it from becoming as good as the best "local" competitors—and from enjoying the market share and profitability associated with that status.

THE CENTRALIZED, FUNCTIONALLY ORIENTED ORGANIZATION

Why are these performance gaps so prevalent? What are their root causes? In our judgment, underlying *all* these problems is the centralized, functionally oriented way in which most Japanese MNCs are organized and managed *in Japan*. Indeed, without addressing the fundamental ways in which the parent company is organized, staffed, and managed, working to close the performance gaps that show up in the United States or Europe will amount to treating the symptoms, not the causes. Although the specifics vary, many of the problems faced by U.S. and European MNCs can be traced to headquarters as well.

The typical Japanese corporate organization is difficult for a *gaijin* (non-Japanese) to understand. Certainly, those aspects that are well known to Westerners—employee/company loyalty, participation of factory workers in making manufacturing improvements, and heavy involvement of middle managers in reaching consensus before decisions are made—have all contributed to the strong performance of the best-known MNCs during the past few decades. Occasionally, a chief executive officer (CEO) such as Mr. Morita of Sony, is a catalyst to propel the employees and the company forward. More often, however, the CEO "presides" over the corporate organism, providing guidance on company philosophy and approving "decisions," most of which have already been made. In this regard, many Japanese executives use the term "middle-up management," meaning that middle managers analyze and formulate decisions and then work them "up" to the CEO as part of the consensus-building process.

Strategically, the typical Japanese MNC has emphasized the design and low-cost manufacture of high-quality products. The collective, consensus-oriented behavior of these companies has been ideally suited to accomplishing these tasks—especially when products could be designed and manufactured in Japan and then exported to an overseas sales subsidiary. Yet, it is precisely this way of behaving that is now handicapping Japanese MNCs in their efforts to achieve the *local* side of globalization in the major geographic markets around the world.

Specifically, five characteristics of Japanese MNCs limit their mastery of the local side of global management:

1. Centralized decision making
2. Functional orientation
3. Upstream focus
4. Consensus orientation
5. Domestic-focused human resource management

The problem is that these aspects of Japanese MNCs cannot just be scrapped. They are part of the fabric that makes these companies great. But they do need to be altered somewhat, and part of that fabric—its global/local balance—does need to be rewoven.

Centralized Decision Making

A product designer in Tokyo decides what color carpet his company should put in a car bound for the United States. A manufacturing manager in Osaka decides how to allocate production of a capacity limited product between the Japanese and the U.S. markets. An export sales manager in Tokyo changes the sales forecast of the U.S. sales and marketing subsidiary before submitting it to production scheduling. A product manager in Tokyo "fights" with the senior marketing executive of the U.S. subsidiary over the features of a new product under development. An attorney in Tokyo (there are a few) decides whether a product liability claim in the United States should be settled or brought to trial. He has never met with the plaintiff or his attorney.

These are examples of centralized decision making—centralized in Japan. They are a remnant of the export era. One Japanese executive I know refers to his U.S. subsidiaries as "children who are now growing up to be teenagers." His intention is to acknowledge and encourage the further development and independence of the U.S. companies. That is not how his U.S.-based managers hear it. To them, his comment is just another sign of the continuing control from Japan over all major decisions.

It is usually not the top executive who clings to centralized decision making. It is the middle management in R&D, manufacturing, sales, finance, and human resources. In the "middle-up" organization, it is middle management that clings most tenaciously to the status quo.

This is not an issue about who has power or authority, but about who has the knowledge needed to reach the right conclusion, to make the right decision. The heavy involvement of middle managers in Japan reduces an MNC's ability to tailor its products, differentiate its marketing, and be responsive to local customer needs elsewhere in the world. In an age of satellite communications and telefaxes, this involvement does not really slow things down. But it does result in getting the wrong answer. In almost every case in my experience where a product was not quite right or where marketing policies did not quite add up, someone in the United States who was close to the customer knew better—and said so. The managers in Japan just did not understand or chose not to listen.

Functional Orientation

At the same time that Japanese MNCs are centrally managed, they are also functionally organized. Only in the very largest and most diverse companies (Toshiba, for example) are the direct reports to the CEO *not* the Executive Vice Presidents of R&D, manufacturing, sales, finance, and "overseas." Each function is itself an organizational pyramid, managed middle up.

Why does this limit effective global management? First, people study, discuss, debate, and decide on things they know something about. An overly functionalized organization spends too much time improving the functions and not enough time understanding how to serve customers better or how to gain competitive advantage. Because of the middle-up approach, senior executives are isolated from cross-functional, as well as customer- and competitor-oriented issues. They are internally—that is, functionally—focused.

This is easily overcome in a small company operating in one region or nation. But not in a multibillion-dollar enterprise serving Japan, the United States, Europe, and a collection of smaller markets. Top managers can stay close to the market and competitive situation in Japan because they live there. They cannot possibly understand what is really going on in the United States, particularly when most of the information they see is processed and packaged by middle managers within their respective functions. Often, there is no top manager who really understands the United States (or Europe) or is responsible for it. And without informed top managers advocating the needs of local customers and markets, the functions will always win out.

Further, as Japanese MNCs recognize the need to extend their local business systems beyond sales and marketing to include manufacturing and R&D, they usually have each headquarters department (function) "give birth" to a U.S. subsidiary. Not surprisingly, this fragmented structure limits the interaction between functions and prevents their integration into a single business system. Even before the U.S. subsidiaries achieve the desired degree of self-sufficiency, they must begin to act as a single business in the way they work together to meet customer needs. The functional organization slows this down.

Upstream Focus

Compounding the centralized, functional orientation of many Japanese MNCs is their strong emphasis on the "upstream" functions of product development, sourcing, and manufacturing. Again, this is both an asset and a liability. The commitment to design and manufacturing has given many of these companies a worldwide edge in quality and cost. Yet a cultural orientation toward designing and making good products does little to support the development of the downstream skills (marketing, sales, distribution, postsales service) critical to local markets.

In the worst cases, the upstream mentality actively works against the development of local downstream skills by devaluing the importance of excellence in these areas and by limiting the investment of money and talent in them. The result—how many times have I heard a Japanese CEO ask, "If we have such a good product and such competitive costs, why isn't our market share higher?"

Consensus-Building Approach

Also working against local market effectiveness is the management-by-consensus approach of most Japanese MNCs. Viewed in isolation, this is a most valuable asset. Our work with clients in all parts of the world suggests that, without consensus, there can be no real understanding of—or commitment to—what needs to get done. As a result, implementation is slow and ineffective. Linked to the centralized, functional orientation of many Japanese MNCs, however, a consensus-based approach makes a company simply too unresponsive. It slows things down and, worse, often results in a compromised, suboptimal solution. The right balance must be struck between speed and consensus.

Human Resource Policies

The human resource policies of Japanese MNCs work against their ability to globalize effectively. These policies affect both the Japanese and non-Japanese employees, as well as their ability to work constructively together.

Many of these companies are limited by the number of talented Japanese "internationalists" on the payroll. There are some notable exceptions. Because of its historically weak position in Japan, Honda placed most of its competitive chips on succeeding in the United States. It has led the way in the development of design and manufacturing resources aimed at the U.S. market and in the deployment of senior executives to the United States. As a result, four of Honda's top five executives (and 14 of its top 20) have lived and worked in the United States. This top-level experience base has greatly facilitated Honda's ability to manage its global/local balance, at least as it pertains to the U.S. market.

In the middle management ranks, the problem is equally pressing. Our Japanese clients have even asked us to help train their middle managers to become more "international." Still, too few of these managers are fluent in English, and too few really want to leave Japan for extended periods of time. In some companies, the "overseas" people are actually considered to be second-class citizens. When it is time for promotions, they often get passed over by those closer to home and, thus, more visible to top management in Japan.

Many Japanese MNCs experience great difficulty in attracting, motivating, and retaining the top U.S. talent they need to perform as sophisticated insiders in the local market. There are many reasons for this, which have been well documented. U.S. pay scales are higher; U.S. managers want a kind of performance feedback that they seldom get from Japanese superiors; they want more involvement in decision making than is often possible; and they want an opportunity to rise to top management. The net result is that, at the local level, many of these companies have second-class employees in many positions—from the field sales representative to the top executive of the U.S. subsidiary. And where there are top-notch people, their performance is limited by the frustration of not being able to do a first-class job in the marketplace.

DEVELOPING GLOBALIZATION SKILLS

The performance gaps faced by Japanese MNCs in the United States, no less than the organizational causes responsible for them, bring sharply into focus the critical importance of developing the skills needed for a company to operate successfully on a global/local basis. Indeed, in working with a handful of Japanese MNCs that are at the forefront of globalization, we have learned that skill-building (rather than traditional modes of reorganization) must be the principal focus for organization change. If an MNC's U.S. subsidiaries for design, manufacturing, and sales/marketing are not working together as one company, simply putting an umbrella organization over them will not cause them to do so. These lessons are relevant to all organizations undergoing change.

There are two broad sets of skills needed to become an effective insider in major markets. These are first, the *local skills* needed at each stage of the local business, and second, the *global management skills* needed for the company to act like a first-class local competitor even though many of the resources used to serve the U.S. market are located elsewhere or shared by other regional markets. In both areas, Japanese MNCs will need to draw on their traditional strengths but will also need to master some elements of typical U.S. corporate know-how. It is the essential process of combining the two strengths, not choosing between them, that creates the hyphenated—Japanese-American—corporation.

Local Functional Skills

Establishing strong, local insider skills means establishing a full U.S. business system that draws on U.S. strengths in marketing and distribution while making the most of Japanese competence in design, manufacturing, and supplier relations. Important as it is, however, this process will not lead to "self-sufficiency."

By definition, a global company keeps some aspects of its business at the global level while decentralizing others to the geographic regions in which it operates. Nissan, Honda, and Toyota, for example, do most of their basic research and component design in Japan. Their product development and engineering functions are also largely centralized, but they are rapidly building smaller groups in the United States and Europe. Each company also maintains a design studio in the United States and Europe. As a result, these companies are developing an increasing number of U.S.-targeted models in their U.S.-based design and development centers. Thus, although they will each have a full business system in the United States, they will (and should) remain heavily dependent on centralized (global) research, design, and engineering resources. The scale economies in these areas prohibit complete regional decentralization.

Nevertheless, they will require strong functional capabilities at all stages of the local business to compete effectively in the U.S. market. In R&D, Japanese MNCs still need to develop local R&D centers that place at least some of the company's technical resources close to the customer. Many Japanese companies are also developing R&D centers in the United States because of the critical shortage of engineers in Japan. (Japan has lots of engineers, but they are all employed.) This problem is fortuitous in that it will force many companies to localize R&D more quickly than they might otherwise have done, thereby accelerating globalization.

As a starting point, these local R&D centers should concentrate on working with the parent organization to adapt and fine-tune products to match U.S. market needs and to "offer" new product concepts to the parent that might not be readily conceived in Japan. Later, these centers will need to take on "cradle-to-grave" product development and engineering responsibilities for at least some of the products destined for the U.S. market. This will be particularly important for those products manufactured here. It will help the MNC to strengthen the critical local linkage between product and process design and to qualify and develop suppliers.

In manufacturing, the process starts with transferring an MNC's basic manufacturing know-how to its U.S. facilities, a task many Japanese MNCs have already accomplished. But this is only the beginning. Next, these organizations must learn to develop and manage local suppliers as they have done in Japan. Otherwise, the full advantages of the Japanese manufacturing system will not be realized in the United States. Later, as local R&D is established, the linkages back into design must be established. The local manufacturing function will also need to link effectively with the company's global manufacturing network, particularly when the U.S. facility is exporting to other markets as well. And manufacturing will have to coordinate smoothly with sister U.S. sales and marketing functions.

In the downstream functions of sales, marketing, and distribution, the critical local skills must be largely acquired rather than transferred from Japan. These are typical U.S. company strengths, which require the intuitive, experience-based knowledge of consumers, intermediaries, and outside advisors that only local managers can possess. As discussed earlier, most Japanese MNCs have already established sales and marketing subsidiaries in the United States yet they are weak in marketing, intermediary management, and even sales force management skills. It is precisely these skills that Japanese MNCs must strengthen.

This means having first-class marketing executives on the payroll. It also means that adequate resources must be provided to develop and manage a high-quality field sales and service organization—an organization with sufficient customer coverage to provide competitive levels of support to intermediaries. MNCs will also need to build a first-class marketing and product management organization and a highly responsive capability for customer service and problem resolution. Finally, as these local marketing skills are strengthened, they will need to be integrated with global marketing activities at headquarters in Japan.

Global Management Skills

The second critical set of skills has to do with the way a company manages itself globally—more specifically, with how it distributes resources, makes decisions, and carries out activities between headquarters in Japan and its "regional business units." I put the term "regional business units" in quotes because they may not be organized as such.

There may, for example, be an R&D subsidiary, a manufacturing subsidiary, and a sales and marketing subsidiary, each reporting to its functional parent on the organization chart. That is okay.

What is important is that the relevant portions of the organization, both in the United States and Japan, *act* as if they were members of the same market-oriented business unit. The trick is to migrate more people from Japan to the United States (taking authority and responsibility with them), and to get those who remain in Japan to play a supporting, rather than an oversight, role.

This is extremely difficult for Japanese MNCs to do. As mentioned earlier, these companies are short on talented, English-language fluent internationalists to serve abroad. But even where there is no shortage, MNCs still find it difficult because it represents a major departure from the middle manager "command and control" model that is so entrenched in many of these companies.

LEARNING BY DOING

How can the capability to manage the delicate balancing act between global headquarters and local control be developed? The CEO cannot just send a cadre of managers to the United States and tell them, "You now have authority to manage our company's affairs in the United States . . . and, by the way, don't do anything that is not entirely consistent with our global strategy or companywide resource constraints." One must develop the skills to manage this way.

In our experience, the best way to accelerate development of new skills is through a series of learning-oriented task forces. These are task forces designed and dedicated to accomplish normal tasks in new ways. The process of actually doing it, rather than being trained how to do it, develops the desired institutional skill. For example, if you want to change the behavior of your sales force from "selling products" to "serving customers," you do not send your sales force to a training class on how to be service oriented. That may be part of the needed medicine, but only a small part.

To develop the new behavior, you must design and implement a model sales call program with real salespeople and their managers and, perhaps, design a "best practices" series of benchmarks for your company. Then you must pilot the program with a few customers or in a few regions. Then you fix it and roll it out—again, through a task force—region by region. You learn by doing.

Developing global management skills is no different. It takes a series of projects or task forces sustained over a period of years, to institutionalize new approaches, behaviors, and systems for running a company. If you simply reorganize it (into, for example, a regional structure) and then tell everyone to "act globally," they will not know what to do.

Some examples of skills that we have seen MNCs learn through task forces are:

- Developing a worldwide product plan that incorporates both the needs of the regions in serving their local markets and the need for achieving scale economies in things like component design, sourcing, and product engineering.

- Developing a five-year business plan for a local market, requiring all functions in the region and headquarters in Japan to work together to develop a fully integrated strategy and implementation approach.

- Designing the first product in a new U.S. R&D center with local management having "special responsibility" to figure out and document how U.S. engineers should coordinate with the basic research group back in Japan.

- Developing a profit model of a local business (including Japan-based costs) so that both headquarters and regional management can readily understand the "total company profit" impact of major decisions affecting product mix, pricing, and volume.

- Revising the company's management information and performance measurement systems to include an integrated perspective built up from financial and physical performance measures from each functional area.

In addition to the preceding "how to" skills, which lend themselves to a learning-oriented task force approach, several "top-down" programs and changes are needed in the development of a truly globally managed organization. These include:

- Changing personnel performance measurement, evaluation, and compensation programs to bring the Japanese and U.S. approaches closer together—and to reward total company, rather than functional, performance.

- Launching human resource programs to accelerate the development of global managers. These might include a variety of hiring, management training, language training, job rotation, and promotion programs aimed at building up the number and the skill levels of "internationalists."

- Accelerating the hiring and promotion of the most talented local executives, as well as putting several of them on the company's board of directors.

Eventually, many Japanese MNCs will have to reorganize to form regional groups for Japan, the United States, and Europe, leaving a small "corporate center" to facilitate global integration. A few leading Japanese MNCs—Sony and Nissan, for example—are already moving toward this form of organization. This, however, is a major task in itself, involving both the formation of regional business units around existing functional subsidiaries, and the realignment and streamlining of corporate headquarters in Japan. It should not be attempted prematurely, nor in the absence of a complementary focus on making required changes in supporting skills and behavior.

The project-based, top-down changes that have been outlined here are not a standard solution for any company. They are examples of the kinds of things that will be needed to move MNCs toward effective global management. They also illustrate the magnitude of the task. Changing the behavior of an enterprise consisting of thousands of employees requires an immensely complex, multiyear process. But companies that believe their capability will, if left to itself, evolve naturally, will discover it to be a multidecade process. By then, it may well be too late.

For Japanese MNCs, in particular, there is the added challenge of preserving the company's Japanese identity while making it more American (or European) in the way it serves local markets. The objective, of course, is not to change it from a Japanese to a U.S. or a European company—or even to make it a "nationalityless" company. It is to marry the best parts of each so that the whole is stronger than any part by itself. For Japanese MNCs, as for those based in the United States or Europe, this is what building a genuinely global organization—a hyphenated corporation—is all about.

11

Winning Strategies in the Competitive Markets of the United States: A Swedish Perspective

Hobart K. Robinson and Magnus Nicolin

Market success in the United States is a prize sought by many Swedish companies. It is clear that Swedish business has invested heavily in the world's premier market during the past 10 years. Over this period, on average 30% of foreign direct investment by Swedish companies was made in U.S. markets. In 1989, Swedish enterprises invested USD 8 billion (close to SEK 50 billion) in the United States—launching strategies, establishing footholds, maintaining interests, and expanding.

Today's America is, moreover, rapidly establishing itself as the market that large companies must capture. For some of today's globally exposed companies, underinvestment in the U.S. market can impede their international growth and hurt their worldwide competitive position.

Yet, investment dollars alone are no guarantee of success. As many large Swedish companies have experienced, the United States is a uniquely challenging environment. Although many have built impressive positions,

At the request of the Swedish/American Chamber of Commerce/The Swedish Trade Council, and Skandinaviska Enskilda Banken North America, McKinsey studied the performance of Swedish companies in the United States over a 10-year period. The study's goals were (1) to define what makes the U.S. market so challenging for Swedish enterprises, and (2) determine what has helped or hindered Swedish companies in their U.S. strategies.

The study team conducted interviews with top management of 15 leading companies at their Swedish headquarters, as well as in their management subsidiaries. These companies were selected as representative in terms of several factors, including size, profitability, strategy (acquisition driven or internal), organization, and number of years in the United States. In addition, the teams, with the valuable assistance of SE Banken North America, researched and analyzed a wide range of financial and economic data.

others have failed to establish a sustained and profitable U.S. presence. Even those who have established strong positions have sometimes done so at considerable and avoidable cost.

What, then, does the United States offer Sweden's largest corporations? What are the barriers they need to overcome? How have Swedish managers coped with the challenges of business in today's "fast, vast" America? What lessons can business leaders draw from these experiences? In particular, what are the implications for business strategy?

U.S. MARKETS: THE REWARDS

By several measures, the United States is the world's largest and most dynamic market.

Size is an obvious attraction. For many industries, the United States accounts for the dominant share of world demand. For example, 45% of all office supplies are sold in the United States. American consumers buy 30% of the world's pharmaceuticals. They buy 30% of the output of automotive manufacturers. They absorb 40% of all telecommunications products and services.

Such a concentration of potential customers also attracts a high level of activity among producers. Many of the world's dominant manufacturing companies—American, Japanese, and European—consider the United States to be pivotal to their business success.

Beyond the size and importance of its markets, the United States offers considerable other advantages to businesses. Many of these result from America's critical mass of management skills, finance, and other resources. Others result from the high level of maturity and development of the markets themselves.

Sweden's pharmaceutical leaders, for example, have had important nonfinancial incentives for their investments in the United States. America sponsors much of the leading edge pharmaceutical research and innovation—fully 75% of world spending on pharmaceutical research and development is made in the United States. Pharmaceutical companies need to draw on the pool of talent that this investment generates. Without a U.S. position, non-American companies cannot compete successfully with the strong U.S. players in the pharmaceutical industry.

By installing research and production facilities in America, Sweden's major pharmaceutical companies can better recruit and retain the skilled researchers and technicians that are important to their development. They also come closer to the universities and institutes, and to important development activity. Being there means joining the network: Not being there slows the exchange of valuable information. Most significantly, not being there can limit companies' access to the ideas that give rise to the next generation of products.

When Swedish companies have made this "investment in intelligence" they have decided on the United States to gain strategic benefits. When a company is interested in developing innovative products that can contribute to long-term advantages, immediate sales success can sometimes be a secondary consideration.

Such front-end business advantages are not limited to the pharma sector. Technology-based companies and even fast-moving consumer goods companies look to the dynamic markets of the United States for innovative products, concepts, and methods.

Similarly attractive is America's financial and management expertise. Companies that avail themselves of the services of innovative professional advisers can reap significant competitive benefits.

In finance, for example, America offers constant exposure to the creativity of the large commercial and investment banking communities. In addition to Wall Street's large pool of bank and stock-based financing, the United States also provides access to venture and high-risk capital.

Also, Swedish companies often find in the United States an outlet for their relatively well-developed industrial organization and operations know-how. Domestic U.S. companies are often less sophisticated in operating management, or suffer from low productivity, inefficient processes, and dated plants and equipment. This situation offers the effective Swedish companies an added dimension of opportunity. Both Asea Brown-Boveri (ABB) and Alfa-Laval, for example, found that recently acquired U.S. companies had plant and equipment three times older and considerably less efficient than comparable European plants. This opened an opportunity for ABB's and Alfa-Laval's managers to use their European experience to drive out the inefficiencies in the U.S. business.

For Swedes, there is an additional attraction to the United States over European target markets. People in business feel more at home with English than with other foreign languages. And Swedes broadly understand the American way of life. Management familiarity and comfort should not be underestimated as a factor in the development of Swedish companies' international strategies. America offers a stimulus that, in itself, is one of the attractions of conducting business there.

U.S. MARKETS: THE BARRIERS

Despite its attractions, the United States is not an easy environment for the outsider. And, as we discuss later, several of Sweden's most respected companies have floundered in their attempts to establish U.S. positions.

Why have many seemingly adequate strategies been upended when faced with American business reality? What makes the United States such a challenge to outsiders, even to the "best in class"?

We have found that three broad characteristics of the American business environment account for most of the confusion and challenge. Managers who are charged with developing their companies' U.S. strategies meet markets that are:

- Diverse
- Costly
- Competitive and complex

The Challenge of Diversity

It is all too easy for Swedish decision makers to view the United States as a single market. But, for business managers, it is clearly a complex of separate markets—geographically, economically, and dynamically. In the Midwest, for example, there is relatively limited spending power and less enthusiasm for imported products (the word "import" might actually be a negative selling point). On the other hand, on the West Coast, imports are "snapped up" by both big industry and individual consumers. Moreover, the U.S. market consists of many separate markets with sufficient buying power to make them an attractive target by themselves—comparable to the leading European markets. Companies that underestimate this diversity invite business problems.

For industrial and commercial purposes, the United States has distinct regions, each with different characteristics. Customers vary in their preferences, they differ in their acceptance of new products, and distribution systems have adapted to different consumer buying patterns.

For some industries and product categories, the diversity sometimes goes beyond even the regional distinctions. For consumer products, for example, geographic segmentation can extend to perhaps 50 markets. Swedish company planners, marketers, and implementers must recognize that separate markets require separate approaches.

In turn, product specifications are sometimes different across the American continent. Because consumers emphasize different product attributes, and because there are many companies ready to tailor their products to local demand, competitors must offer very distinctive products to win. This means that, in many industries, companies will face different competitive environments with different players and different buying factors in different regions.

In addition, the federal and state authorities often impose divergent requirements on companies, products, liabilities, packaging, pricing, and reporting. The "United States" can be a labyrinth of regulations and attitudes.

The Barrier of Cost

Costs for outsiders can be high. For companies choosing to build their own operations, there are obviously significant start-up expenditures. And for those opting to acquire businesses, there are substantial premiums to consider—foreign buyers tend to pay acquisition premiums that are higher than those that domestic American companies pay. For example, between 1976 and 1988, the average premium paid by non-U.S. companies for acquisitions in America was 49% above market value; for domestic American companies, the average premium was only 35%.

But even ongoing business expenses can be relatively high. Swedish managers in most industrial and commercial sectors must expect substantially higher costs for marketing, insurance, legal services, and recruitment in their U.S. subsidiaries. As a result, profit margins can be threatened.

Marketing, for example, may require significantly higher spending. American companies' spending on advertising amounts to 2.5% of gross national product—twice as high as the spending in Sweden. Getting noticed against the tide of media messages requires skillful, organized campaigns—and money.

One Swedish consumer products company, for example, increased its advertising budget by 30% and still did not generate sufficient response among its target group. In contrast, the company's Japanese competitors in the same U.S. market spent up to 70% more. Because competitors spend aggressively, most players need to spend large sums to keep brand awareness alive. Furthermore, companies must spend intelligently, focusing on a more narrowly defined and competitively distinct message than in Europe.

Professional service costs are another considerable expense. A Swedish pharmaceutical company incurred legal expenses four times higher in America than in Sweden. A Swedish engineering company had legal expenses five times higher than in Sweden. (Both comparisons are adjusted for differing sales volume.)

Product liability claims, for example, have been well beyond Swedish levels and, as a result, insurance premiums are very high. Fees for expert counsel can also bring problems—partly because of the higher incidence of legal action taken by suppliers, customers, competitors, and shareholders; and partly because outsiders to the United States typically need a lot of qualified and continuous advice.

Similarly, Swedish companies face extraordinary costs to recruit and retain management personnel. The managing director of one Swedish player states: "I can't compete with the large U. S. companies for the top candidates." Says another Swedish executive in the United States, "If you can't find a way to provide stock options, it will be difficult to get good managers."

To overcome this obstacle, some Swedish companies have found it necessary to break with Swedish practice in compensation arrangements for their U.S. subsidiary managers. One Sweden-based company, for example, offered a U.S. division manager an unusually attractive compensation package, including an innovative use of "shadow options"—an artificial stock option for the division. Not only is the division manager better compensated than the U.S. subsidiary's chief executive but he is also better compensated than the Group chief executive in Sweden.

The Forces of Competition and Complexity

The markets of the United States are dynamic, competitive, and complex. Outsiders face considerable challenges in meeting the requirements of success in such an environment.

Product innovation is one of the areas that can challenge even the most competitive producers. The United States often leads developments, setting standards that later reach other parts of the globe. And, because U.S. competitors are often well informed of market innovations and quick to copy winning concepts, few products and commercial ideas enjoy long periods free of rivals. Technological and business developments can quickly outpace even well-prepared companies.

The ready availability of capital also spurs competition from small start-up companies. Established players therefore have to compete not only with big established players but also with small newer companies.

Our research shows that, in most industries, companies contend with between two and four times as many active competitors as in Sweden. This can be explained by the behavior of the typical company. For example, an executive at a midsize Swedish engineering company stated: "We have to be in the United States market to remain viable as a global competitor." A small Japanese manufacturer of electronic equipment said: "In our second year of business, we sold more than 50% of our production in America."

Local companies are also well aware of the importance of holding a strong U.S. position. One midsized American high-tech company considered its domestic business to be "our 'bread and butter'—we won't do anything internationally that could endanger our position at home."

In short, both outsiders and American domestic companies are intent on placing U.S. markets high on their priorities. So competition for position is intense.

So too, the complexity of marketing and distribution in the United States can present problems. In Sweden, managers typically deal with only one, or few distribution channels. In the United States, they must often confront a complex of channel choices that requires considerable skill and time to handle. Many of these channels may overlap with each other, raising issues of channel competition and effective resource use.

SWEDEN INC.—THE EXPERIENCES

Many of Sweden's premier companies have been active in the United States over a long period. In evaluating their success in American markets, we have looked at two dimensions: (1) strategic market position; and (2) average U.S. profitability compared to group profitability.

Market Position

Success in achieving penetration of available market segments varied widely between the companies in our investigation. Also within companies the success of different business units has sometimes varied. All the companies surveyed showed wide gaps between their most and least successful business units.

Profit

As with strategic market positions, profitability varied greatly between and within companies. For the surveyed group as a whole, financial success (as measured by consistency of profits) has been limited. Although early returns should not always be expected (start-up costs after all are an investment in future opportunities) our figures indicate that American units of Swedish companies are less profitable than their groups overall (Exhibit 11.1). From our interviews with company managers, it appears that, even when adjusting for transfer pricing, the overall picture remains the same—with only a few players showing significant improvement.

For most companies, the operating results of their American activities over the past 5 to 10 years have been disappointing. Nevertheless, most companies have been able to build impressive strategic positions and are well respected by local competition, customers, and suppliers. Others have not been so successful and have had meager returns for the large investments in money and time.

What are the reasons for this mixed success? Why have some companies and business units been so much better at interpreting the demands

PERCENTAGE POINT DIFFERENCE IN OPERATING MARGINS*
BETWEEN GROUP AND US SUBSIDIARIES, COMPANIES A–K

* Average 5-year operating profit before appropriations, taxes and interest divided by average gross sales 1984–1988.

Exhibit 11.1   U.S. results are lower than group results. *Source:* S-E-Banken; McKinsey analysis.

of the difficult U.S. market? What lessons can companies draw from this? In the final section, we explore these questions.

DEVELOPING A WINNING APPROACH
TO THE U.S. MARKET

There is no single answer to what constitutes a winning strategy. But, the success of some companies and business units can be attributed to their consistent approach—doing things right all the time, not some of the time. Our investigation suggests that successful entry and growth requires, at a minimum, effective management in the following areas:

- Concentrate efforts and investments on a well-defined, viable strategic thrust
- Get downstream activities (distribution, marketing, sales, and after-sales service) right
- Forge effective links to the corporate center
- Use a dynamic approach
- Acquire, rather than build, market position

Concentrate Efforts on a Well-Defined, Viable Strategic Thrust

Just as a high-performance engine needs to fire on all its cylinders, a U.S. thrust needs the business strategy equivalent of five cylinders to maximize its performance. On the evidence of our investigations, these are: (1) a business advantage that is unique to the United States market; (2) a clear idea of how to market in a highly segmented environment; (3) products that are adapted to U.S. requirements; (4) a medium- or long-term strategic focus; and (5) realistic, rather than wishful, attitudes toward opportunities.

Our work suggests that the degree to which these requirements have been fulfilled has varied widely. The following examples may shed some light on how important these requirements are, and why failure to comply may foretell problems.

Unique U.S. Advantage

White/Electrolux, for example, drew considerable benefit from its careful assessment of its competitive position. The company came to a clear understanding of what it needed to do to fulfill its competitive strategy: "We will be the largest producer to get economies of scale—consolidating plants, standardizing components, but not features and design." Interestingly, the strategy was successfully implemented by local American managers who were brought into the company through previous acquisitions.

In some cases, Swedish companies have failed to foresee the power of competitors, or have overestimated their own advantages. One company, for example, was taken offguard by the ferocious competitive climate: "Large companies teamed up to support small manufacturers against us." Moreover, the apparent superiority of its product was not enough to withstand competition from established technologies, since buyers did not recognize its claimed benefits.

Recognition of Regional Differences

AGA, an industrial gas producer, provides a good example of the importance of regional differences in the United States. AGA was able to spearhead its U.S. business by concentrating on a single region—the Midwest. Another company also tried a regional approach to sell its products to the Northeastern geographical segment. In this case, because regional segmentation was less significant than other segmentation criteria, the approach did not succeed. So, the lesson is that there is no substitute for a thorough and correct assessment of the fundamentals of how products are used and how distribution and support must be organized to serve the market effectively.

Adaptation of Products

To build a U.S. position, it is important to adapt products and clearly understand the market requirements. One Swedish packaging competitor, for example, overestimated its prospective customers' willingness to accept European products. They offered a one-liter package instead of the standard American quart or gallon measures. This unfamiliar product was shunned by U.S. buyers.

The U.S. market is often driven by criteria that are surprisingly different from the European market. While in many cases the European technology or approach may be considered superior, it typically takes a well-orchestrated approach and a lot of time to convert the U.S. end user.

Medium- or Long-Term Focus

The U.S. market is complex and competitive. This means, among other things, that strategies must be pursued with consistency over long periods of time. If it takes 5 years to penetrate the French market, it may take 10 years to do the same in America. Ericsson, for example, invested heavily and consistently in its central office equipment business unit for more than 10 years before achieving some success.

Realistic Goals

Finally, the strategy needs to be realistic. One consumer product company expected to get 5% of the U.S. business. "We have 20% in Europe; it should be easy to secure 5% in the United States." The lesson here seems to be that the competitive, diverse character of the United States makes it difficult to achieve a nationwide position quickly. A goal of, say, 10% in the Northeast would have been more realistic than the 5% nationwide.

Furthermore, a low market share, say 2%, in the gigantic U.S. market may seem tempting for many companies. In most cases, however, this is unrealistic since effective coverage is difficult if the 2% is spread across the country. As a result, one Swedish company has developed a more realistic target for market share: "If we can't realistically get 20% in a segment, we will exit."

Get Downstream Activities Right

Many of Sweden's industrial and commercial success stories, at home and in export markets, have their origins in Swedish skills in "upstream" activities such as R&D, design, and production. For example, Swedish product design has traditionally received deserved attention for its innovation and functionality. Similarly, in product manufacturing, Sweden has been able to maintain a high international standard—leading many industries in factory automation and even in productivity growth.

Yet, the United States, as several Swedish companies have discovered, requires also very strong "downstream" skills to match winning products to the complexity of U.S. markets. To build strong downstream skills, companies must (1) manage complex and diverse distribution systems, (2) focus marketing to cut through the media hailstorm, (3) manage sales effectively, and (4) manage responsiveness of after-sales service.

Manage Complex and Diverse Distribution Systems

Distribution systems in American markets are complex. In addition, companies must often concurrently manage dissimilar distribution systems in different regions (Exhibit 11.2). This may amount to devising and evolving ten different strategies, each needing to be closely monitored.

Also, the style of managing distribution must often be adapted and made very collaborative. Distributors, for example, are usually more powerful than in Europe and often "control" their regions. One company got firsthand experience of this a few years ago. It enjoyed strong and close working relationships with the end user in Sweden and tried to adopt a similar approach in America, bypassing local distributors. It quickly found, however, that the distributors controlled access to end users in many areas. To avoid losing established customers, it had to backpedal on its approach. Interestingly, the company eventually succeeded in negotiating a mutually beneficial arrangement with its distributors, giving it direct access to the end users and giving distributors a small margin of the sales.

Another Swedish company on the other hand was, from an early moment, aware of the importance and power of local distributors and dealers. The company set out to communicate with, educate, and support its dealers in an effort to improve not only coverage, but also quality and dealer effectiveness. This program made the company's dealers the most

EXAMPLE: FOUR REGIONS

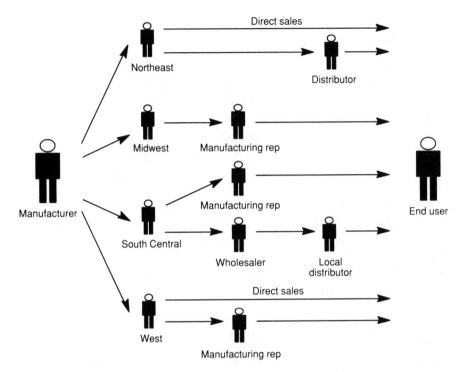

Exhibit 11.2 Distribution management must cope with regional differences.

highly rated in the U.S. and greatly contributed to its success in the mid-1980s. It has also helped cushion the company when the product line lost competitiveness in recent years.

The successful companies thus devote their time and effort to aggressively implementing regional distribution structures and to building very strong relationships with all the parties in the distribution system.

Focus Marketing to Cut Through the Media Hailstorm

Not only is the amount of media spending higher in the United States, it is also very difficult to cut through the clutter of messages targeted at the consumer. To succeed, companies must spend advertising funds intelligently, focusing on a more narrow message or theme than in Europe.

The lesson here is that marketing funds can easily be wasted in the U.S. market unless the company has a distinct message or innovative approach. Increasing the marketing budget may be part of the solution, but not all of the solution.

Manage Sales Effectively

Many companies and business units enter the market and immediately establish their own sales force. Yet, effective coverage in many industries often requires a large number of salespeople and revenues of $100 to $200 million per year. One Swedish player attempted to cover the United States with its own sales force but quickly realized that the coverage was insufficient and expensive. In contrast, another Swedish company in the same industry secured effective sales coverage through major acquisitions.

The sales effort in the competitive U.S. market also needs to go down the line to effectively impact all influencers of the buying decision. Furthermore, the complex distribution structure needs to be activated to ensure sufficient attention and aggressiveness from distributors. These penetration requirements clearly create more work for an already stretched sales force.

Manage Responsive After-Sales Service

The market is particularly demanding in regard to functionality. For example, construction equipment that does not maximize uptime is unattractive. Ergonomics, safety, and performance are irrelevant if the supplier cannot guarantee rapid service and shipment of spare parts. This makes it tough for a foreign entrant since quality after-sales service often results in an expensive organization.

The U.S. customer is demanding and so suppliers must guarantee effective support. For some products and services, the support can be organized locally or regionally, but for products that are used across the country, it is necessary to establish a nationwide support structure. To make this economically viable, a company must often merge with an established player or establish a joint venture.

Forge Effective Links to the Corporate Center

Some companies have operated with insufficient linkages between the parent and the U.S. subsidiary. The special challenges of U.S. markets require appropriate lines of communication across the Atlantic.

Unless the company develops an effective answer to the issue of linking corporate and subsidiary management, critical tasks will likely be neglected or be performed inefficiently. Lines of authority need to be made clear, and mechanisms must be created to ensure rapid decision making without incurring untoward costs. The principal objectives of the effective link are to ensure (1) open communications and (2) sufficient support from the parent and coordination of, principally, upstream activities.

Open Communication

Open communication is critical to ensuring that the parent sufficiently adapts products, provides support, produces sufficient quantities, and so on.

A transportation equipment manufacturer, for example, had poor communication between parent and subsidiary on U.S. demand forecasts. Partly as a result of this, the parent overinvested in new production capacity. Quality communication can be facilitated in many ways using an array of linking devices. These could range across board representation, policy committees, task forces at several levels, formal reporting/communication systems, daily fax contacts, or informal but frequent phone conversations. This exchange of information also needs to take place in high-level, strategic decision making to ensure sufficient adaptation to U.S. market requirements. One competitor recognized this aspect of the U.S. market needs and subsequently included its U.S. country manager (as the only country manager) in its President's Advisory Council on corporate policy.

Communications and execution are sometimes weakened by divergent management styles, cultures, and approaches. Several companies have, for example, appointed well-qualified managers from Europe to the U.S. subsidiary only to see them get mired in the unfamiliar complexities of the U.S. market. Proven success in Europe is not necessarily transferable—as nearly half the interviewed companies attested.

Some companies have employed American managers but failed to formalize their important links to the Swedish network. Without these links, problems can quickly arise. In particular, differences in management style can create barriers.

For example, the Swedish tradition of consensus and loose reporting responsibilities can be discomfiting for American Managers. As one Swedish chief executive said, "A CEO is expected to use his own judgment to temper decisions." In contrast, an American chief executive officer asserted, "I will take all the freedom I can get, and if the

Swedish board is hands-off (as they are) that is a lot of freedom." And as one of our more candid interviewees claimed, "You can't trust a U.S. CEO to give you bad news." With such possible divergences of attitude, misreadings of responsibilities can surface at awkward moments and derail execution. It is thus important to take steps to prevent poor communication, whether it results from a lack of procedures and devices or stems from cultural differences.

Support from Parent or Division

Successful companies have in the past 10 years shifted operating power to divisions. Linkages will primarily be between parent divisions and local divisions—with headquarters playing a smaller direct role in subsidiary management. Likewise, on the U.S. side, the holding company has a smaller role as "country head" but in many cases an expanded role in other areas, such as mediating between division management and the local division. Support from the parent or division is particularly important in the early stages of a market entry or when introducing new products. As noted, it needs to be consistent over a long time to ensure effective results.

In the more integrated stand-alone local subsidiary, the need for outright support lessens and the need for coordination increases. Coordination of upstream activities like R&D and production is particularly important.

Use a Dynamic Approach

The way U.S. activities are managed must evolve dynamically over time. This includes (1) the relationship between the center and the local company, (2) the role of the local (holding) structure, and (3) the style and skills of local managers.

The Relationship between Parent and Local Company

Two drivers determine what relationship is required; first, the strategic significance of the U.S. market; second, the degree of integration or level of local skills. Integration can be considered along an axis: at one extreme, a sales operation; at the other extreme, a fully integrated business system, including research and development, manufacturing, and distribution.

The relationship may start with a "trading post" that needs to be managed hands-on with specific sales targets. Most Swedish subsidiaries have however been integrated with strong local skills in the United States—a market that most companies consider to be of high strategic significance. This means that a U.S. subsidiary should be managed very differently from, for example, a Finnish subsidiary (including systems, investments, managerial independence). Typically, the U.S. subsidiary would need to be managed as an equal partner (Exhibit 11.3).

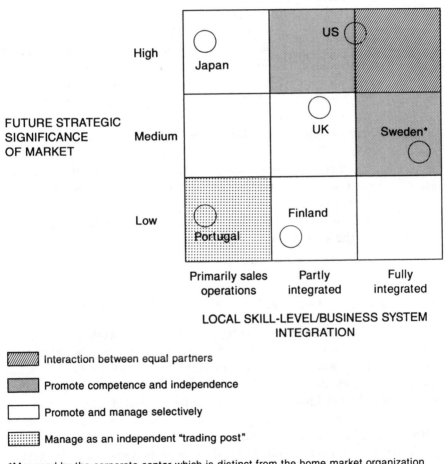

FUTURE STRATEGIC SIGNIFICANCE OF MARKET

High / Medium / Low

Japan — US — Sweden* — UK — Finland — Portugal

Primarily sales operations / Partly integrated / Fully integrated

LOCAL SKILL-LEVEL/BUSINESS SYSTEM INTEGRATION

Interaction between equal partners

Promote competence and independence

Promote and manage selectively

Manage as an independent "trading post"

*Managed by the corporate center which is distinct from the home market organization

Exhibit 11.3   In the U.S. market, companies may need to be managed as "equal partners." *Source:* McKinsey analysis.

The Role of the Local Structure

Local roles may need to change in the course of building a position in the United States (Exhibit 11.4). For a small company, or in the earliest phase of establishing a U.S. presence, subsidiaries are often managed from the home base in Sweden. The role of the holding company is therefore to provide support. As activities grow, local U.S. coordination becomes more important. In some cases, this geographic focus may need to take precedence over centralized business unit management.

Eventually, there may be advantages to allowing the U.S. units to assume a leading role in specific divisions. This might be the case in pharmaceuticals, office equipment, or other areas where the United States clearly leads market or product development.

Similarly, access to technology or raw materials may suggest a lead role for the U.S. subsidiary. The move by the management team of a Sandvik division from Sweden to Detroit is a good example of a company adapting to market requirements. Sandvik concluded that the key factors for success of the division were better served from a U.S. platform.

The adaptation needs to be driven by evolving market requirements, local skill levels, and the like. Many companies have, however, changed strategies, structures, and approaches not as a result of market conditions, but rather because of poor performance. This has often been interpreted to have been caused by the wrong strategy, the wrong manager, or the wrong sales force. While these factors may have contributed to the poor performance, the root cause is more often a poor understanding of the customers' needs.

Style and Skills of Managers

The complexities of the markets previously discussed dictate that the overall skill level of local managers must be high. Furthermore, the skills need to evolve with the demands of the market. For a market entry, the CEO should have strong experience or an understanding of how the parent operates. He should also know how to ensure effective and efficient support for products, funding, and management time. This needs to be complemented with a strong U.S.-experienced marketing and sales executive.

As the venture evolves and the local company becomes more integrated and skilled, the CEO's success depends on managing local complexity while maintaining good coordination with the parent. The CEO position is often better suited to a U.S. national or someone with extensive U.S.

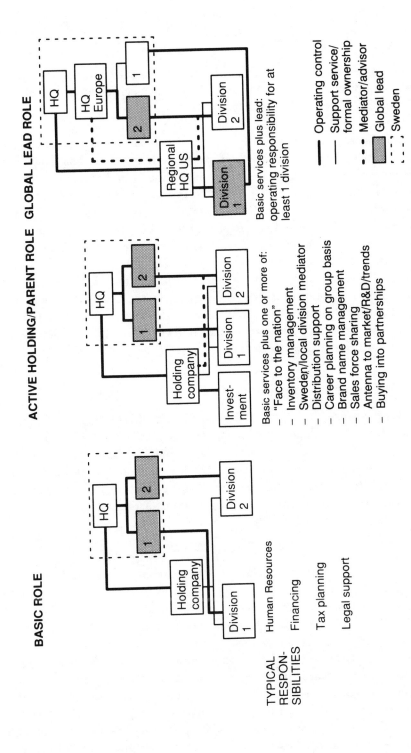

Exhibit 11.4 Sample U.S. holding/parent company roles. *Source:* Company interviews; McKinsey analysis.

BASIC ROLE

HQ

Holding company

Division 1

1

2

Division 2

TYPICAL RESPON-SIBILITIES

Human Resources

Financing

Tax planning

Legal support

ACTIVE HOLDING/PARENT ROLE

HQ

Holding company

Investment

Division 1

1

2

Division 2

Basic services plus one or more of:
– "Face to the nation"
– Inventory management
– Sweden/local division mediator
– Distribution support
– Career planning on group basis
– Brand name management
– Sales force sharing
– Antenna to market/R&D/trends
– Buying into partnerships

GLOBAL LEAD ROLE

HQ

HQ Europe

Regional HQ US

1

2

Division 1

Division 2

Basic services plus lead:
operating responsibility for at
least 1 division

— Operating control
— Support service/ formal ownership
---- Mediator/advisor
▨ Global lead
⌐⌐⌐ Sweden

company experience. On the other hand, U.S. executives with no experience in Swedish management principles or the specific corporate culture will probably experience some frustration.

Therefore, building the right skills and experience may entail significant training or career management. For example, companies may need to familiarize a newly hired American chief executive with the parent company's ways of doing things. This could mean asking the incoming manager to undertake an extended immersion program in Sweden. Similarly, a Swedish executive transferring to America may need similar immersion in U.S. business practice and culture. Early exposure to the United States—traveling, living, communicating—may be a worthwhile investment for a senior manager. Although the cost of such immersion can be high in expenses and man-hours, the cost of possible management failure may warrant it.

In sum, a successfully managed company in the United States is one that follows and addresses changing market requirements and that is prepared to constantly adapt at the parent level, in the local structure, in staffing, and in many other areas.

Growth Through Acquisitions

Since 1984, acquisitions have contributed roughly 40% of the growth generated by the 14 companies in our survey (A–L in Figure 11.5). The approaches used and successes have been mixed. We have found that (1) companies using acquisition-driven strategies are more successful, (2) successful acquirers use a well developed preacquisition evaluation approach, and (3) successful postacquisition integration is fast-paced.

Acquisition-Driven Strategies Are More Successful

Swedish companies that have chosen acquisition as their growth strategy have generally had better results (Exhibit 11.5).

This finding may be somewhat surprising, especially in view of the costs and difficulties of making acquisitions. However, the explanation could be that the "hardware" of the acquisition deal—fixed assets in the United States—may be the somewhat less important element. In many cases, the "software" of the deal is more significant—quick access to an established position, immediate understanding of how those markets are served, and a skilled local management team. Such "software" elements of a deal can be acquired through acquisition relatively inexpensively—certainly in relation to the cost of building those skills internally. Of course, such advantages

COMPANIES A–L, 1984–88

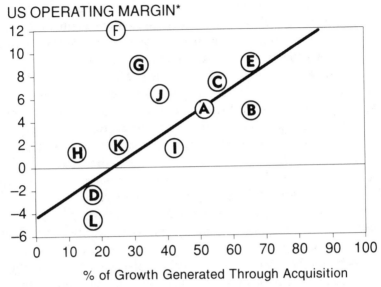

US OPERATING MARGIN*

% of Growth Generated Through Acquisition

* Average 5-year operating profit before appropriations, taxes, and interest divided by average gross sales over the last 5 years

Exhibit 11.5 Acquisition-based growth strategies have been more profitable. *Source:* McKinsey analysis.

must be weighed against the acquisition price and the management challenge of bringing a new subsidiary under the parent group's control.

Furthermore, and for obvious reasons, the success of the acquisition approach depends on the availability of suitable companies. In some industries, the acquisition volume in recent years has depleted the stock of attractive candidates. In other industries, restructuring activity has already gone as far as antitrust authorities will permit. In situations where full acquisition of fully integrated companies may not be possible or desirable, companies can still acquire pieces of the important "software side" of a business. This might entail buying into the distribution system or buying critical management skills.

Successful Preacquisition Strategies

Successful companies make acquisition evaluation building on three dimensions: the strategic thrust, industry evolution, and desired management skills. Furthermore, successful companies acquire related businesses.

This finding mirrors the conclusions of a 1987 McKinsey survey of 97 acquisitions in the United Kingdom and the United States (where related acquisitions were successful almost twice as often as unrelated acquisitions) as well as our more recent analysis of cross-border acquisitions by the largest 150 companies in the United States, Europe, and Japan.

Moreover, the best managers must be given responsibility for running acquired companies, and they must be well acquainted with the strategic thrust. In addition, successful acquisitions are instigated in the line organization but receive support from an experienced staff function. Two of Sweden's largest companies, for example, successfully managed all their U.S. acquisitions through a dedicated acquisition team that acted on the direction of the business group management.

Preacquisition assessments in successful companies are never hasty; rather, they evolve over several years. This allows managers to develop a feel for which companies would fit, and what conditions are right. As a former deputy managing director put it: "You just have to wait for the flow of deals." Finally, as with all acquisition management, a rigorous, focused, and complete approach is needed to extract the full value of the investment.

Successful Postacquisition Integration

Postacquisition integration is exceedingly important to secure a successful result. Integration in winning companies is fast-paced and emphasizes as many improvement dimensions as possible. Specifically it focuses on:

- Functional improvements to the acquired company, for example, in scale and technology.

- Financial improvements, including financial synergies, spin-offs, innovative equity placement strategies.

- Managerial improvements in both subsidiary and parent. This might include putting tested managers into the acquired company on a long or short term basis. It might also mean exploiting the skills of acquired managers—to develop the required strategy changes in the merged business units, or to help improve the performance of other business units.

In our experience, companies that drive through more improvements—functional, financial, and managerial—at the critical period immediately after acquisition are more successful (Exhibit 11.6).

No. of improvement dimensions used*	No. of acquisitions in survey	% assessed to be successful**
0	12	◯ 0
1	11	◕ 73
2	12	◕ 92
3	5	● 100

* Functional, financial, or managerial changes that lift the combined value of the integrated companies beyond their separate values.
** Return on capital invested exceeded cost of capital.

Exhibit 11.6 Driving through integration using several dimensions increases acquisition success. *Source:* McKinsey & Co. survey "Making Successful U.S. Acquisitions"; survey encompassed 52 related acquisitions by Scandinavian companies.

In summary, a well-executed approach can increase chances of success where acquisition is chosen as the growth strategy. Three factors seem to explain why the more successful Swedish companies in the United States have been those that have driven their growth with acquisitions: (1) It ensures access to an existing skill base; (2) it normally provides instant access to distribution; and (3) it simplifies the difficult task of becoming a market "insider."

For many Swedish players, success in the competitive markets of the United States will depend on how well management addresses the challenges of diversity, cost, complexity, and competition.

For Swedish companies, an investment in the United States is only in part an investment in a market opportunity. For many, it is also an investment in an international position. To get on top—and stay on top—of the dynamics of an increasingly global business, companies must achieve success in the critical U.S. market. The U.S. market must therefore be managed exceedingly well since mistakes not only hurt the U.S. position but the global position as well. To ensure success, management must commit strongly and consistently over a long period of time.

For smaller companies or divisions of major companies, the global requirements may be less important. These companies may instead view the U.S. market as an opportunity to build sales and revenue. Furthermore, smaller companies may not be able to buy their way into the market, but rather will have to invest persistently and consistently over long periods of time.

Although most of the companies we surveyed for this report are large, the findings presented in this piece are broadly relevant to smaller companies. In fact, the challenges created by the huge size of the market may be even greater for the small company. This will tend to put even more emphasis on the need to cooperate with local companies, to work well with distributors, to make effective use of advertising, and to use innovative compensation systems to secure competent local management.

12

Making Successful Acquisitions: United States

WILLIAM E. HOOVER, JR.

Driven by a falling dollar, mature home markets, and an accelerating trend toward globalization, Scandinavian companies are acquiring an increasing number of U.S. companies.

But how many of these deals are likely to work? Less than half, according to our examination of Scandinavian U.S. acquisitions. Out of 52 deals made between 1970 and the mid-1980s, only 20 met a strict criterion of success: that the return on capital invested exceed the cost of capital.

While this result is similar to those of surveys of U.S. firms buying U.S. firms, the lack of success has often been more traumatic for Scandinavian buyers, due to the relative size of the losses, drain on management resources, and blows to prestige.

This accentuates the importance of understanding: What makes for a successful U.S. acquisition? What distinguishes winners from losers? In a study of the acquisition practices of 11 leading Scandinavian companies in a broad range of industries, complemented with the experiences of investment bankers and the consulting community, we found successful acquisitions to have five common characteristics.

Acquiror characteristics

**Predetermined U.S.
Strategic Platform**

- Superior and
  transferrable
  product/concept
- Major position in niche
- Relevant distribution
  channel
- Calculated industry
  risk

Process characteristics

Fact-Based and Systematic Evaluation	**Price-Sensitive and Creative Negotiation**	**Rapid and Differentiated Integration**
• Functional levers • Financial levers • Managerial levers	• Non-competitive bidding • Walkaway price • Creative structuring of deal	• Immediate integration • International functional and financial integration • Local managerial integration

**Highly Skilled and
Aggressively Managed
Acquisition Team**

- Strong financial
  orientation
- Significant resource
  commitment
- Multifunctionally
  skilled staff
- Clear and aggressive
  goal setting

Exhibit 12.1   The winning acquisition system.

These five factors, which we think apply not only to Scandinavians but also to other European acquirers of U.S. firms, explain whether and how a prospective acquirer should pursue a U.S. acquisition (Exhibit 12.1):

- Predetermined U.S. strategic platform
- Financially oriented and aggressively managed acquisition project team
- Fact-based and systematic evaluation of performance-improving levers
- Price-sensitive and creative negotiation
- Rapid and differentiated integration

PREDETERMINED STRATEGIC PLATFORM

Successful U.S. acquisitions are consistently driven by a predetermined, longer term, and ongoing strategic program. It reflects a unique clarity about the purpose of U.S. presence and how to go about it; the specific acquisition remains an instrument of implementation rather than a "once-in-a-lifetime" opportunity. These programs are typically built up around four elements:

- A superior and transferable product or concept
- Gaining major market share
- Targeting a relevant distribution channel
- Assessing industry risk and predicting industry performance changes

Superior and Transferable Product or Concept

A superior and transferable product or concept is key to justifying the high costs and significant difficulties in capturing the benefits of a U.S. acquisition. This is not just a matter of making small improvements, for example, by cutting overhead costs by 5% to 10%; successful acquirers transfer products or concepts that generate improvements in performance by 30% and upward. Such improvements are required to justify the substantial costs of U.S. acquisitions, and a critical evaluation of the superiority and transferability of the product or concept is key to realizing them.

On the cost side, a premium over market value of about 40% and a P/E ratio of 20 has typically been paid for foreign acquisitions of U.S. companies. In addition to this premium, Scandinavian companies that carry out acquisitions in order to introduce new products on the U.S. market often experience significantly higher introduction costs than expected. Advertising expenditures, for example, are about twice as high in the United States as they are in Scandinavia. Product liability costs are far higher. In order to offset these additional cost elements, it is necessary to achieve substantial improvements in the acquired company's returns.

On the benefit side, several Scandinavian companies have tried to introduce new products or concepts only to find that U.S. consumers prefer vastly different products or that improving the acquired company's performance is more complex or less sustainable than expected. Volvo, for example, unexpectedly found that its modular trucks were a far cry from what U.S. truck buyers wanted. They wanted their trucks customized right down to the details. The sheer size of U.S. customers (a typical U.S. truck operator has 500 to 3,000 trucks) gave the buyers a power unknown in Europe.

Improved Market Share

Gaining major market share also represents a key success factor—in fact, we found 85% of the acquisitions resulted in a major share position (i.e., putting the combined entity in the top 4). This does not imply, however, that one necessarily has to go big or national: Most successful U.S. acquirers have focused on a niche.

AGA—a large Swedish gas company—built its very successful U.S. entry strategy around this notion. It took a strong position in the Midwest of the United States through the acquisition of Burdox; a geographical niche that fitted well with AGA's distribution skills and was small enough to be manageable and affordable to enter. "It is totally wrong to think of the United States as one country," says AGA's CEO Marcus Storch, "it is really four or five."

This approach contrasts strongly with the classical unsuccessful approach of going for 3% of a huge total by buying a laggard national company (because one cannot afford a leading one) without having the turnaround skills to get the company back on track. Again, Volvo is instructive. When it bought White Motor (a number six player), their combined share was still under 10%, and Volvo has spent a decade trying to push it up a few points. Might it not have been better to simply buy the number two or three earlier, if it had been available?

Relevant Distribution Channel

Targeting a relevant distribution channel is critical to success for most Scandinavian U.S. acquirers, since they often carry out acquisitions to exercise high-quality product synergies; that is, the introduction of new or the repositioning of existing products. The typical U.S. distribution channel is on average larger, the number of channels for distributing a product higher, and the average channel more focused than in Europe. As a consequence, almost 50% of Scandinavian companies currently present in the United States have organized their distribution network differently than in Europe. Acquisition failures result from lack of advance attention to these differences:

- *Wrong distributor.* Superfos failed to achieve the expected distribution synergies in the Royster acquisition because the acquired company's distributors did not sell the same wide range of products as Superfos did in Denmark. The U.S. distributors turned out to be much more specialized—thus greatly limiting the ability of Superfos to fill out the U.S. network it bought.

- *Wrong acquired salesforce.* Swedish Match hoped to transfer a very successful European marketing strategy to the United States, by shifting the direction of the acquired salesforce of Universal Match. However, getting the salesforce to call on a whole different set of customers and, in fact, to change their selling habits (including appropriate attire) proved extremely difficult.

Industry Risk and Performance Changes

Assessing industry risk and predicting industry performance changes are essential to the timing and pricing decisions in an environment of high and increasing volatility of profitabilities for many industries. Very few value-added products or concepts are strong enough to outweigh the impact of deteriorating industry economics.

Several Scandinavian U.S. acquisitions were made at the peak of a cycle or before the full effects of structural overcapacity had been felt. With overoptimistic market forecasts drawn from extrapolation of past trends, the downturns had disastrous consequences. Elkem, for example, acquired Union Carbide's ferroalloys division on the brink of an industry sales decline, at a price representing an in-perpetuity discounting of peak earnings. By the end of 1986, the total estimated loss amounted to a sum approximately equal to Elkem's total market capitalization.

Certainly, no one can make definite predictions on future industry performance. But if management knows where the industry is, and identifies the forces driving it, it is in a much better position to make the acquisition timing and pricing decisions accordingly.

Apart from providing the strategic rationale for an acquisition, the strategy platform, per se, has helped successful acquirers to maintain perspective in a fast moving situation, while still allowing a rapid strike:

- *Being patient.* This is the best approach because there is continuous scrutinizing of the acquisition market until a good deal appears (almost 80% of all U.S. acquisitions are initiated by the seller and not by the buyer) rather than a three-month intensive screening effort (Exhibit 12.2). "At Esselte," says Bengt Strandberg, Deputy Managing Director, "we don't see much value in screening. There is a value in screening very early on if you are not clear who all the players are, but other than that you just have to wait for the flow of deals."

- *Remaining selective and defusing pressure.* This is necessary because you must say no far more often than you say yes. "You need a broad vision of what you want, then cast your net, let it be known you are looking, and wait for the right one to pop up at the right time, and say no to a lot in the meantime," says Hans Werthén, Chairman of Electrolux.

- *Moving fast when the deal appears.* As one chief executive officer (CEO) commented: "You have to cover the water with a fairly broad net, let the world know you are interested, then be willing to act very quickly and decisively when the opportunity comes along."

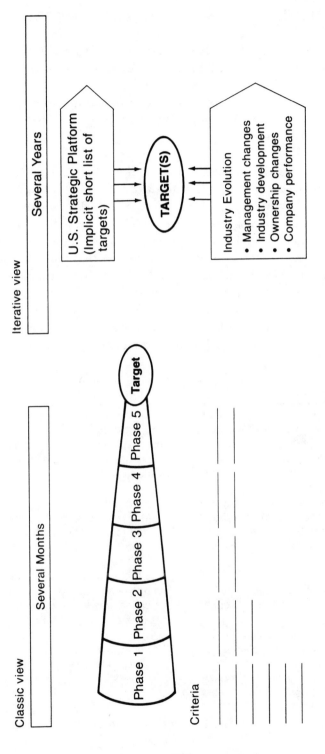

Classic view

Iterative view

Several Months

Several Years

Phase 1 Phase 2 Phase 3 Phase 4 Phase 5

Target

Criteria

U.S. Strategic Platform
(Implicit short list of
targets)

TARGET(S)

Industry Evolution
• Management changes
• Industry development
• Ownership changes
• Company performance

Exhibit 12.2 Classic sequential screening versus iterative process.

FINANCIALLY ORIENTED AND AGGRESSIVELY MANAGED ACQUISITION PROJECT TEAM

Successful acquirers have a surprisingly consistent acquisition project organization, despite vastly different sizes and types of businesses and acquisition projects. They are typically characterized by:

1. *A strong financial orientation.* Most acquirers have a strategic vision and a strategic rationale for their acquisitions. Characteristic of the successful acquirer, however, is that financial objectives also remain a key priority, and values and management style spell out the way the acquisition is going to fulfill these objectives (Exhibit 12.3). Profits—rather than growth, risk diversification, or excess cash motives—are the main criterion by which the viability of the acquisition is judged. The thrifty financial orientation of the winners contrasted sharply with the empire-building notions ("We have to be in the United States at any cost") of the less successful. Conversely, the poor acquirer too often pursues a deal based on a strategic vision that has never been tested on its bottom-line implications.

Financial Orientation	Empire Builder Orientation
"I carried out the financial evaluation of the acquisition myself—it is the combination of experience and penny-pinching which makes an acquisition create profits."	"You have to understand that these were prestige projects, often the personal ideas of management, and that management had a lot of their own ego tied up in them."
"With the prices you have to pay in the U.S. (for acquisitions), it is the marginal savings that count—if you can't exploit those you better forget the deal."	"We wanted to be the biggest in the world in our industry and therefore needed to be in the U.S. . . . in retrospect it was all quite romantic."
"Higher return on equity is our only goal—growth is just an instrument."	"The failure was due to a bad board member—he created euphoria among his colleagues about the acquisition because of his personal ambitions."
"I always translate acquisition proposals into financial implications before I make a deal—if it doesn't generate returns which cover a risky cost of capital, I don't do it."	"We bought it with a lot of high hopes and flimsy ideas of strategy."

Exhibit 12.3   Acquisition motives. *Source:* Interviews.

2. *Significant resource commitment.* This commitment must be made by successful acquirers. Involvement starts at the top, but covers man-years of effort down the line until the end of the project. Up to 20 man-years in the prenegotiation phase, and up to 80 man-years in the postnegotiation phase, are being spent on one candidate. Furthermore, seasoned top management are heavily involved throughout the whole process. They spearhead the development of a U.S. strategy, remain closely involved in the evaluation and negotiation process, and spend a considerable amount of time in the integration process.

The value of this involvement cannot be underestimated, given the significant challenges that an acquisition represents: multiple stakeholders need to be balanced, complex strategic and operational issues have to be resolved, substantial tactical skills are required, and significant sums are at stake. "Only with long business experience do you know how to smell a rat," says Einar Sissener, CEO of Apothekernes Laboratorium, the Norwegian pharmaceutical company.

3. *Multifunctionally skilled staff.* Experience along three lines is involved in success. On the functional side, marketing, finance, and manufacturing people analyze issues such as quality of, and required investments in, acquired plants; carry out finance and tax modeling; and resolve brand advertising and channel management issues. On the geographic side, U.S.-based staff is heavily involved if the acquirer has already established a presence in the United States. This provides the necessary insight into local conditions.

Finally, on the organizational side, the staff composition shifts during the acquisition process. In the prenegotiation phase, project teams normally consist of acquirer staff; in the integration phase, staff from the acquired organization play a vital role—indeed, they do most of the work. However, functional specialists and strategy liaisons from the acquirer also remain heavily involved in this part of the process. They make sure that the integration teams stay in line with the acquirer's strategy and have access to the acquirer's management and skills.

4. *Clear mandates and aggressive goal setting.* These factors guide successful acquisition teams. As one CEO commented: "Start the task force off by giving a one-page description of the project, highlight the options and, if possible, give a clear hypothesis on which option is favorable." Similarly, successful acquisitions are managed through aggressive goal setting which often forces people to take a totally new look at their business. "We had a 45% repair ratio in our business, and when we started were asked to cut it by half. I thought it was damn near impossible, but

in fact was able to cut if to 27% over a two-year period." Another Scandinavian executive commented: "We set extremely aggressive targets for our integration teams, probably well above what is feasible."

FACT-BASED AND SYSTEMATIC EVALUATION OF PERFORMANCE IMPROVING LEVERS

A U.S. entry and development strategy is a prerequisite for identifying attractive acquisition candidates. Several U.S. acquirers wrongly assume, however, that most of the job is done as soon as the strategy is in place, and that target-specific evaluation becomes an unimportant exercise once negotiations are initiated. On the contrary, the continuous evaluation carried out by companies that have made successful acquisitions can best be described as a "count-the-pennies" approach. Vision is complemented with facts. Improvement opportunities are explored and documented in detail, as are their implications on investments, cash flows and maximum bidding price. The winning evaluation is structured around three improvement levers: functional, financial, and managerial.

Lever 1: Functional Improvements

The first lever consists of functional improvements. These are obtained by leveraging existing or jointly developed business strengths. AGA, for example, capitalized on this lever in the acquisition of Burdox by transferring its gas bottling technology, distribution systems such as computer-controlled bottle-tracking systems, and fleet-maintenance programs. Together, these improvements quintupled Burdox's postacquisition cash flows. When Alfa Laval acquired Cashin (a small food processing manufacturer), the product lines of the two companies were closely integrated. Cashin's products were sold through Alfa's distribution system in Europe, while Cashin's marketing approach was expanded to a system approach to facilitate the sales of Alfa's engineering and installation services in the United States.

Normally, these kinds of improvement opportunities are identified and evaluated by breaking down areas of potential integration benefits into the various activities of the value-added chain or business system and by simulating the consolidated operations of the two companies. This process explores issues such as how volume can be consolidated in the various factories, what product lines can be transferred, what factories can be closed, and what kind of customer distribution arrangements can be made.

One word of caution: Most acquirers overestimate the expected synergies significantly and vastly underestimate required investments. For example, most acquirers buying poorly or even moderately performing companies can expect to have to invest considerable sums in updating plants and equipment. Testing the feasibility of synergies, including the cost of obtaining them, is vital. "Despite the fact that we have made more than 100 acquisitions, we still overestimate the synergies. As a rule of thumb, we therefore take only half of the synergies assessed, and double the cost of realizing them," says Leif Johansson, Managing Director at Electrolux.

Lever 2: Financial Improvements

As a second lever, creative use of financial improvement opportunities characterizes many successful acquisitions. Analysis of own, the existing owner's, and alternative freestanding and inside investors' valuation of the candidate, as well as of the opportunities for financial synergies, serves as the basis for identifying opportunities for four types of financial improvements (Exhibit 12.4).

1. *Making a deal that captures hidden value.* Such deals are based on a positive gap between the acquirer's baseline valuation of the candidate "as is," and the current shareholders' valuation of their stock. In most cases, this would imply that the buyer knows more about the business than the seller, something that is most likely to happen where a holding company or a conglomerate is selling out one of its businesses.

This was, for instance, the case when Apothekernes Laboratorium acquired S.B. Penicks' bacitracin business. Apothekernes Laboratorium made a deal based on superior insight into the U.S. market, which enabled it to estimate correctly that the business had a higher "as is" value than the seller had estimated. However, this sort of deal can be expected to be rare, particularly for acquirers who do not have excellent insight into U.S. conditions. Many acquirers who think they have made "a deal" turn out to be wrong.

2. *Reselling stock at a premium.* This is accomplished by selling stock at a spread relative to value to acquirer to a different set of investors and/ or with a new equity marketing strategy. Apothekernes Laboratorium,

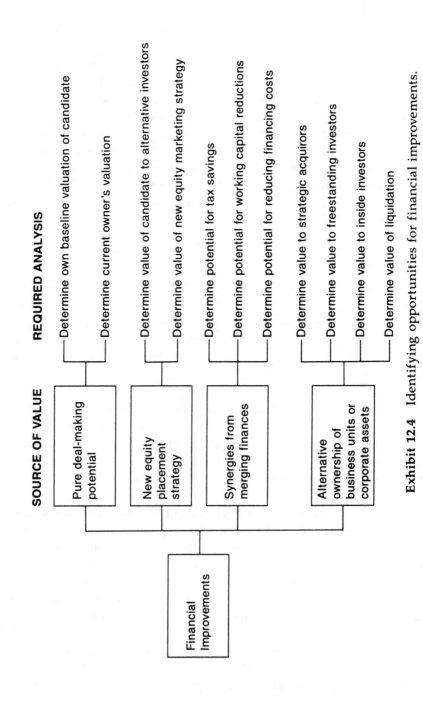

Exhibit 12.4 Identifying opportunities for financial improvements.

for example, went public with 40% of an acquired company and managed through this transaction to recover two thirds of the acquisition cost.

3. *Exploiting financial synergies.* These are created from tax savings, working capital reductions, and reductions of financial costs. In the Dymo acquisition, for example, Esselte recovered 10% of the acquisition price by offsetting current earnings against Dymo's forward tax losses.

4. *Spinning off business units at a higher price than value in use.* Electrolux and Esselte's strategy for example, has been to exit the noncore parts of the business that they have acquired. After Esselte acquired Dymo, three business units that did not fit Esselte's strategy and accounted for 7% Dymo cash flows, were sold off. In total, this allowed Esselte to recover about 50% of the acquisition cost.

Lever 3: Managerial Improvements

With the third lever, the managerial lever, improvements are made to strengthen the stand-alone performance of the acquired company. This is achieved by bringing in managers as discussion partners to existing management, or as active managers for a shorter or longer period as necessary. Electrolux, for example, has consistently exercised this lever in more than 300 acquisitions worldwide. It buys underperforming companies and revitalizes them by replacing nonperforming management and exercising substantial performance pressures. It is usually in turnaround situations that the managerial lever is required most clearly.

The most promising candidate for success is an acquisition in which a clear value added along one or more of these levers can be identified prior to the negotiation. In fact, the probability of success in any acquisition appears to increase strongly with the number of improvement levers applied. In the cases where two or more improvement levers were identified and employed, all but one of the acquisitions were successful, while all acquisitions where none was employed turned out to be failures. In the cases where only one lever was exercised, our study shows that this was usually the functional lever.

PRICE-SENSITIVE AND CREATIVE NEGOTIATION

Successful acquirers negotiate in a disciplined but creative way. This strong discipline is designed not only to energize and concentrate the acquisition team efforts but also to generate marginal dollars. Good negotiation efforts typically have three characteristics:

1. *Avoid competitive bidding situations.* Competitive bidding situations were identified by several successful top executives as one of the surest ways of stacking the odds against creating acquisition value. "You have to avoid auction situations: The United States is full of third parties like investment banks, whose main goal is to get the price up and create auction situations," says an experienced U.S. acquirer. To avoid such situations, the acquirers typically position themselves as the best buyer. Good business relationships or a strong reputation often make them the exclusive counterpart in a deal.

Some good acquirers spend years cultivating these relationships in the hopes of buying some day. They also move quickly. Getting in first and making a quick decision is critical to avoiding the influx of more buyers into the bidding process. At Esselte, the Executive Vice President, Bengt Strandberg, was the front-end deal cutter who did the evaluations and negotiations in many acquisitions, while the President was the "back-office" driver who handled the Board, secured the funds, and prepared the necessary documents at home. This setup, in combination with business relationships that were developed over a number of years, allowed Esselte to act very quickly in the acquisition of Dymo, when it became clear that the company could be taken over. In fact, Esselte prepared a bid over a weekend, made the bid on the following Monday, and even managed to respond to a counterbid on the Wednesday with a new bid that went through.

To avoid competitive bidding situations, Scandinavian acquirers also let it be known they are interested so that the seller approaches them. Taking the first move (i.e., informing the market about your interest in buying) gives much higher chances for exclusivity than having the seller openly invite bids.

2. *Establish a firm walkaway price.* This helps prevent successful acquirers from becoming macho in a bidding process—letting the desire to buy overshadow economic sense. As one CEO commented: "You have to say 'no' more than you say 'yes'. . . you have to go in with a cut-off price. . . you have to be willing to lose. You have to treat the whole thing as a stock market arbitrageur who can make a few points one day but must be willing to see a lot of deals go away." Further, since most deals do turn out as failures, one should be happy to say no to most of them and feel good about it.

3. *Structure a creative deal.* Analytical skills might bring you far, but it is surprising to observe how "small" unique ways of approaching the seller

often appear to make the difference. Successful acquirers provide "the small big extras." Reading the cards of the other party—their concerns, what they want for their families, and what would be required to protect their ego—may make the whole difference.

Furthermore, one may be able to split and rule, "We got the management of the target division on board—they understood that we knew the business better than their owner. They basically worked for us rather than the holding company." This was the case when Swedish Match acquired a division of GAF, which made flooring material. The acquisition team basically got to know the division better than their owners and gained the division's confidence in the process. This, together with their "open book" tactical estimate of the division's value, enabled them to argue the price down significantly.

The winner is characterized by negotiation strategies that are heavily focused on reducing and controlling acquisition cost, whereas the less successful accept asking prices and justify premiums with false synergies.

RAPID AND DIFFERENTIATED INTEGRATION

Unless the acquired company is integrated functionally, financially, or managerially, the likelihood of shareholder wealth creation is very low. At the other extreme, careless and insensitive integration can wipe out the culture of the acquired company, destroy its skill base, and cause losses in market share. Three factors appear to make the difference between success and failure in managing integration:

1. *Immediate integration.* Successful acquirers do not waste time when integrating. Typically, they have well-functioning systems that they impose on Day 2, and they manage to be back to normal business after 6 to 12 months, despite relatively drastic changes. "We make the changes immediately. Regardless of how big a turnaround we have in front of us— the acquirer of a company must be back in normal operations never later than a year after the acquisition," says a Scandinavian executive.

Such immediate action is achieved by applying carefully preplanned programs, setting demanding targets for the acquisition teams, keeping the integration phase very short-term oriented and applying symbolic gestures as a way of getting things done (e.g., moving out of headquarters buildings very quickly and eliminating executive parking spaces).

The value of this rapid action is twofold: First, it allows immediate improvements in cash flows; and, second, an acquired organization is more receptive to change just after the deal. As one top executive commented: "You have to move fast. The danger of not doing it rapidly is that nothing will happen. The more you wait, the harder it becomes to make changes."

2. *International consolidation of techniques and assets.* This allows acquirers to capture functional and financial synergies (Exhibit 12.5). Furthermore, it signals the strategic interdependence of the acquiring and the acquired companies.

On the one hand, techniques are transferred to improve productivity and to facilitate communication and control. For example, most successful acquirers immediately implement corporate-wide accounting systems that allow a common language to be developed and internal comparisons to be made fairly quickly: "We put in our accounting and control system. I would not say it is a key factor, but it certainly helped the success," says acquisition artist Bengt Strandberg of Esselte.

VALUE-ADDED
LEVERS

	Techniques	Assets
Functional	• Inventory control • Production scheduling • Production technologies	• Product lines • Plant and equipment
Financial	• Accounting systems • Budgeting systems • Financing techniques	• Receivables • Inventories • Pension plans • Debt • Tax shields
Managerial	• Structure • Salaries and compensation • Performance control • Management techniques	• Managers

TYPES OF INTEGRATION

☐ International content   ▨ Local content

Exhibit 12.5   Integration management framework.

On the other hand, assets of the acquiring and the acquired companies are combined to eliminate redundant resources and jointly utilize existing resources. Esselte, for example, closed the entire Dymo headquarters by merging it with existing operations in the United States.

Notably, the good acquirers are not willing to debate the quality of their techniques or approaches (although they will incorporate good ideas). Their attitude is much more "We need improvements rapidly and we will do it our way."

3. *Local integration of management.* Contrary to common belief, winning acquirers normally do not make sweeping managerial changes at the time of the takeover, but maintain a high U.S. and company-specific managerial content. Most acquirers appear to agree on the risks of replacing local U.S. staff with Scandinavians: "If there is a common flaw in the acquisitions, it is in bringing in Scandinavian management and trying to run the company in another way," says a Swedish investment banker in the United States, who has handled several of the major acquisitions over the past few years.

Furthermore, they promote from within. In fact, achieving quick turnaround and meeting aggressive goals in the integration phase are often used as a test of the acquired management. If these goals are not acted on, the acquirers then change the management.

As a final measure of management integration actions, incentive-based compensation is applied. The typical heavier emphasis on social control in Scandinavian companies' control systems appears to be less effective in a U.S. environment for two reasons: Physical distances make social control hard to pursue, and U.S. managers are used to tight performance controls and rapid feedback on performance. Contrary to common Scandinavian practice, successful acquirers therefore use financial incentives linked to company performance. As one acquisition advisor with extensive experience in Scandinavian U.S. acquisitions noted: "The key to successful acquisition lies in providing proper incentives for the local management team."

Making a U.S. acquisition is a substantial challenge; the pitfalls are many, but overcoming them may be highly rewarding. Carefully formulating a U.S. strategic platform, supporting it through a highly skilled and aggressively managed acquisition team, and executing it firmly represent the strongest approach for making a company an acquisition manager rather than a acquisition gambler.

13

Alliance versus Acquisition: Strategic Choices for European "National Champions"

Roger Abravanel and David Ernst

Much of the current worldwide activity in cross-border alliances and acquisitions is taking place in Europe. Many alliances and acquisitions have been done by Europe's national champions—companies that earn a third or more of their total revenues and profits in their home countries and that have long enjoyed formal or informal government protection. (See Exhibit 13.1.) But much of this activity is unsustainable. National diversification and defensive mergers and acquisitions in local markets often fail because they do not address the fundamental gap in competitiveness, based on skills and global—rather than national—scale, that frequently separates such champions from their foreign competitors. Attempted cross-border mergers in already-concentrated businesses such as tires (Pirelli and Conti, for example) bring tough organizational problems that are not easily justified by the additional scale. There have been many cross-border alliances and acquisitions in businesses where the

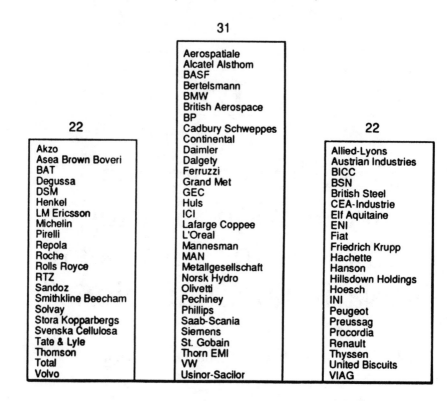

	31	
22	Aerospatiale	**22**
Akzo	Alcatel Alsthom	Allied-Lyons
Asea Brown Boveri	BASF	Austrian Industries
BAT	Bertelsmann	BICC
Degussa	BMW	BSN
DSM	British Aerospace	British Steel
Henkel	BP	CEA-Industrie
LM Ericsson	Cadbury Schweppes	Elf Aquitaine
Michelin	Continental	ENI
Pirelli	Daimler	Fiat
Repola	Dalgety	Friedrich Krupp
Roche	Ferruzzi	Hachette
Rolls Royce	Grand Met	Hanson
RTZ	GEC	Hillsdown Holdings
Sandoz	Huls	Hoesch
Smithkline Beecham	ICI	INI
Solvay	Lafarge Coppee	Peugeot
Stora Kopparbergs	L'Oreal	Preussag
Svenska Cellulosa	Mannesman	Procordia
Tate & Lyle	MAN	Renault
Thomson	Metallgesellschaft	Thyssen
Total	Norsk Hydro	United Biscuits
Volvo	Olivetti	VIAG
	Pechiney	
	Phillips	
	Saab-Scania	
	Siemens	
	St. Gobain	
	Thorn EMI	
	VW	
	Usinor-Sacilor	

Home country less than 30%	**Home country 30–49%**	**Home country greater than 50%**

Exhibit 13.1 Home versus total revenues—Top 75 European companies that reported a country breakdown of sales, 1990.

main opportunities for synergies are in narrow geographic markets. Finally, many weak national champions have pursued multiple alliance strategies that are inappropriate and that may complicate an eventual divestiture.

Much of this activity does not work out because of flawed strategic thinking. For many CEOs, the critical question is whether, through alliances and acquisitions, to be a leader in the process of restructuring their industries or to sell out and exit. This is a question of fundamental importance. But it is not the place to begin. First comes a hard-headed reassessment of industry dynamics in terms of the scale and skills that will be needed to compete, along with an assessment of how competitive position will change in the face of much tougher competitors and customers.

NATURE OF BUSINESS

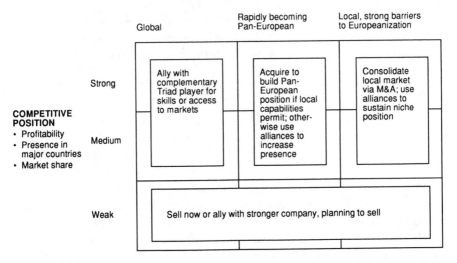

Exhibit 13.2 Menu of alliance and acquisition options (illustrative).

For national champions with viable competitive positions, *whether the business in question is global, Pan-European, or local is critical for determining the relative attractiveness of alliances and acquisitions, and for selecting partners.*

- In *global* businesses, alliances with non-European partners to improve skills or to get access to new markets—while sharing fixed costs—are often the most attractive option.

- In *Pan-European* businesses, acquisitions within Europe to bolster scale and leverage superior skills are the preferred option for companies with existing multiple-country positions. Where outright acquisitions are not possible (because of regulation or lack of experience), alliances tend to be either a good first step on the way to acquisition or a good way to learn how to enter the market independently.

- In *local* businesses, the most attractive option is often to dominate the home market through acquisitions. (See Exhibit 13.2.)

VIABILITY

In industries that are being deregulated or opened to new competitors, historical or even current profitability does not accurately portray underlying competitiveness. The advent of 1992, deregulation, and new competition from global players will alter the playing field dramatically. Only players who have a clear understanding of their true competitive position can respond accordingly. Therefore *before* approaching alliances or acquisitions, the first step for European players at risk is to reassess their competitive position along the following dimensions.

Profitability

European companies that depend heavily on home markets must ask themselves how they will measure up in terms of profitability after markets open to new competitors. A McKinsey survey indicates that Japanese executives across all industries view Europe as the major arena for expansion in the 1990s (Exhibit 13.3). In fact, cumulative Japanese direct foreign investment in Europe nearly tripled between 1987 and 1990, reaching a level of almost $60 billion. This expanded Japanese presence will have a significant impact on several major European industries. In the mid-1980s, the European automotive industry, for example, was on average earning returns twice those of the Japanese; one automaker was even three times as profitable as Toyota. However, these figures are not a legitimate indicator of real competitive position, because protection of some national markets allowed high-capacity utilization and relatively high prices for autos. See the box, "Autos—Battleground of the 1990s," for an assessment of the impact of Japanese transplants on the profitability of European automotive companies (Exhibits 13.4 and 13.5).

Product/Customer Attractiveness

Deregulation, as was the case in the United States, often changes the attractiveness of specific product or customer segments. The liberalization of store operating hours in Italy will, for example, make self-service gas stations combined with minimarts more profitable than today's full-service-only gas stations. The players best able to understand the impact of deregulation on specific product and segment profitability will be better equipped to run their base businesses and to plan and execute alliances and acquisitions. Their choice of partners will be based on attractiveness in *tomorrow's* competitive environment.

Market Share

High current domestic market share does not necessarily imply a strong position tomorrow against competitors that are "not visible" today. A case in

EUROPE 1992 SEEN AS

Number of responses

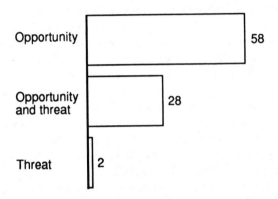

Opportunity — 58

Opportunity and threat — 28

Threat — 2

MAIN FOCUS FOR EXPANSION

Number of responses

☐ Last 5-10 years
▨ Next 10 years

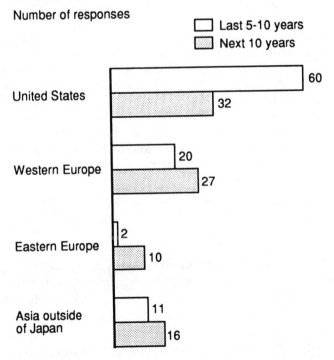

United States — 60 / 32

Western Europe — 20 / 27

Eastern Europe — 2 / 10

Asia outside of Japan — 11 / 16

Exhibit 13.3 Top Japanese companies—Perspective on Europe. *Source:* McKinsey surveys of 90 executives from 25 leading Japanese companies.

———————— **Autos: Battleground of the 1990s** ————————

As is well known, all the major Japanese auto players are already establishing transplant operations in Europe. The transplants are expected to be significantly more cost-competitive than European automakers on average, although not at world-class (that is, Japanese local production) standards. An example of the large competitive gap: European carmakers require an average of 36 to 37 hours to assemble a car, but Japanese transplants in the United Kingdom are expected to achieve levels of about 20 hours per car (similar to Japanese transplants in the United States). Beyond their cost position, the Japanese transplants will also bring shorter product development cycles (average product age: 2.2 years for Japanese models, vs. 5 to 7 years for European models) and high-quality manufacturing (see Exhibit 13.4).

At the same time that transplants are adding low-cost capacity, European OEMs are also building their low-cost capability, mostly by taking over and restructuring Eastern European plants. Some of this capacity will be targeted at Western European markets.

What is not so well known is the huge size of the likely impact on European car producers and component manufacturers. By the end of the 1990s, this overcapacity, coupled with the growing Japanese market share, could result in up to $100 billion of additional debt for European OEMs, as well as up to 500,000 unemployed between the automakers and their component suppliers (see Exhibit 13.5). This is equivalent to the employment of two European automakers. This situation could be even worse after 1999, when further growth of Japanese market share is likely.

══

point: Many European construction equipment companies in the 1980s looked only at Caterpillar as a key competitor and underestimated Komatsu, Hitachi, and Sumitomo. This is an easy mistake to make. In industry after industry, European champions are being threatened on their home turf for the first time: in white goods, Whirlpool-Phillips and Electrolux-Zanussi are challenging Thomson in France, Merloni in Italy, and Siemens-Bosch in Germany. This was not the case 5 or 10 years ago.

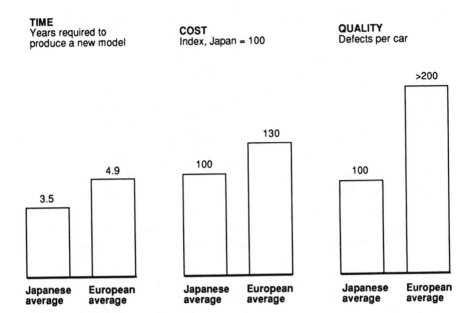

Exhibit 13.4   Competitive advantage of Japanese automakers. *Source:* Industry data; McKinsey analysis.

Customer Satisfaction

For European companies in protected industries, current measures of customer satisfaction may be misleading because customers have not yet been exposed to the high levels of product and service quality that competitors are capable of offering. This caution applies not only in businesses where

Major restructuring challenges . . .

- Loss of market share as Japanese OEMs expand share to at least 16-19% by 1999
- Cost of developing new models
- Expenses of plant closures and layoffs

. . . will result in large financial losses

- European auto industry return on sales:
  1989-1990: 5 to 8%
  1991-2000: -2 to -5%
- Increase in debt of up to $100 billion between 1991-2000

Exhibit 13.5   European automotive industry under pressure.

government procurement is important, but also in industrial oligopolies and businesses that are now protected by trade barriers.

One company in a process chemical business, a leader with 40% to 50% market share, which was regularly monitoring customer satisfaction with the help of an outside research firm, surprisingly found that customers rated *all* players very highly. However, when the company launched an in-depth effort to "live through the customer's experience," they found that many customers were dissatisfied, and subsequently they were able to identify numerous service improvement opportunities. In one case, a customer was experiencing frequent maintenance problems on a storage tank, which had caused slowdowns in its production schedules. A joint team, consisting of staff from the supplier and the customer, found that filling each storage tank to an ideal capacity could reduce maintenance problems by up to 80%. Because of the oligopolistic nature of the business, suppliers had avoided competing for customers based on price or service. In this situation, customers were not aware of the potential for improved service levels.

The availability of new products and services will distort the old proxies for customer satisfaction even more. Today, only about 45 Japanese auto models are available in Europe versus 90 in Japan. This means Japanese OEMs have the opportunity to significantly enhance the choice of models they offer in Europe—an opportunity for which they are preparing by rapidly expanding their distribution systems. A broader choice of models, together with an expanded service and distribution system, are expected to lead to a sharp drop in measured customer satisfaction with European OEMs, paradoxically just when the European OEMs could otherwise expect benefits from their massive efforts in total quality management and reducing time to market.

For some European players, a dynamic competitive assessment will suggest that the gaps in skills and scale relative to global or Pan-European players are simply too great to close. Selling to a strong buyer may be the best approach. This is already happening: nearly 300 of the 500 largest European companies in 1989 were not on the list in 1991. Many have been merged or sold. For weak companies, alliances are not a way to *avoid* sale. If anything, they complicate or even prevent an eventual sale. The evidence shows that most alliances *between* weak partners are doomed to failure.

Having done a careful viability analysis, managers can then assess which alliance or acquisition strategies make the most sense in addressing their companies' gaps in skills or scale.

Global: Ally with Non-Europeans

In industries such as computers, earth-moving equipment, and autos, where presence in multiple regions of the Triad provides a competitive advantage, *many local or regional European companies face a large competitive gap between themselves and their global competitors.* In such cases, alliances with geographically complementary players of similar strength are the most attractive way to access markets and skills rapidly—and to share the huge investments that are required. *Non-European* companies are usually better able than European ones to provide the needed access to global markets in concentrated businesses. Alliances are usually a better first step here than merger and acquisition because European national champions often do not have the market presence and cross-border postmerger integration experience required to succeed at cross-border M&A.

The Himont joint venture, formed on a 50-50 basis by Montedison and Hercules in 1983, is an example of an alliance between geographically complementary partners. Montedison used the alliance to build global presence at a stage when it did not yet have the presence to acquire comfortably in the United States. Prior to the joint venture, Montedison held about 17% of European polypropylene capacity and had a minimal position in the United States. Hercules, with clients mostly in the United States and Canada, had a 13% share of world polypropylene capacity. Montedison provided technology, European access, and capital to the venture. Hercules provided U.S. capacity and U.S. marketing capabilities.

The combination of Montedison's proprietary process technology and Hercules' capabilities in marketing, as well as worldwide presence, propelled Himont, subsequently acquired by Montedison, to a global leadership position with approximately 20% of the world polypropylene market. Another 40% of world polypropylene production is accounted for by companies operating under Himont license, which is based on Montedison's technology.

A Trojan Horse?

Many European managers are concerned that alliances can easily become a "Trojan horse" to allow a competitor to enter their market. Their concern is justified, especially since most alliances are temporary. Some lead to mergers between the partners; others to unplanned divestitures or to an eventual separation in which the stronger partner, having used the alliance to learn, is better positioned than before. Because the dangers are real, these managers should be careful to minimize their risks by selecting partners who are of similar strength and who are not likely to become direct competitors. They can also maximize their bargaining power within the alliance by investing in their own core business and by raising the value of their contribution to the joint venture.

The Fiat/Hitachi joint venture has allowed partners of similar position to achieve global scale in the hydraulic excavator business (which is an important segment of the earth moving equipment business) with much less risk—and expense—than would have been possible for either with a go-it-alone strategy. Hitachi was an attractive partner for Fiat-Allis because it was strong in hydraulic excavators, but lacked the full product line necessary to control European distribution of earthmoving equipment. The fact that Hitachi was not, like Komatsu or Caterpillar, a dominant competitor in the global market for construction equipment made for a more even balance of power. (See Exhibit 13.6.) By allying with Hitachi, Fiat significantly strengthened both its technological skills and its position in a global business.

Lucas, a world leader in technology for brakes, has also been able to increase its global presence via an alliance with Sumitomo Electric. In the United States, Lucas-Sumitomo share a 50-50 joint venture in brakes. Lucas also cooperates with Sumitomo in the Japanese brake market.

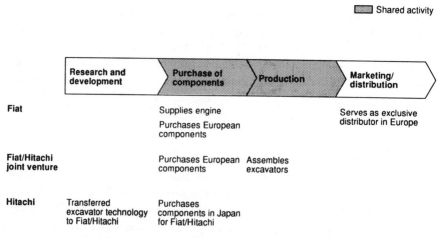

Exhibit 13.6 Fiat-Hitachi joint venture.

For each of these European companies—Montedison, Fiat, and Lucas—an alliance was more attractive than other options: an outright acquisition would have been too expensive or risky. In addition, for Montedison, the joint venture also facilitated an eventual acquisition.

What is common in each of these cases is that a European company forged a broad alliance with a *single* non-European partner. In general, we have found that national champions trying to develop global presence do best when they concentrate on one (or a few) global alliance(s) focused on filling critical gaps in their core business. Some global players—like GEC and IBM—have used multiple alliances to develop technologies, products, and market presence. Succeeding at even a single alliance, however, takes a lot of time and effort. Simultaneously pursuing multiple alliances is a dangerous approach for European national champions—especially those that are also trying to improve their core businesses or that have little past experience with alliances. Pursuing multiple alliances can also complicate an eventual sale by creating a competitive conflict with the potential buyer.

In all of these examples, the partner was not a European player. *Alliances between European national champions should be viewed with skepticism because they are also natural competitors.* Moreover, alliances between them are unlikely to offer the market access or skill-based opportunities that are available from global companies.

Similarly, merger and acquisition in global businesses on an *intra*-European basis—even where allowed by antitrust laws—will not often bring the same possibilities for performance improvement that can be gained by alliances with non-European partners (for example, the Japanese in autos or in electronics). Mergers between European players can bring additional scale, but they are also likely to bring massive integration problems.

Emerging Markets

For threatened European players in global businesses, acquisitions in Eastern Europe or other emerging markets are not an alternative to gaining world-class competitiveness in the core markets of the United States, Japan, and Western Europe. Because of the time, money, and other resources required to achieve significant returns in new markets, they should be pursued only *if and when* the competitive position in core markets is assured. For example, given their competitive strengths, it often may make more sense for the Japanese rather than European automotive manufacturers to enter Eastern Europe; witness Honda's recent decision to invest in the former Soviet Union. Yet many European companies are focusing heavily on opportunities in Eastern Europe. The 10 largest ventures announced by European companies in Poland, Hungary, and Czechoslovakia alone would absorb about one third of all 1991 cross-border merger-and-acquisition spending by European companies. For some investors, this capital would be better spent in core markets.

PAN-EUROPEAN: ACQUIRE WITHIN EUROPE

The options for national players in businesses that are or are rapidly becoming Pan-European—like paper, chemicals, and process industries—are substantially different than for players in global businesses. It makes sense for players in global businesses to concentrate on allying with non-European players. By contrast, companies in Pan-European businesses need to think most about acquisitions *within* Europe as a way of generating meaningful scale economies or leveraging skills.

Companies with a strong position at home and a presence in multiple European countries should consider a "concentric" acquisition program, where early acquisitions in home and nearby countries serve as a platform for later acquisitions elsewhere in Europe. But there are obstacles. Barriers such as "friendly" shareholders or government regulations can sometimes prevent outright takeovers. Moreover, not all players have the European presence necessary to make acquisitions work. Under these circumstances, alliances can be a good way to develop an insider position in advance of further investments.

Merlin Gerin built leadership in electrical equipment via a series of acquisitions, first by developing a platform in "nearby" countries (Gardy in Benelux and Spain, Magrini in Italy), then in Germany (Weckmann), and finally by acquiring in the United Kingdom and the United States (Square D). In the process, it has grown from a national company into a global corporation, achieving an average return on equity of 21% in the second half of the 1980s and sales growth of nearly 20% each year.

Similarly, Arjo Wiggins Appleton (AWA), a merger between Arjomari-Prioux and Wiggins Teape Appleton (WTA), has created a Pan-European power in paper. During the mid 1980s, Arjomari of France grew rapidly. Its 15 or so acquisitions in France, Spain, the United Kingdom, Germany, and Italy, more than doubled its net sales between 1983 and 1988 and supported an average ROE of 32%. In late 1990, after the spin-off of WTA from BAT,

Arjomari-Prioux merged with WTA to create AWA, with worldwide sales estimated at $4.5 billion.

The merger created a strong paper distribution network in Europe, which is particularly important for protecting competitive position in quality papers, a high value-added and fast growing segment. The breadth of the combined companies' product range in uncoated fine papers will make AWA attractive to independent merchants, who are particularly important in the German market. Added scale in manufacturing will allow the rationalization and specialization of production across the more than 20 European mills operated by the merged companies, as well as bring additional clout to the purchasing function.

Leverage Skills

Even where businesses are still subject to significant regulation and are not heavily affected by 1992, the ability to leverage skills across countries can make Pan-European strategies attractive. For example, Ferruzzi, which was an Italian trading and farming company in the 1950s and 1960s, has built a leadership position in agribusiness, despite continuing regulation of the industry via the Common Agricultural Policy. Largely through acquisition, its revenues have grown at a 55% annual rate in recent years, increasing from $660 million in 1985 to $9.2 billion in 1990. Its strategy has been to leverage its corporate skills in trading and processing and its strong position in the sugar and oilseed crushing businesses in Italy and France. First, it expanded in Southern Europe in core and very closely-related businesses such as starch and oil, and then it built a broader European and (for selected products) global position.

Ferruzzi bought Eridania, Italy's largest sugar producer, to enter the sugar business in the early 1980s. In 1985, building on an existing stake, Ferruzzi gained control of Beghin-Say, France's largest sugar producer. Using these acquisitions as a platform and source of cash, Ferruzzi then made a series of very closely related acquisitions, mostly cross-border within Europe: CPC's European starch business, Central Soya, Lesieur/Koipe, Kelsa, the oilseed crushing businesses of Continental Grain, and Ducros. Ferruzzi has added value to these businesses through restructuring and by cutting costs. It has also improved returns by combining the complementary trading and processing businesses—for example, by exploiting the cost differentials of raw products across countries. Net income (as consolidated in Eridania) has grown more than tenfold between 1985 and 1989.

Balancing Act

Acquisitions in Pan-European businesses are complicated by the need to build scale economies and improve performance while also balancing stakeholder sensitivities to postmerger integration across multiple countries. Electrolux's strategy in the food service equipment business over the past several years shows how this balance can work.

After more than 15 acquisitions across Europe in the food service equipment business, Electrolux now has a European market share of more than 30% and achieved an estimated return on net assets of 28% in 1991. By 1989, this business of Electrolux had grown to the point where it encompassed 46 independent companies, 25 factories in eight countries, and 30 brands—many of which competed with each other (Exhibit 13.7).

The task to deal with this level of complexity was entrusted to Zanussi Grandi Impianti, as Electrolux's global center of competence in food service equipment.The new CEO, Gianfranco Zoppas, launched a three-phase program to fully realize the potential of European integration through factory rationalization, Pan-European coordination of product development, and consolidation of national sales networks. The approach explicitly recognized the potential for local sensitivity across various elements of the business (Exhibit 13.8). In the first phase, several Pan-European

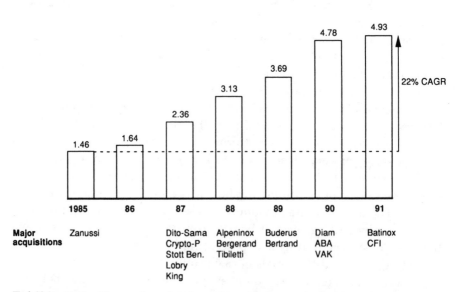

Exhibit 13.7 Electrolux food service and vending (net sales, billion Swedish kroner).

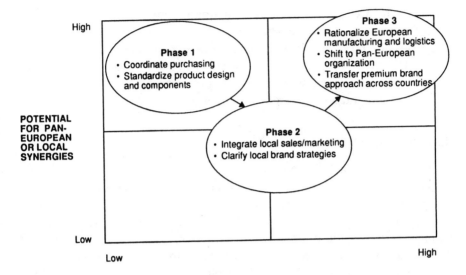

Exhibit 13.8 Electrolux FSE—Approach to Pan-European integration.

work teams were created to generate "early wins" in areas that had high potential for performance improvements but little stakeholder sensitivity: purchasing, standardization of components and subassemblies, and preliminary coordination of product development. The real achievement of this first phase was to plant the seeds for a common Pan-European culture between companies that previously has been rivals.

In the second phase, from 1989 to 1991, country managers were given the responsibility for improving sales and marketing across the complex product line within each country. This was a huge task, which included clarifying brand positions to avoid cannibalization and product complexity, filling product gaps, strengthening relationships with dealers based on improved product position, and rationalizing the multiple sales and marketing staffs that had been built up through acquisition. These tasks were carried out on a local basis and thus posed less of a risk in terms of employee sensitivity than if they had been imposed from the "outside."

Only in the third phase, now getting under way, are the more "obvious" steps of pursuing Pan-European factory rationalization, strengthening R&D coordination, and building a Pan-European organization being tackled. Performance measurements are being modified to reflect contributions to Pan-European performance: for most managers, a portion of compensation is tied to Pan-European product line results. Product group leaders, who are responsible for product development and management of core factories, are being evaluated both on time-to-market in multiple countries and on their role in helping country managers improve local cost levels. The sales and marketing responsibilities of country managers continue to be emphasized, while they are encouraged to close uncompetitive local factories and sources from lower-cost "core" factories.

Enhance Power

In Pan-European acquisition programs, enhancing the power of key managers in the target company—rather than a predatory, acquirer-takes-full-control approach—can be critical to success. These managers have the skills that are necessary to run the target company. Electrolux, after acquiring Zanussi Catering, leveraged the latter's strengths to grow throughout Europe. Zanussi, with over 50% market share in Italy, also had significant export sales throughout Europe. Electrolux built on these export relationships to establish footholds in Germany, France, and the United Kingdom and to make further acquisitions in these countries. The Zanussi Grandi Impianti company led the development of a Pan-European "value-for-money" brand and became the core factory for dishwashers and other important products throughout Europe.

Other Strategies

Although these examples show the benefits of using acquisitions to build scale in Pan-European businesses, they do not suggest that acquisition is the *only* strategy. Many European players that do not yet have substantial positions outside their own countries should consider alliances as a first step to building Pan-European presence. An example is the Thyssen-Beltrame joint venture formed in 1991 to operate a minimill for producing bar steel in Germany.

A joint venture with Thyssen gave Beltrame, a leading minimill player in Italy, access to other European markets, as well as the necessary know-how to manage in Germany that only a native company could offer. Beltrame took a 60% stake in Thyssen's existing Oberhausen plant. Thyssen contributed the facility and will take half of the output of the plant, in addition to providing 230,000 tons per year of scrap metal for input. Beltrame will contribute its superior production technology, revamp the rolling mill, and operate the business.

Besides entry into the German market, the joint venture also allows Beltrame to start with lower volume and lower risk because Thyssen will take half the volume of the plant. Prior to the joint venture, the production of small steel bars had almost disappeared from Germany because of the high cost of making them in integrated steel mills. To get around these costs, scrap metal would be transported from Germany to minimills in other countries for production of bars, and reimported into Germany—all of which added substantially to transportion costs, which production at Oberhausen will allow Beltrame to avoid.

Minority stakes in parent companies, which account for approximately 25% of all the linkages between European companies, are another form of alliance that can build access to new markets. Examples include the many cross-shareholdings among food and beverage companies. Minority stakes can also provide an "introduction" in Pan-European businesses, particularly in closed markets where a straight acquisition would not be possible. However, these "financial alliances" provide little or none of the consolidation potential available from merger and acquisition. Nor can they provide the benefits of an autonomous joint venture with a clear charter. This underscores the importance of clarifying the objectives of minority stakes at the outset: Are they a step toward acquisition or divestiture?

LOCAL: CONSOLIDATE AT HOME

For businesses where the natural scale is national or subregional, the same strategic advice holds true as for Pan-European businesses: pursue acquisitions to generate scale and market power in the relevant market arena.

Despite hundreds of European cross-border mergers and acquisitions (M&A) in retail banking, the natural scale of such combinations is less than Pan-European. Not surprisingly, little of this M&A activity has been a clear success; most has led to average or below-average profitability. Indeed, not one of the cross-border banking acquisitions in Europe was among the top 10 players in a major market. As a result, the market share of foreign-owned banks did not increase in most European markets between 1985 and 1990. (See Exhibit 13.9.) The reason why these cross-border mergers have met with such mixed results is that retail banking is still a local business; hence, the benefits of integration are mostly local: branch reconfiguration, local market power, consolidation of computer systems. What applies to retail banking also applies to many other retail businesses.

For other local businesses like insurance, cement, and retailing, a more attractive option for strong local players is often to push for *domestic* leadership through M&A. In banking, about 70% of all European

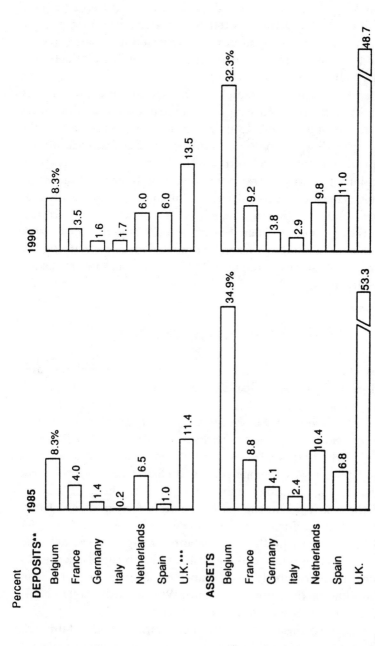

Percent

DEPOSITS**

ASSETS

*Foreign commercial and savings bank branches and subsidiaries, including banks with "local" names but majority owned by foreigners
**Current accounts, savings, and time deposits
***U.K. sterling based deposits only

Exhibit 13.9 Market share of foreign-owned banks* in different markets. *Source:* National banking statistics; McKinsey analysis.

246

M&A between 1985 and 1991 was executed on a national (not intra-EC or international) basis. In the Dutch banking sector, for example, the top three players increased their share of total deposits to 72% in 1989 from 39% in 1985. Examples include the Amro/ABN and NMB/Postbank mergers.

Some companies in local businesses are forming cross-border alliances to take an "option on the future" in case deregulation or other forces accelerate the move toward Pan-European competition. These strategies often have low upfront costs, but what we said about minority shareholders applies here as well: how will these alliances be managed so as to ultimately generate synergies? Or, will they represent purely financial investments?

Some companies in local businesses are pursuing cross-border M&A, sometimes even pointing to the complementarity between the partners as a sign of "good fit." Unfortunately, cross-border M&A in local businesses are likely to succeed only if the two companies are multilocal companies with overlapping geographic positions (hence providing the potential for local consolidation) or the acquirer is purchasing undervalued assets. Complementarity, which is a plus in cross-border alliances in global businesses, can be a strong negative in M&A in local businesses.

Companies seeking to remain independent may choose to form partnerships that support specialist product/distribution positions by cooperating on individual functions or lines of business. In banking, most of these transactions have taken the form of cross-border minority stakes or domestic joint ventures. Compagnie Bancaire, the largest specialist personal financial services provider in Europe, competes in leasing, consumer finance, mortgages, real estate, insurance, and fund management, most of which are local businesses. Since the early 1980s, it has expanded in specific lines of business using targeted cross-border joint ventures: examples are leasing (through joint ventures with savings banks in Belgium and Italy) and consumer finance (through joint ventures with banks or retailers in Belgium, Italy, the Netherlands, Spain, and Switzerland).

EUROPEAN RESTRUCTURING: THE NEXT PHASE

Many European countries have had a less-efficient market for corporate control than the United States. Restrictions on "outside" acquisitions have encouraged the use of M&A for diversification on a domestic basis, since relatively few attractive European companies can be acquired in core businesses abroad. Meanwhile, friendly shareholders and less demanding capital markets have sometimes led to cross-border alliances among European companies that would otherwise be competitors.

Looking ahead, we expect shareholder demands to help support a convergence in the intensity of competition between the more- and less-protected countries within Europe and between Europe and the United States. This convergence, driven in part by the single market directives and deregulation, will be accelerated by the actions of global players that are already insiders in Europe, although often non-EC European companies. In fact, three of the best-known restructurers of European industry—Asea Brown Boveri, Nestlé, and Electrolux—are based in Switzerland or Sweden.

Alliances and acquisitions will continue to reshape Europe, but the pattern of linkages will be very different from that of the past because of a more efficient market for corporate control and more demanding shareholders. In global businesses that are unblocking, there will be fewer domestic mergers and acquisitions, more Triad alliances, and a few "unthinkable" sales of national champions. In addition, there will be many more European acquisitions in businesses that are becoming Pan-European, and continued consolidation on a domestic basis in local businesses. There will also be fewer minority stakes, as restrictions to outright acquisitions diminish.

The pace of restructuring will be greatest in those countries and businesses where the levels of protection have long been highest and where privitization programs are just starting. Thus, for example, we would expect the number of acquisitions to grow sharply in Germany and Italy.

As they adjust to more demanding customers and financial stakeholders, European managers will face the challenge of developing an "unregulated" perspective on their competitive position—a perspective based on newly demanding European (or even global) customers, not on the traditional, "friendly," national customers. They will also need to change the spectacles through which they view current and potential allies. As competition becomes less avoidable, many former partners may become direct competitors. And many former competitors, including the Japanese, may become global allies. As always, choosing the right strategy depends, first and foremost, on developing a clear understanding of how industries actually compete—not of how the conventional wisdom says they do.

14

Strategic Choices for Newly Opened Markets

Joel Bleeke

Markets are opening around the world. In Eastern Europe, Asia, and North America, trade walls that have stood for decades are crumbling in the face of political unrest and technological innovation. Because of these changes, a do-or-die atmosphere is driving many European, Japanese, and U.S. companies to become broad-based competitors. And in the deal-oriented atmosphere that has ensued, aggressive competitors are often forced to make critical decisions fast on whether and how to expand into uncharted terrain.

Fortunately, a valuable map is available: U.S. companies' experience with deregulation over the past 20 years. That experience shows clearly the pattern of competitive dynamics that unfolds when artificial constraints are suddenly lifted and new entrants are allowed to rush in. Consequently, it provides useful lessons not only for markets' opening because of regulatory changes but also for markets such as telecommunications,

Author's note: I thank my colleague David Ernst for his contribution to this article.

semiconductors, and autos, which are becoming global in response to technological or other discontinuities.

Perhaps the most important of these lessons has to do with time. The U.S. companies' experience shows that managers who look only to the years immediately surrounding 1992—or any other market opening—will make irreparable mistakes. Because the competitive environment changes twice—once when the market opens and again about five years later—a 10 year roadmap is essential.

This road map will direct many large competitors away from their traditional roles as broad-line players into new, more profitable roles as low-cost entrants, focused-segment marketers, or providers of shared utilities. And for many, the map will include significant changes in course, since the actions required to survive in the early years of a market's opening are not the same as those that bring success in the second phase of open-market competition.

These lessons derive from a year-long study of the managerial implications of deregulation in U.S. airlines, financial services, long-distance telephone service, central-office switching, trucking, and railroads. The first part of this study involved a detailed assessment of the dynamics in each industry from its deregulation to the present (including an analysis of structural costs, industry cost curves, industry profitability, new entries, and exits). In the second part, my colleagues and I examined the management strategies of profitable and unprofitable companies to uncover common patterns. (The strategic choices we considered included pricing, breadth of product or service offerings, cost-reduction activities, and marketing strategies.)

In some ways, the opening of Europe and other global markets may be even more traumatic than U.S. deregulation. New entrants will not only be fledgling companies like People Express but also powerful organizations like American Airlines and Deutsche Bank. Given histories of local protection and the large number of strong across-the-board players that are planning to build beyond their national franchises, the competition (especially among global companies) may be far more painful than it was in the United States, where deregulation was largely a domestic event. The fact that major Japanese companies are planning investments that will meet local-content requirements—often at lower cost than existing European facilities—leads to that conclusion. So does the wave of cross-border merger and acquisition activity that has already begun, allowing less time for managers to think through their long-term game plans. Indeed, the strong alliances that are already forming across Europe suggest that the competitive situation may soon be dominated by powerful, broad-based competitors holding a series of local oligopolies and making new entry extremely difficult and costly.

Despite the differences, the U.S. experience with deregulation shows how the opening of once restricted markets leads to a new competitive world. Whether the market is in Canada, Eastern Europe, Asia, or the European Community matters less than the competitive dynamic its opening unleashes. And in that competitive dynamic, undifferentiated size matters less than the strategic choices thoughtful managers make.

THE COMPETITIVE DYNAMICS
OF DEREGULATION

Deregulation in the United States began in 1975, when the Securities and Exchange Commission abolished fixed rates for U.S. securities brokers. Before long, other industries were coping with deregulation as well: airlines in 1978, trucking and railroads in 1980, banking and telecommunications at intervals throughout the 1980s. In every instance, we can see the same set of competitive dynamics play itself out:

- While the number of new entrants can be staggering, nearly all soon fail—along with many large existing competitors. No fewer than 215 new air carriers entered the market in the 10 years following deregulation, compared with *no* new FAA-certified carriers in the preceding 40 years. But fewer than one third of the new entrants and fewer than half (44%) of the existing competitors survived those 10 years as independent entities. Arguably, none of the new carriers have distinctive strong franchises today. In trucking the story was much the same. From a steady level of 17,000 truckers in the 1960s and 1970s, the number of competitors rose to over 37,000 in 1987. At the same time, more than 72 companies, accounting for over $2 billion or 16% of industry revenues, shut down between 1980 and 1982 alone.

- Industry profitability deteriorates rapidly as new entrants shatter pricing for all competitors for at least five years. The surprise is not entrants' starkly lower costs. (On average these were 40% to 50% below competitors' chiefly because the new companies carried less baggage such as seniority agreements, outmoded factories, and expensive distribution systems.) The surprise is new entrants' ability to destroy market pricing for everyone, even if they take only 10% to 15% of total market share. In the securities industry, for example, discount brokers captured less than 20% of consumer volume, but they forced a 30% reduction in market prices. Prices in the central-office and PBX-switching markets fell by 40% to 50%, yet low-cost entrants captured no more than 25% of the total market share.

- The most attractive business segments often become the least attractive—and vice versa—as competitors all flock to the same markets and cross-subsidies unwind. In telecommunications, prices on the previously most profitable business, long-distance service, dropped 38% between 1984 and 1988, while prices on local service rose 43%. In airlines, prices on high-density, longer haul routes (like the Chicago to New York corridor) fell by 42%, while prices on previously less profitable, short-haul secondary routes climbed sharply. In the retail brokerage business, prices on institutional transactions dropped 30% on average in the year after deregulation, while prices on consumer transactions fell only 4%. In short, what appear to be less attractive strategies before deregulation often pay off after deregulation as savvy competitors avoid the rush of new entrants and anticipate the large price changes (both up and down) that soon occur.

- Variation in profitability between the best and worst performers widens dramatically and remains high. In time, the spread reflects the strongest companies' ability to gain on weaker competitors by rebuilding their franchises. From 1984 to 1988, for example, American Airlines earned $1.5 billion while Pan Am lost over $950 million. (As a benchmark, the nine largest carriers had aggregate profits of approximately $3.5 billion during this period.) But during the first five or so years, the variation occurs because the weak get weaker, not because the strong become more profitable. In the first three years after deregulation, for example, the least profitable railroads suffered massive losses (on the order of returns of negative 10% to 50%) after just about breaking even in the previous five years.

- Merger and acquisition activity often occurs in compressed waves that are driven by the demonstration effect of other acquisitions and by pressure to keep up with rivals that are doubling in size and/ or scope. The first wave focuses on consolidating weak players, the second wave on combining the strong. In the brokerage industry, second-tier firms (numbers 11 to 25 in market share) grew rapidly in the three years surrounding deregulation by acquiring weaker competitors. But after raising its market share from 14% to 26%, this group began to lose ground before a second wave of acquisitions among the industry's largest firms.

- Only a small number of companies (no more than five to seven in the industries we examined) can remain broad-based competitors. Most are forced to narrow their product range and spin off noncore activities to survive. The reasons are mostly financial: at the same time that profits are falling and cross-subsidies are unwinding, the cost of competing in each segment shoots up as new entrants increase competitive pressure and force established companies to invest heavily to improve productivity, research and development, marketing, and customer service. Given these pressures, many companies choose—or find it necessary—to focus on core activities in which they have strong skills and a competitive advantage.

  The result is much greater segmentation within the industry, with each segment requiring its own set of skills and a distinctive business system. The trucking industry, for example, now consists of integrated less-than-truckload shippers, stand-alone, full-load carriers offering no consolidation services, and truck lessors. In brokerage, competitors have emerged to create related but distinct businesses in research, trading, and retail distribution.

STRATEGIES FOR SURVIVAL, STRATEGIES FOR SUCCESS

Looking back on 20 years of deregulation, four distinct types of companies were able to survive and build profitable, sustainable market positions. They are broad-based distribution companies that offer a wide range of products and services over an extensive geographic area; low-cost entrants that migrated over time to become specialty or customer segment-focused providers; focused-segment marketers that emphasize high levels of service at relatively high prices or target a very specific, defensible customer group; and shared utilities that focus on making economies of scale available to a large number of small competitors.

Except for some high-end marketers, successful companies in each of these categories pursued very different strategies in the first few years of deregulation than they did thereafter. Why the change in course?

Changes in industry structure—and the innovations and initiative of sharp-witted managers.

In all the industries we studied, the early years of deregulation were characterized by shakeouts, restructuring, and the consolidation of position among survivors. During this period, flexibility (especially pricing flexibility) is the key to survival. Then the competitive situation changes. After five years of intense competition, the strain on industry performance has forced many of the weaker companies to exit. Larger companies have figured out how to offer low-cost products and services to compete with new rivals. The price gap between new entrants and existing companies has also diminished as the latter's cost-cutting efforts take effect. The result: New entries decline, the industry consolidates, and competition shifts away from purely price-based behavior. In this second phase, which is continuing in many industries today, leading companies move to build new oligopolies that can be every bit as powerful as those eliminated by deregulation. Exhibit 14.1 summarizes the key strategic choices these companies made.

Broad-based distribution companies are deregulation's equivalent of large, multinational organizations. As a rule, more companies seek this role than are able to play it. Following deposit deregulation in 1981, for example, an informal survey of executives at the nation's largest banks showed that nearly all expected to be broad-based competitors 10 years after deregulation. Yet, of necessity, most of the group moved away from broad-based competition throughout the 1980s, shedding overseas operations and, in several cases, selling consumer operations such as mortgage and credit card processing.

Broad-based competitors that did succeed understood their pricing in detail and were able to eliminate cross-subsidies and disaggregate pricing if competition demanded it. Equally important, they conserved resources and were willing to bide their time in moving to dominate their markets. Early critical actions for companies seeking this role include the following.

1. *Improving pricing capability.* Effective competitors assess the price sensitivity and underlying costs of serving specific customer segments and adjust pricing to protect these segments from new low-cost players. AT&T's price reductions for high-volume business customers reflected its recognition that these relationships were endangered by MCI's and Sprint's targeted marketing efforts. American Airlines became a leader in yield management by hiring a staff of over 100 people to manage the

	Broad-Based Distribution Company	Low-Cost New Entrant	Focused Segment Marketer	Shared Utility
Key Actions Early On	• Cut costs • Differentiate service • Improve pricing capabilities • Increase marketing, product development • Don't overcommit early	• Target the most profitable segments • Eliminate structural costs • Focus on price-sensitive customers and price-oriented advertising • Outsource to limit the scope of operations • Don't grow too fast	• Target nonprice-sensitive segments • Bundle products • Develop customer information systems • Build personal relationships	• Identify separable, scale-intensive functions • Sign up development partners to share costs, provide inputs • Build a core set of clients
Five Years Later	• Develop new oligopolies • Use detailed pricing as a strategic weapon • Preempt competitors via strategic alliances	• Move up the service-price ladder • Identify new riches • Maintain cost advantages • Avoid competing in the core markets of broad-based competitors	• Continue to emphasize early actions • Selectively expand into related segments • Improve customer service • Expand product features to support price	• Become the industry standard by building share • Ensure participation and use by industry players, often by selling minority interests • Move to a high-service, high-price position while increasing customer dependence on the shared utility
Examples	American Airlines Merrill Lynch	Midway Airlines Charles Schwab	Hambrecht & Quist Northern Trust Goldman, Sachs	SABRE SWIFT Telerate Reuters

Exhibit 14.1 After deregulation, strategies change.

mix of seats and fares. While making it hard for business travelers to take advantage of cut-rate fares, American also moved to gain their loyalty by introducing the frequent flyer program.

2. *Cut structural costs.* In no instance could established broad-based companies reduce their costs to match those of low-cost entrants. But they could and did cut costs substantially. AT&T's employment has dropped roughly 20% after divestiture. American Airlines was among the first to introduce a two-tier wage structure, paying new pilots, flight attendants, and mechanics up to 50% less than industry averages.

3. *Shift quickly toward new ways of differentiating service.* U.S. Sprint aggressively installed digital fiber networks to provide high-quality service between major cities. Yellow Freight System improved its ability to consolidate less-than-truckload shipments by expanding from 248 trucking terminals in 1980 to 440 terminals in 1982. Federal Express introduced a computerized bar code system to track packages.

4. *Conserve capital to maintain flexibility.* The most costly mistake broad-based competitors made was overcommitting capital through acquisitions, major equipment purchases, or entry into new markets, leaving themselves too thin a cushion to weather the profit storm. IU International, for example, expanded rapidly in the less-than-truckload business by acquiring Ryder and Pacific Intermountain Express. After losing over $125 million in two years trying to build a national carrier, the business was divested.

United hurt its competitive position in airlines by its costly acquisitions of Hertz and Westin. These nonairline holdings were sold in 1987, but by then American had been able to outpace United's growth in revenue passenger miles due in part to this diversion. In contrast to United's capital-consuming acquisitions, American grew mostly from within, conserving its cash to build existing businesses and using affiliations rather than acquisitions to extend its reach.

The key point is that during the profit squeeze that follows deregulation, capital markets often close for new funding because of low industry profitability. As a result, capital becomes scarce in deregulating industries, and conserving capital during the early years is essential for survival. This is less true later on, however, when a different set of strategic choices becomes critical for success. Of these, the most important is identifying new ways to increase market clout and to develop new local oligopolies.

At first, as we have seen, low-cost entrants and focused-segment marketers threaten existing broadline players, and many giants topple as they fail to react quickly enough. But it is crucial not to underestimate the power of large competitors over time to make big better again. In the deregulated airline industry, the use of hub control, computerized yield-management systems, and frequent flyer programs have been powerful tools for competitors to regain clout and pricing power. The top eight airlines controlled 94% of revenue passenger miles in 1988, compared with 80% before deregulation. (By 1988, American alone accounted for about 20% of the airline industry's market value compared with approximately 7% in 1978.) Local oligopolies are also apparent at many major hubs: in St. Louis, TWA controlled 82% of the traffic in 1988 compared with 43% in 1979. The same year, USAir controlled 36 of Pittsburgh's 51 gates and held an 85% market share compared with 48% in 1979. By 1990, United and American represented 80% of the flights from Chicago's O'Hare.

The reemergence of oligopolies is also evident in the securities industry, where the top 25 firms increased their share of capital to 63% in 1985 compared with 51% in 1980 and 43% on "May Day" in 1975. At the same time, these firms made deep pockets more important by escalating the role of risk capital in securities trading and mergers and acquisitions. In trucking, the top 10 less-than-truckload carriers held a 50% market share in 1987 compared with 35% in 1980, enabling them to gain economies of scale by leveraging their spending on freight terminals and information systems.

In rebuilding market power, finely detailed pricing capabilities continue to play a critical role. Pricing can be used defensively, to protect profits by discouraging competitors who enter home turf, and offensively, to maximize profitability from uncontested markets. In airlines, this kind of capability makes the chances of a new entrant modeled on People Express virtually nil. By 1981, the 600,000 fares incorporated in American's computer system in 1977 had risen to 1.6 million, allowing it to meet low prices for selected routes and passenger segments without endangering its broad revenue base. Similarly, truckers filed over 1.2 million tariffs in 1987 compared with an average of 185,000 independent tariffs per year in the early 1980s.

Low-cost new entrants were the catalyst for the competitive battles that followed deregulation. But successful entrants almost always migrated relatively quickly to specialty or segment-focused competition rather than pursue a pure low-cost strategy. Among the reasons for changing strategy were the reactions of existing competitors, the appearance of "faster guns" with even lower cost structures, and the slow-but-steady rise of the companies' own structural costs.

As we have seen, low-cost entrants compete with cost structures that are fundamentally different from those of existing competitors. They have lower wage schedules, more flexible employment arrangements, and often no unions. Simpler manufacturing and distribution systems eliminate many costs of complexity. Low-cost entrants streamline their businesses and leave decisions to line managers supported by little or no staff. They also tend to outsource products and supplies. Discount brokers let clearing agents handle many of their transactions, for example, rather than build their own internal systems. Similarly, low-cost airlines avoided building computer systems, leased gates, and paid other carriers to handle their maintenance. Over time, of course, new entrants begin to develop their own structural costs as employees become more senior and facilities age. But successful players in deregulated industries continue to control expenses tightly, even when they are no longer competing on price alone.

Other critical choices that low-cost entrants make early on are to target the most profitable segments of a business—those that are cross-subsidizing other segments—and to focus on price and price advertising. In their early years, low-cost entrants are no-frills suppliers. They do not offer service, just rock-bottom price. In addition, they manage their growth. People Express failed in part because it expanded too quickly, consuming capital that was needed later to support price competition. By the end of 1985, less than five years after its founding, People Express had grown to 3,400 employees and 78 planes with enough seats to rank as the ninth largest airline in the United States. Capacity doubled in 1984 alone, and the acquisitions continued in 1985 and 1986. Yet by the end of 1984, earlier profits had already given way to red ink as the airline was unable to fill its seats even at loss-leader fares.

The most dangerous mistake low-cost entrants can make is to take on broad-based competitors in their sensitive core markets where their larger rivals will use all their resources to defend their turfs. Most new entrants are bruised severely when the giants react, and all but a few fail. Midway Airlines's attempt to enter the Milwaukee–Chicago market illustrates the power of pricing against new entrants. On Monday, May 1, 1989, Midway began offering jet service from Milwaukee to its own hub at Midway Airport in Chicago. On Thursday, June 8, Midway cut its Milwaukee fares to increase its passenger loads. But Milwaukee is a hub for Northwest Airlines. By Tuesday, June 13, Northwest had not only matched Midway's fares but also cut *all* its fares on flights to and from Midway. By Friday,

June 16, Midway was forced to cut back its promotion in Milwaukee to restore its pricing in Chicago.

Longer term, the key to survival for low-cost players lies in finding a viable migration route to a position as a broad-based competitor (as MCI has done) or a focused-segment provider.

Implicit in this migration, of course, is movement up the service-price ladder. While maintaining acceptable prices, Charles Schwab now offers a range of money market and mutual funds, retirement accounts, and CDs as well as customer help lines and quotation services that increase cost but still offer a reasonable price-value trade-off. U.S. Sprint features the superior quality of fiber-optic lines. MCI has systematically built skills in new product areas like "800" lines and international service, while marketing heavily to profitable corporate customers and keeping a tight hold on headquarters expense.

Focused-segment marketers target a specific set of customers or products, emphasizing, at relatively high prices, service levels that are unavailable elsewhere. Because success in pursuing this strategy largely depends on identifying the right niche and building strong personal relationships, many companies do not need to shift direction five years out. They can continue to develop initiatives that are effective early on.

In general, the closer the personal relationship in the sales channel between the customer and the provider, the less price sensitive the customer (and segment) is likely to be. Once these customers have been identified, segment marketers often develop a broad range of products for the customer group and encourage cross-selling. Bundling products and increasing product complexity help segment marketers by reducing price sensitivity and by creating opportunities to deepen personal relationships. Sales of corporate banking services to middle-market customers by regional banks are a good example of such product bundling.

Successful focused-segment marketers also develop customer information systems with an emphasis on databases and customer profitability levels. The relationship databases used by regional banks for upscale accounts, the customer files that make frequent flyer programs possible, and Merrill Lynch's Cash Management Account for its securities customers are all good examples of such systems.

Other essential pieces of this strategy include (1) selectively expanding beyond existing segments into closely related segments or markets, as many regional banks have done in rolling up local community banks; (2) identifying new approaches and ways to measure service performance such as turnaround time, reprocess time, and error logs; and (3) developing new product features such as the extended product guarantees, car rental insurance, and high credit limits that now come with costly credit cards to support a premium price. In every instance, the intent is the same: to lock in attractive customers through product attributes and customized service.

Shared utilities are the last—and newest—of the strategic groups that emerged from deregulation. Shared utilities offer new entrants and other competitors the advantages of scale by sharing costs across many companies. They are usually created as competitive pressures generate demand for new information, services, or inputs that cannot be met by small, individual companies. Relatively few places for shared utilities exist in each industry. But for those companies that can identify and capitalize on an opportunity, the strategy is most attractive.

Ironically, in the years immediately following deregulation, many observers predicted that only a few large companies would survive in each industry. But these observers never imagined the growth of shared utilities that would make many of the advantages of size available to everyone. Telerate, for example, provides government bond and foreign exchange quotations and financial market news instantly around the world from its home in New York, thereby making it possible for small- and medium-size traders to have many of the information advantages that come from scale. Telerate's average return on equity between 1985 and 1988 was more than 20%.

Similarly, Centex Telemanagement, a telecommunications remarketer in California, became one of Pacific Bell's top customers, purchasing telephone time in large blocks and reselling it to smaller companies at attractive rates.

The first step for a would-be shared utility is to identify discrete functions with heavy fixed costs that cannot easily be developed in-house by new or small competitors. Computer expenses are often the basis for a shared utility like Dallas-based Hogan Systems, set up to provide systems support for small- and medium-size commercial banks.

Next comes signing up development partners to help build the utility by sharing costs or contributing proprietary information. Most deregulation-inspired shared utilities had such partners in their early years. Telerate shared development with a U.S. primary securities dealer, in part to get access to real-time trading information. Globex, the utility for off-hours futures and options trading, established links with Reuters, the Chicago Mercantile Exchange, and the Chicago Board of Trade. Equally critical is building a set of core clients among the utility's largest users and working to ensure their loyalty through superior service. Telerate's early penetration of major trading rooms was a key to its later success.

As the service gains momentum, making sure that it becomes the industry standard is crucial. For many utilities, that means growing fast enough to meet the demands of customers and build a large installed base. Even though many customers initially had complaints about Telerate's service, it became the industry standard because it could handle extremely rapid growth in the number of terminals, information sources, and customers it had outstanding.

Unhappily for most competitors, shared utilities are natural monopolies. So while they offer attractive opportunities during the first phase of open-market activity, eventually less effective producers are driven out of business by the scale required for satisfactory performance. Those that are largest, with the greatest ability to spread costs across a broad base, survive. The rest do not. This shakeout is now occurring in airline computer reservation systems. It is also taking place in global rating of debt securities, where the strength of Moody's and Standard & Poor's has made it hard for European-based and Asian-based entrants to prosper.

Because they dominate their markets, shared utilities have great pricing flexibility and often generate extraordinary returns. As a result, they can easily become the target of envy, prompting powerful customers to consider creating a rival. In fact, a consortium of securities firms and investment banks has recently been discussing the possibility of creating a new shared utility to compete with Telerate and Reuters in the market for U.S. government securities pricing information.

To avoid encouraging rivals and to support their revenue base, utilities often move to supply high levels of customer service and personal contact in exchange for their high price. They also seek to lock in their product or service: for example, by expanding the number of individual users who receive their services at a given company. Selling part of the shared utility to customers and suppliers may also help to ensure continued use and profitability while reducing the resentment associated with high returns.

WHEN GLOBAL MARKETS OPEN

The patterns of competition that characterized deregulation in the United States are already emerging in Western Europe. In the airline industry, early liberalization of flights between London and Amsterdam led to a 37% increase in capacity and an effective drop in prices of 16% on what had been a highly profitable route. Ryanair, a new low-cost player, entered the Dublin–London market with round-trip fares approximately half those of Aer Lingus. Trans European Airways, Europe's second largest charter airline, applied to fly scheduled routes at discount prices out of Belgium.

The wave of merger, acquisition, and alliance activity that followed U.S. deregulation is also well underway. In Europe, M&A and alliances have grown at an annual rate of approximately 25% since 1985. Air France has acquired control of UTA and Air Inter to become the largest airline in continental Europe. Similar alliances are emerging in telecommunications and financial services, suggesting that the powerful series of local oligopolies that characterize the second phase of open-market competition are already developing. In the Netherlands, for example, the top three banking players increased their share of deposits to 72% in 1989 from 39% in 1985.

Europe's competitive evolution is also being speeded up by the fact that many of the new entrants are mighty international competitors like Honda or American Airlines and because of the rapid expansion of global companies such as Electrolux and ABB. These competitors will be able to capitalize quickly on current differences in global efficiency across markets. Pilots of some continental European airlines, for example, are paid, on average, more than twice what their counterparts at major U.S. airlines receive. Yet the productivity of U.S. airlines, measured by revenue passenger miles per employee, is more than double that of the European airlines. As markets open, these differences will be largely equalized.

Similarly, the North American Free Trade Agreement has already intensified competition for many U.S., Canadian, and Mexican companies. For example, one Mexican home products company seeking to broaden its North American position found that the largest U.S. companies had already formed JVs or established their own operations in Mexico, threatening the companies' home market and preempting the possibilities for expanding into the United States.

The exact dynamics of market openings will vary, of course, from country to country. But the new competitive structure that market opening creates remains the same, not only for deregulating markets but also for markets experiencing other discontinuities. The oil crisis of the 1970s, for example, made possible a rush of new Japanese auto entrants into the United States. And while these companies initially entered as low-cost players, they soon recognized the need to migrate to positions as focused-segment marketers and broad-based competitors in order to survive as others entered with even lower costs.

Whether in Eastern Europe, the EC, Asia, Mexico, or the United States, opening markets will cause rapid changes in the character of profitable companies as cost cutting, pricing, and market segmentation become far more important than undifferentiated size. Managers who use the lessons of U.S. deregulation wisely should be able to avoid many of the hard landings that so often surround market openings.

15

Alliances in Europe: Collusion or Cooperation

Herbert A. Henzler

What makes economic sense for an individual company is not necessarily best for the economy as a whole. Arguing in this vein, policy makers such as the president of the Germany Anti-trust Agency have been trumpeting the dangers they see emerging from the strategic alliances now so prevalent in global businesses. Hiding behind the new-fangled "strategic alliance," do we find nothing other than the familiar evil of worldwide industrial cartels? Is cooperation and harmonization of interests among alliance partners simply collusion in a flimsy disguise?

These fears are understandable but unfounded. Indeed alliances can be and have been abused. But the fact that many alliances wind up a failure for both partners indicates that alliances in and of themselves do not engender price gouging or bestow unfair competitive advantages. Alliances are not even distant cousins of cartels. On the contrary, if properly designed, alliances provide companies with their best chance to compete in the global market place by improving skills, gaining access to new markets, and increasing scale. Alliances can make companies *and* markets more competitive and give companies a unique opportunity to learn.

NOT CARTELS

Adam Smith captured present-day suspicions about cooperation among competitors in "The Wealth of Nations": "People of the same trade seldom meet together even for merriment and diversion, but the conversation ends in a conspiracy against the public, or on some contrivance to raise prices." The critics are actually assuming a twofold restraint of competition: First, it is assumed that the partners in an alliance will avoid competing with each other; second it is assumed that, in consequence, the intensity of overall international competition will diminish. Neither stands up to critical examination.

Alliances differ in essential characteristics from cartels and their anticompetitive ilk: Whereas the contracting parties in cartel agreements lay down prices, terms, territories, and much more in extremely precise detail to preserve the status quo, most successful alliances are aimed at *new* products, markets, or businesses. In contrast to cartels, alliances create more options for customers at more favorable terms.

Alliances do not restrict competition between partners or in markets as a whole. Alliances are temporary arrangements and they can de facto be dissolved at any time unilaterally, when one of the partners has achieved its goal. To gain entry in the Japanese pharmaceutical market, Sandoz allied itself with Sankyo and Bayer with Takedo. Eventually when they were firmly planted in the new market both Sandoz and Bayer withdrew from their alliances. Both are now ranked among the top 20 companies in the Japanese pharmaceuticals industry and are competing vigorously against each other and their old partners.

But even if the partners in an alliance, for a time, were to pursue peaceful coexistence, it still does not automatically follow that global competition would decline. For various alliances are in strong competition with each other. In fact, alliances often have the effect of heightening competition, by making the member companies more potent market participants.

Thus, in the early 1980s, the rapid development of the Eurobond market was substantially advanced by the alliance between First Boston and Crédit Suisse. These two companies, which until then had operated in separate competitive arenas, linked up to bundle their complementary strengths: First Boston opened up access to the issuers of corporate bonds in the United States and contributed superior skills in shaping innovative financial instruments; Crédit Suisse, on the other hand, had access to European investors. Later, when First Boston ran into difficulties in its home market, Crédit Suisse bought up its share of their joint venture. Today, the

Eurobond markets are very competitive, very liquid, and very efficient; neither the First Boston–Crédit Suisse alliance nor Crédit Suisse alone has dampened competition.

To claim that competitive intensity is reduced, you have to believe that a large number of small national competitors always makes for a better market than a few strong ones. This preference may have made sense at a time before markets became global and existed only on a national level. Numerous impediments made the national markets incontestable from abroad and so each country needed many competitors in each market to provide protection from monopoly pricing. This view, however, fails to do justice to the new realities of global competition. Because fixed costs are so high, entering, let alone winning, in the global market for products such as computers, autos, airplanes, pharmaceuticals, chemicals, and many other products requires scale larger than most single-country markets can support.

Nor does a small number of global competitors imply a cartel—even if interlinked by alliances. There are only a handful of competitors in the jet engine and semiconductor business. All the companies have multiple alliances with both suppliers and direct competitors, yet competition is still intense.

A CHANCE TO LEARN

Even where an alliance is designed to serve specific functions such as production and marketing, it often involves a much more extensive transfer of knowledge. The day-to-day contact of alliances is by far the best way for companies to acquire complex background knowledge that cannot be learned from manuals or from observation at a distance. Behind the sales and research results, which allow the success of the alliance to be quantified, is hidden the whole range of personal and professional exchanges that provide new stimulation and substantially contribute to the building up and revitalizing of skills and proficiencies in both partners. Since it is not reflected in tangible indicators, this essential enrichment of a company's internal human capital frequently goes unnoticed.

Ford's 13-year alliance with Mazda illustrates this subtle but important transfer. Mazda teaches Ford about lean manufacturing and engineering, while Ford teaches Mazda about design, finance, and international marketing. Ford's Hermosillo, Mexico, plant, which assembles the top-performing Mercury Tracer, is modeled on Mazda's superefficient factory in Hofu,

Japan. One of every four Ford cars sold in the United States last year benefited from some degree of Mazda involvement, while two of every five Mazdas showed the Ford stamp.

Learning is not synonymous with giving away proprietary knowledge. When a Japanese and a European manufacturer of semiconductor equipment cooperated in a research alliance in order to challenge the world market leader in their field, it was clear to both of them that they could only gain possession of the vital top technology quickly enough if they joined forces.

At the same time, each of the partners in this high-tech alliance had serious misgivings that his own technological know-how could be drained against his wishes in the course of the collaboration. The necessary security was achieved through agreeing on somewhat complicated but effective procedural rules: The alliance was given its own laboratory, to which only a selected group of persons had access. Specially nominated "border patrols" supervised what research know-how was made available to whom. The partial opening of company boundaries for a potential rival requires a very high degree of trust and real two-way exchange of ideas and information. Partners must work at maintaining the balance of this mutual give-and-take.

The learning that comes with strategic alliances actually contributes to raising the welfare of the world economy. Just as international trade tends to equalize factor price differences, so strategic alliances work toward equalizing worldwide knowledge. Alliances allow the transport between companies of knowledge that is too complex to be covered by traditional instruments such as patent or license agreements. Superior know-how that was once only embedded in specific locations—like Silicon Valley—will become transferable thanks to strategic alliances.

The most important benefit of alliances is not the dissolution of economic cartels, but the destruction of cartels of knowledge. Alliances accelerate learning. Close contact with other companies challenges the entrenched position of a company's traditional ways of thinking and doing things. A confrontation with alternative points of view can have a revolutionary effect, remaking existing patterns of thought and releasing innovative forces not unlike a paradigm change in science. This free exchange of ideas is the best hope for the future of the world's economy.

Postscript:
A Look Ahead

Joel Bleeke and David Ernst

Global corporations of the future will be rather like amoebas. This single-celled aquatic animal is among the most ancient life-forms on earth. It gets all its nourishment directly from its environment through its permeable outer walls. These walls define the creature as distinct from its environment, but allow much of what is inside to flow out and much of what is outside to come in. The amoeba is always changing shape, taking and giving with the surroundings, yet it always retains its integrity and identity as a unique creature.

To be truly global and not merely "big," organizations of the future must hold this permeability as one of their highest values. When managers enter a new market, they should first ask these questions: "How is business here different? What do I need to learn?" They have to seek partners who can share costs and swap skills and access to markets. In the fluid global marketplace, it is no longer possible or desirable for single organizations to be entirely self-sufficient. Collaboration is the value of the future. Alliances are the structure of the future.

This has enormous impact on corporate strategy. It makes the world very complex, because there is no single valid rule book for all markets. As this book has demonstrated, alliances are based on arbitraging the unique differences between markets and partners. And so it is impossible to standardize an approach to the topic. Managers at the corporate center must be able to tolerate and in fact encourage variation: 10 different markets, 10 different partners, 10 different organization charts, 10 reporting systems, and so on. Policies and procedures must be fluid. The word *schizophrenia* has negative connotations, but it captures this idea that truly global organization must entertain two seemingly contradictory aspects—a strong identity, along with an openness to different ways of doing business, to the values of different cultures and localities.

This duality is going to be very difficult for many of the "global" companies of today. Companies with a sales-based culture, where senior executives all come from a sales background, will have a particularly hard time adapting to this new collaborative world. Such companies see the world as "us and them." They reject ideas from the outside world, even if the concept is helpful. They find it hard to live without standardization. They find it hard to collaborate with partners. Deep down, they are trying to convert everyone to their own way of doing things. This makes them inflexible and confrontational. They don't know how to communicate and work with the outside world on its own terms. They cannot be like the amoeba, with its permeable walls and changing shape, its openness to take from every environment. These companies may survive because they are large and powerful, but they will cease to be leaders.

Index

Note: Bold entries indicate tables or figures.